A JOURNEY THROUGH THE BOOK OF ECCLESIASTES

SOMETHING MORE

LIVING WELL IN A BROKEN WORLD

FROM THE AUTHOR OF *EVEN THE MONSTERS*

DARYL POTTER

PAPER STONE
PRESS

Paper Stone Press
Oakville, ON, Canada
www.paperstonepress.com
Published: September 2024

Copyright © 2024 by Daryl Potter

Oakville, Ontario, Canada

Paperback: 978-1-990388-13-2
Hardcover: 978-1-990388-14-9
eBook: 978-1-990388-16-3
Audiobook: 978-1-990388-15-6

The epigraph is from Mere Christianity *by C.S. Lewis, copyright ©*
1952 by MacMillian Publishing Company, p. 129.

Structural editing services provided by
Christine Gordon Manley of Rosemount Writing and Editing Services

Developmental editing as well as stylistic and copy editing by
Amelia Winters of Amelia Winters Editing

Proofreading by
S. Robin Larin of Robin Editorial

Cover design and typeset by
Damonza

For Jackson,
my dearly loved son.

I would fight lions barehanded for you.

If I find in myself a desire
which no experience in this world can satisfy,
the most probable explanation is that
I was made for another world.

C.S. Lewis

A JOURNEY THROUGH THE BOOK OF ECCLESIASTES

SOMETHING MORE

LIVING WELL IN A BROKEN WORLD

CONTENTS

A PERSONAL INTRODUCTION

"Dad, why am I here?"

A refreshing wave of cool air washed over us as my nine-year-old son and I escaped August's heat and humidity into air-conditioned bliss. The Oakville, Ontario Home Depot stood tall and open before us—paint and tools and hardware as far as the eye could see. The building is one of my happy places.

"Why are you at this store?" I asked. He knew why we were in the store. His tone carried a searching quality. "Or why are you here on this earth, in this life?"

"Yeah, what am I alive for?" he responded. "What's the purpose of me being born?"

If you're thinking, *No, that is not a conversation a nine-year-old boy starts with his dad*, well, you'll have to take my word for it. It was not unusual for Jackson to ask me a philosophical question, and learning how to answer him has been a joy to practice over the years. Earlier that year, his older sister had spoken her last words. She suffers from a degenerative medical condition, one that delayed her ability to speak and then stole it away by age twelve. As a result, having one child who can still engage with me verbally is not something I take for granted.

So my nine-year-old son asked me a grown-up question.

"There are two answers to that question," I answered. "There is the ultimate answer that focuses on the eternal, and then there is a simpler answer that focuses on this life here on earth. The ultimate eternal answer is that God created you to have a beautiful relationship with him forever. The whole Bible talks about that. It can get complicated in places, but that's the basic idea."

Remember, I'm talking to a nine-year-old here.

"The simpler answer applies mostly to just this life and is the focus of the book of Ecclesiastes. It just so happens that I'm going to start a sermon series on Ecclesiastes next month."

I have no memory of what we talked about next. I don't know if we got distracted by other shoppers, if Jackson switched topics to something Pokémon related, or if the conversation continued for another twenty unrecorded minutes of father-son philosophizing while we shopped for power tools or angle brackets or number eight two-and-a-half-inch flat-head, square-drive construction screws. (If it was the latter, we probably bought the yellow zinc variety. I seem to have a lot more of those than I need.)

Before we go on, I'd like to clarify one thing. I mentioned that I'd prepared a sermon series on Ecclesiastes. I am not, however, a preacher by occupation. I did my undergraduate degree in liberal studies, which allowed me to jam a large volume of religious studies and history into my degree. I have studied the Greek of Alexander and the New Testament. I've unpacked the various Anabaptist and Calvinist schools of theology, explored by foot and sailed the places that today we call the Holy Land and its surrounding geography, but the preaching thing was strictly voluntary.

The practice of passionate study, however, has been a consistent part of my life since childhood. Like my son, I started wrestling with existential questions and faith topics from my preteen years. I find this material intensely interesting, and I love making it practical and relatable. This vein of investigation grips me the way sports grip some of my friends.

Supporting this introspective quality, I moved out of my parent's home at thirteen. It was a practical arrangement—my father had secured me a twelve-hour night-shift job at an old creaky farmhouse some miles from our place. While still essentially a child myself, I became the night nurse for the farmhouse couple, a brother and sister in their nineties. Bedpans, sponge baths, salves for wounds that would not heal, soiled bedsheets, and cleaning dentures for this couple were my introduction to some of the challenges of old age. The job took me away from home from 6:30 p.m. till 7:30 a.m. seven nights a week, 365 days a year from age thirteen to seventeen. I learned to raise myself while dealing with a spilled urinal or other problem at 2 or 3 a.m. This seemed like a good idea to my parents. I think boarding school would have been better. At least I would have had teachers and peers.

The oddly cold nature of my home life, unfortunately, mirrored my relationship with spiritual matters. Home and religion were intellectual constructs but not deeply attractive experiences. Bible study gripped me for its meaning but not its emotion.

I quit the nursing job at seventeen. In response to me sleeping at home again, my parents began charging me rent. As a result, I got my own apartment at eighteen, as soon as I was old enough to sign my own lease. That separation from my parents proved insufficient, so less than a year later, I moved from California to Canada. Shortly thereafter, I formally abandoned Christianity and became an atheist. I've written elsewhere about how I came back to faith in my early twenties.[1] With that return to faith, Bible study transformed from an intellectual interest to an emotionally engaging source of deep meaning.

In my early thirties, however, that faith was challenged once more. The birth of our daughter, her immediate medical problems, and a cascade of other calamities that followed tore apart my understanding of God and the sense of self I had established.

There's a book in the Bible called Job, which is the landmark text for Christians, Jews, and Muslims on the topic of unjust suffering. I began a serious study of that book after our daughter's birth, desperate to find answers to deep questions regarding suffering and pain. The result of that study was a new faith foundation that didn't take away pain but taught me how to survive what had previously seemed unendurable. As a secondary result of that study, I published a book that combined memoir with biblical commentary on Job to explain what I had discovered.[2]

However, once I was done with Job, mere survival was not enough to see me through the rest of my life. I needed something more than survival. I needed to know how to live day to day and not just endure. Thus began my study of Ecclesiastes.

If Job is the book in the Bible on unjust suffering, Ecclesiastes is the book on existential suffering.[3] Said differently, Ecclesiastes is a book narrowly focused on the meaning of life—in this life, right now. Ecclesiastes doesn't

---

1   Daryl Potter, *Even the Monsters: Living with Grief, Loss, and Depression*, 2nd ed. (Oakville, ON: Paper Stone Press, 2022).

2   Potter, *Even the Monsters*.

3   I am indebted to Leslie Pashuk (Registered Psychotherapist and MThS), who pointed out this distinction in private conversation.

concern itself much with matters of salvation, heaven, or eternity. Ecclesiastes wants to know how to live now on this planet, even when conditions are less than ideal. Pick your sphere of interest—political controversies, environmental challenges, social ills, psychological pain, misogyny, economic oppression, war, death, and disease—Ecclesiastes covers it all and more. The world is broken. The book pulls no punches on that score, but in response, it teaches us how to live well in a broken world.

Job taught me how to survive the monsters life sometimes throws at us. I needed Ecclesiastes, however, to teach me how to do more than survive. Ecclesiastes was the flower planted on Job's foundation that taught me how to enjoy life again.

A few days after my philosophical conversation with Jackson in the hardware store, I had a conversation with a friend of mine. Let's call him George. I had known George for over two decades in another city over four thousand kilometers away. George had just come to town for a visit. It was great to see him, but then it became clear that George was in rough shape. I had not seen George in person for a long time, and the things George shared with me caught me off guard.

George was in his mid-forties, married, and a mature career-oriented guy. His kids were grown and on their own now. By all accounts, he had made a success of himself. But he approached me on that visit with tears in his eyes, and to cut a long story short, a lot of bad stuff had happened. He was at a stage where it seemed he didn't want to live anymore. He started sharing with me his lack of dreams, his emptiness, and his feelings of despair. He no longer had any goals or desires. Depression, it seemed, was only part of it.

George had read my book on Job, which had helped him sort through his feelings about God and his sense of injustice. But, like me after I'd finished writing the book, he needed to know what came next. He needed something more.

As George talked, I listened. While I listened, I also talked to myself. *This is serious*, I thought. *George is in pain, but I have no idea how to help him. I'm not a doctor or a psychologist or a therapist.*

George kept talking. I kept listening. I also started silently praying. The prayer went something like this: *God, please help me help your boy because I have no idea what to say to him.*

If you're thinking, *That's your genius prayer in a crisis?*, my honest answer is yes. That's about it. I can be articulate on paper, but my wife will be the first to attest that I can get a bit tongue-tied in an emotional jam.

At least I knew what not to do. I knew not to say, "Well, you've got heaven to look forward to, George." That would suggest that he was right: life was, at best, an empty disappointment, and all he could hope for was to hurry up and die. A middle-aged adult on the edge of a nervous breakdown needs something more immediate than an after-death consolation prize to get them through the day.

So I prayed. Then it came to me: *I've been studying Ecclesiastes for a long time now. Ecclesiastes is not a book about heaven. Ecclesiastes is a book about how to live this life, here and now, today.*

Ecclesiastes had everything my friend needed. And so, in ten minutes, right there on the spot, with no notes, I gave him the entire sermon series— not just the first sermon scheduled for delivery a few weeks later, but the whole series, the whole book of Ecclesiastes, in ten minutes.

There was George, in crisis, suddenly subjected to my ten-minute survey of Ecclesiastes. He got the whole thing, cover to cover, in one uninterrupted go. I have no memory of what I said precisely or how I organized my points, but he was glowing by the end of my speech. His tears were gone. You could see a sparkle in his eyes.

Ecclesiastes is not a book that gives pat answers. There is no A plus B equals C in this book. Ecclesiastes is instead a gut-level reality check on how life really works and an open door to a new way of thinking and being. George's eyes didn't sparkle because he had the solution to life's riddle. His eyes sparkled because he suddenly saw the path forward in a completely different light—one focused on now and not some mysterious beyond-the-grave promise of heaven.

George still had his work cut out for him after this talk. All I could do in ten minutes was crack open Ecclesiastes and get him started. It was up to him to take his walking stick and bravely step through that door.

My conversations with Jackson and George reinforced for me the importance of revealing the message of Ecclesiastes not just for me but also for those I loved. George did not have academic interests and was unlikely to read a traditional commentary. And how long would it take for my son to be old enough to really dig into this ancient text and understand its modern applications? I'd rather he understood these things early in life and not wait until his fifties, as was my case.

Modern life cries out for the kind of understanding that Ecclesiastes was written to provide. However, that ancient text has become obscure. The foreign nature of ancient poetry, translation complexities, and a bias in academic literature toward obscure and, frankly, boring language conspires to hide God's treasure beneath layers. For many, Ecclesiastes has become either inaccessible or misunderstood. As a result, unlike my book on Job, which was an accident of personal study, I intended for this text on Ecclesiastes to become a book from the beginning.

This book is a journey. It unfolds according to a natural progression, weaving memoir and commentary together as it unveils truth and practical tools for living. Ecclesiastes makes false starts and then backs up to correct the record as its author honestly explores the reality of human experience in this life. The passions of youth are unpacked with wiser eyes later in life, and thus the contradictions revealed here are part of the book's charm.

Life is not neat. It does not conform to a formula. As a result, this book is not an internet article on the ten keys to a better life. While I've included a section called "Life Lessons Summary" at the end, that is not a checklist to work through. Likewise, jumping ahead to sections of topical interest may help a little, but that approach won't give you the best results. Ecclesiastes is a lived experience that aims to adjust how we think about reality and how we approach living well despite the brokenness evident in the world around us. Nothing is off limits. Sex, politics, and religion are all up for investigation and debate in Ecclesiastes. The topics flow from one to another, and we'll engage with them as they appear, but their order matters. The book's ideas, images, and evolving metaphors build on each other in sequence.

Ecclesiastes is for the soul that wants to know how to live now. Heaven can wait. This book asks how I should live on Tuesday afternoon when things around me go right or wrong or take unexpected turns that defy understanding. Then it teaches us how to live again on Wednesday when dawn brings yet new experiences or emotions.

The reader of Ecclesiastes will come away with a mindset—a framework for living well in a broken world regardless of the unique circumstances of our lives and times and individual days. The book is a rich and, in some places, controversial work, and it will be fun to unpack its layers.

I've come back to Ecclesiastes again and again for over forty years now. For the past decade, I have studied it intensely, unpacking the original

Hebrew grammar with the aid of translation tools and commentaries written by Protestant, Catholic, Jewish, and secular scholars. I've quizzed preachers, doctors, therapists, bankers, craftsmen, farmers, artists, fishermen, nurses, programmers, and mechanics, testing the lessons found in Ecclesiastes against the reality of their own lived experiences and mine. For the single or paired, parents or childless, young or old, rich or poor, God's own book on how to live in a broken world has proven its worth. It's a pleasure to share those lessons now with you.

"Why am I here? What am I alive for? What's the purpose of me being born?" my son asked.

"How do I keep living when there's nothing further to look forward to?" my friend George asked.

And I wondered, *How do I do more than just survive this life? How can I live well in my broken world?*

Ecclesiastes answers all these questions. Let's tackle this wonderful book together.

PART ONE

A HEART'S HUNGER LEADS TO A SEARCH

1

THE AUTHOR OF ECCLESIASTES

A LITTLE OVER three decades before Jackson asked me his "What am I here for?" meaning-of-life question, I was about the same age as him and busy thinking about how to get more sugar in my diet.

When I was growing up, our household was a firmly whole- and natural-foods house. Processed foods were not stocked, and sweets were usually only found in whatever fruits were in season or had been canned the previous year. Our pantry did have a plentiful supply of the ingredients necessary to make just about whatever sort of cookie, pie, or cake a kid might crave, but they were purchased and stored, as far as I could tell, just to collect them. Compounding what I saw as the sugar shortage in my world, strictness ruled our household. Asking for treats was not an option. As a result, we ate healthy and as a kid, I hated it.

One day my parents went into town with my sister, and I was left on my own in the house. The sugar cravings that day were high. Looking back, I suppose that a normal preteen boy would have simply raided the pantry to scoop sugar into our unsweetened iced tea or found some similar low-effort solution. However, for me, ambition was an early quality.

Instead of starting with the pantry, I started with the recipe drawer. There, I found a promising handwritten guide to making German chocolate cake. Perfect. Never having baked or cooked anything in my life before, I went through the kitchen finding all of the listed ingredients and then set to work making a full cake pan of gloriously sweet German chocolate cake.

Considerations about the trouble I'd be in when everyone got home were drowned out by the siren call of sugar.

The handwritten recipe recorded everything in old imperial measurements. "Pounds" was written the usual shorthand way as "lbs" and so on.

I went to work. I measured carefully. I followed the recipe exactly. I preheated the oven perfectly. I timed its entry and exit with precision. I was going to eat cake, and I was going to eat a lot of cake before the rest of the family got home. For me, this was a preteen sugar heist of epic proportions.

My attempt was a complete disaster. Experienced bakers will right away have wondered, "Who measures cake recipe ingredients in pounds?" Nobody, unless you're running an industrial bakery. The items accounted for in teaspoons were appropriately abbreviated as "tsp." Tablespoons should have been "tbs," but someone forgot to cross the *T*. So "tbs" became "lbs," and my sheet pan German chocolate cake consumed several pounds of butter and cocoa and, relatively speaking, not much else. The end product was an oily soup. Likewise, cocoa is quite light—I needed a lot of it to start doling it out in pounds. The half cup or so of sugar never had a chance against pounds of bitter cocoa. Looking back, I have no idea how I even measured the cocoa. The bathroom scale maybe?

I have an aunt, who we'll discuss later, who would have laughed at my mistake, corrected the handwritten recipe card, and taken everyone out for ice cream with a sparkle in her eye. Alas, that was not the house I grew up in. The experience, however, did teach me a lot about recipes. I learned to question who wrote them and if they were any good at baking before committing resources to executing their demands.

Studying Ecclesiastes brings up a similar concern. The book claims to unpack the meaning of life and to teach us how to live well in a broken world. Those are big topics. So who wrote this book? And do they know what they're talking about?

Fortunately for our study, the first thing we encounter in Ecclesiastes is a claim of authorship. Ecclesiastes 1:1 states,

¹ *The words of the Teacher of the Assembly, David's son, king in Jerusalem:*[4]

For most of my life, I believed that the famous King Solomon had been

---

4   Unless otherwise indicated, all biblical quotations are taken from the Common English Bible (CEB).

the author of Ecclesiastes. This first verse seemed to support that idea since Solomon was one of David's better-known sons.

When I began to seriously study this book, I consulted numerous commentaries as well as a translator's handbook, and many of them assured me that in the original Hebrew, the language emphasizes that the author was in fact *the* son of David, not *a* son of David.[5] In other words, the author was David's most prominent son, the one who succeeded him on the throne—Solomon.

Jewish and early Christian tradition also identified this son as Solomon, my Sunday school teachers taught it that way to me as a child, and most Bibles with brief introductions to the biblical books put him down as the author as well. There are references to Solomon's reign, wealth, and wisdom later in the book, which also support that claim. As a result, my childhood understanding looked solid.

It didn't take me long, however, to stumble into a jungle of modern criticism that took issue with the idea that Solomon was the literal author. The reasoning in these texts was complex, even for scholarly articles, and it took some serious effort on my part not to quit my study at verse one. Making practical head or tail of academic infighting quickly becomes exhausting.[6]

However, here I'm focused on what God is communicating to us through the book of Ecclesiastes in light of the events of Solomon's life—his activities, accomplishments, and failures. From that standpoint, it doesn't matter if Solomon was the literal writer. Solomon could have spoken these teachings aloud, and a listener could have digested his words and written them down years later. Perhaps Solomon wrote several texts and a later editor stitched those various unpublished works together into this book. How God put the book's message together is beside the point. The scholarly jungle awaits if you're interested in that kind of study.

However, once you boil all that theory, analysis, and outright speculation down and emerge from the academic jungle with a conclusion on the authorship, the same profoundly engaging and surprising book awaits. The

---

5   Graham S. Ogden and Lynell Zogbo, *A Handbook on Ecclesiastes* (New York: United Bible Societies, 1998), p. 20.

6   Solomon himself says essentially the same thing at the end of Ecclesiastes in 12:12.

book takes an unflinching look at life and offers wisdom as relevant today as when it was written. And the writer, whether it was literally Solomon or not, wants us to read this book through the lens of Solomon's life and experience. As a result, identifying whose hand held the pen is pointless for practical readers.

All that to say, I'm going to call the author Solomon from now on because it's a helpful approach to understanding what God is trying to communicate here, regardless of the mechanics of how the book was physically penned and edited.

Why Solomon?

So who was this guy and why put him in charge of writing a book about the meaning of life? We'll need to dive into a bit of history here to answer that question, but bear with me. This guy has an interesting biography.

Solomon was born in the eleventh century BCE with the proverbial silver spoon in his mouth. Around the time of his birth, his father, David, finalized the last conquest of his reign by taking the Ammonite city of Rabbah.[7] The crown he took from that defeated king was made of seventy-five pounds of gold (about thirty-four kilograms) plus precious stones.[8] I think that a crown that heavy might have been a strategic blunder. It may have served the Ammonite king better, politically and medically, to have spent more effort working on nation building and international relations rather than devising a crown the weight of a child. Regardless, David conquered the Ammonites, and Israel became the region's powerhouse.

But what was it like growing up in that context in David's palace?

I can imagine Solomon talking with someone at some point about how his parents met. He may have asked one of his parents, his nurse, or perhaps one of his older half siblings. *Wait—Solomon had half siblings?* you might ask. Yeah, well, that's where Solomon's silver spoon starts to look a little tarnished.

Solomon's mom was David's eighth wife. Right away, you know there must be a story there. That story gets even more dramatic when we remember Solomon's mom's name was Bathsheba. This marriage was originally an

---

7   See 2 Samuel 12 for the full story.

8   2 Samuel 12:30, NIV.

adulterous affair that led to the murder of Bathsheba's first husband and the death of David and Bathsheba's first child, Solomon's older full sibling.

This discussion could quickly morph into endless digressions about David's family line, so let's not get too lost in the backstory. A few highlights, though, will help paint the picture of Solomon's not-so-silver-spoon childhood. First, his older half brother Amnon raped his half sister Tamar. David, as both father and king, did nothing about this horrible crime. Another half brother named Absalom eventually took matters into his own hands, murdered Amnon, and then led an armed rebellion against his father.[9] Absalom briefly overthrew the throne before losing a key battle and dying at the hands of David's men.[10]

Solomon's dad was a poet, a king, and the warrior famous for killing Goliath, which sounds cool, but his home life was a mess. Actually, his home life was criminal, but let's move on from this extreme domestic dysfunction.[11]

The second book of Samuel introduces God's view of the newborn Solomon, despite the circumstances of his birth.

The Lord loved him [25] *and sent word by the prophet Nathan to name him Jedidiah because of the Lord's grace.*

2 SAMUEL 12:24B–25

As the CEB notes, the name "Jedidiah" means "Loved by the Lord."[12] The poor kid would need God's love to survive his family life.

And right there, I think, is one key reason why God chose Solomon as his point of view for Ecclesiastes. Modern psychology offers much insight into how growing up in a dysfunctional family can shape a heart's hunger

---

9   See 2 Samuel 13 for the full story.

10   See 2 Samuel 15–18 for the story of Absalom's revolt and eventual defeat.

11   For readers offended by this unflattering portrayal of David's family life, in addition to reading 2 Samuel carefully, you may find value in North Coast Church's excellent forty-six-week sermon series on this topic. It is available online at this site and address: "David: The Pride, Priorities, and Passions in the Palace; 1st & 2nd Samuel," North Coast Church (website), uploaded January 8–November 19, 2022, *https://www.northcoastchurch.com/david-1st-2nd-samuel/*.

12   2 Samuel 12:25, CEB footnote b.

later in life. God didn't need modern psychology to know this. God made the human heart. God chose Solomon when he was just a newborn.

But there's more. First Kings provides further insight into how Solomon's good character and bad upbringing comingled in both positive and negative ways.

On the negative side of the ledger, Solomon kicked off his reign by embarking on several violations of God's law: he murdered a half brother for political reasons,[13] married the daughter of the Egyptian Pharaoh Shoshenq I,[14] and conscripted tens of thousands into forced labor gangs to help him achieve his personal and political ambitions.[15] Think slaves operating in mines and other dangerous, back-breaking, inhuman conditions, and you get the idea of how ruthless Solomon could be.

The positive side of Solomon's ledger is also a bit of a mixed story. For example:

> [3] *Now Solomon loved the Lord by walking in the laws of his father David, with the exception that he also sacrificed and burned incense at the shrines.*
>
> 1 KINGS 3:3

So was he worshipping God at these shrines? In other words, did he have the right idea but the wrong procedure? Or was he worshipping idols at these shrines? The passage doesn't say, but it does make it clear that this was a flaw. He loved God and was doing well at this early stage, except for this detail.

Regardless, God demonstrates his characteristic grace by coming to Solomon with an amazing offer. In 1 Kings 3:5, God says to Solomon, "Ask whatever you wish, and I'll give it to you." Solomon asks for wisdom, and

---

13   1 Kings 2:25.

14   1 Kings 3:1.

15   1 Kings 9:15–21.

¹⁰ It pleased the Lord that Solomon had made this request. ¹¹ God said to him, "Because you have asked for this instead of requesting long life, wealth, or victory over your enemies— asking for discernment so as to acquire good judgment— ¹² I will now do just what you said. Look, I hereby give you a wise and understanding mind. There has been no one like you before now, nor will there be anyone like you afterward. ¹³ I now also give you what you didn't ask for: wealth and fame. There won't be a king like you as long as you live. ¹⁴ And if you walk in my ways and obey my laws and commands, just as your father David did, then I will give you a very long life."

1 KINGS 3:10–14

The result was a wealthy, famous man renowned for physical and intellectual achievements in areas as diverse as architecture, landscape and interior design, botany, literature, zoology, entomology, international relations, and ornithology.[16]

He also went a bit bananas in the marriage department and a few other areas of life, but we'll talk about that later. The bottom line for our purposes is that he was a guy from an incredibly dysfunctional family who somehow found favor in God's eyes and was blessed in adulthood with every resource imaginable to make meaning out of his earthly life. Ecclesiastes records this eminently qualified man's search for earthly meaning.

As we'll discover as we go through this book, Solomon was not only rich, wise, and famous—he was also a detail-oriented guy. If Solomon had written a recipe for a fancy chocolate cake, he'd have noted the measurements accurately. This is a guy who knew how to put a life plan together.

---

16   For example, see 1 Kings 4:29–34.

2

HEVEL AND THE MEANING OF LIFE

THE ONE THING I'll say in favor of the pre-internet world of handwritten recipe cards is that they got straight to the point. Unlike modern foodie blogs, the German chocolate cake's three-by-five-inch recipe card stated right up front what kind of cake it was trying to help you bake and then immediately listed the ingredients and directions. There was no preamble about the history of Germany, cultural significance of cakes, or how cocoa is processed in various parts of the world.

In the introduction, I described Ecclesiastes as a flower planted on Job's foundation. Job offers lessons on survival and Ecclesiastes provides guidance on practical living. But would Solomon agree with such use of his material? And if so, does he divulge life's secrets early in Ecclesiastes, or does he like to spend a lot of time in preamble before he gets to his point?

It turns out that Solomon was a no-nonsense sort of guy who states his conclusion right at the beginning.

> ² *Perfectly pointless, says the Teacher, perfectly pointless.*
> *Everything is pointless.*
>
> ECCLESIASTES 1:2

Pointless? If everything is not only pointless but "perfectly pointless," then this clearly isn't a book that will teach us anything about practical living or the meaning of life unless depression is our goal. Solomon perhaps needed a therapist, and I needed to find another source of inspiration.

If that's what Solomon meant to communicate at the start of his book, my study would have ended at verse two.

On the surface, my study did seem to be in trouble. Solomon repeats himself twelve verses later: "everything is pointless" (1:14). Chapter one uses that "pointless" word four times. When we get to chapter two, we might hope that Solomon backs off this defeated assessment of reality, but instead, he doubles down on his theme, using the word "pointless" eight times.

Ecclesiastes is only twelve chapters long, and in these twelve chapters, "pointless" shows up a total of thirty-four times. The root word and its derivatives appear thirty-eight times in the original Hebrew.[17] Defining everything as "pointless" is the primary theme of Solomon's book.[18]

Some readers may be more familiar with other translations of the word that the Common English Bible (CEB) translates as "pointless." The New International Version (NIV) translates the Hebrew as "meaningless," as do at least two other English translations. The King James Version (KJV) renders it as "vanity," the most common choice, appearing in at least seventeen English translations. Three translations, including our chosen CEB version, use "pointless." This all adds up to a rather bleak theme for a book I hoped would help me understand how to live life better in this complicated and often troublesome world.

If everything is perfectly pointless, useless, meaningless, or vain, then why bother reading the book of Ecclesiastes at all? If we take Solomon's words at face value, Ecclesiastes is just another useless, pointless, and meaningless thing. There is no help for us here or anywhere.

Ah, but here is where our study gets very interesting.

In the original Hebrew, the word we're discussing, is *hevel*. The term is translated as "pointless" by the CEB, but that is not the word's literal meaning. *Hevel* is the ancient Hebrew word for "breath." It can also mean "vapor."[19] For those of you from cold climates, think about how we can see our breath on a wintry day, and the vapor definition makes perfect sense.

---

17   Ogden and Zogbo, *A Handbook on Ecclesiastes*, p. 2.

18   William P. Brown, *Ecclesiastes: Interpretation; A Commentary for Teaching and Preaching* (Louisville: Westminster John Knox Press, 2011), p. 21.

19   Except where otherwise noted, all references to other Old Testament uses of *hevel* in this chapter are courtesy of Ogden and Zogbo, *A Handbook on Ecclesiastes*, p. 3.

Here is the word *hevel* in a passage from Isaiah that discusses idol worship:

> *13 When you cry out,*
>   *let those things you've gathered save you!*
> *The wind will lift them all;*
>   *one breath will take them away,*
>
> *but those taking refuge in me will inherit the land and possess*
> *my holy mountain.*
>
> ISAIAH 57:13

Do you see the word "pointless" or its synonyms anywhere in the above quote? No. It's not there. In Isaiah, the CEB and other English translations correctly translate *hevel* as "breath."

Occasionally, translators will get a bit creative when they translate *hevel*. In the following example, the translators swapped out "breath" in favor of the more evocative phrase "puff of air."

> *33 So God brought their days to an end,*
>   *like a puff of air,*
>   *and their years in total ruin.*
>
> PSALM 78:33

Here's another example where the translation is even more creative.

> *6 Those who gain treasure with lies*
>   *are like a drifting fog, leading to death.*
>
> PROVERBS 21:6

"Drifting fog" here is the Hebrew word *hevel*. Presumably, the translators were thinking of the "vapor" option in their translator's handbook and assumed a cold day for Proverbs 21.

Here are two more examples. One sticks with translating *hevel* as "breath," and the other returns to that creative "puff of air" option.

> *⁹ Human beings are nothing but a breath.*
> *Human beings are nothing but lies.*
> *They don't even register on a scale;*
> *taken all together they are lighter than a breath!*
>
> PSALM 62:9

> *⁴ Humans are like a puff of air;*
> *their days go by like a shadow.*
>
> PSALM 144:4[20]

Let's pause for a minute, return to Ecclesiastes, and reread this key verse with this proper definition in mind.

> *² Perfectly breath, says the Teacher, perfectly breath. Everything is breath.*
>
> ECCLESIASTES 1:2

Okay, that sounds weird. Perfectly breath? What in the world is that supposed to mean?

Alright, we've got another translation problem. The word "perfectly" isn't in the original Hebrew text either. Here is what is in the Hebrew text:

> *² Hevel of hevels, says the Teacher, hevel of hevels. Everything is hevel.*
>
> ECCLESIASTES 1:2

Hevel of *hevels*. Breath of breaths. Repeating two words, first in the singular, then in the plural, is an ancient Hebrew way of saying that something is the ultimate of its kind—for example, the king of kings, song of songs, and lord of lords.

Solomon starts his book by saying this is the biggest breath there is. This is the ultimate breath, and by the way, everything is breath. Everything. This is huge. This is the most profound breath of them all.

---

20   For this example, I am indebted to: Michael V. Fox, *The JPS Bible Commentary: Ecclesiastes* (Philadelphia: The Jewish Publication Society, 2004), p. 3.

Oh. Okay, let's put that in English again, but this time in a way that conveys Solomon's original intention.

> [2] *Breath of breaths, says the Teacher, breath of breaths. Everything is breath.*
>
> ECCLESIASTES 1:2

Okay, now I've got a question for you. Is breath pointless?

Umm. No. Without breath, you die.

Is it meaningless? Again, no.

Is it vain or useless? Okay, you get the idea.

So what happened in our English Bibles? How did "breath of breaths, the ultimate breath, the biggest breath there is, the king of all breaths, everything is this super important breath" suddenly become pointless, meaningless, and all the other bad choices in our English translations?

To answer that question, you'd have to return to the late Roman Empire, where a young village lad named Jerome of Stridon was busy being a rebellious schoolboy and getting involved in scandalous sexual escapades.[21] He did learn Latin but did poorly at Greek and didn't learn any Hebrew at all.

Eventually, Jerome converted to Christianity, after which he travelled to a place that today we call northern Syria to start a life that, for the sake of simplicity, we'll describe as a monk's life. Curiously, he spent his Sundays in local crypts—underground graveyard tunnels—paying his respects to Christian martyrs to appease his conscience for his schoolboy misdeeds. How knocking around decaying bones in pitch-black darkness resolved old regrets is a matter you'd have to discuss with Jerome.[22]

Along the way, Jerome belatedly studied Greek, then finally Hebrew, made his way back to Rome, got connected to the pope, was commissioned to do an original translation of the entire Bible into Latin, and eventually was declared a saint. He achieved sainthood despite the notice that "Jerome's

---

21 For the biographical sketch of Jerome that follows, I am indebted to: Robert Payne, *The Fathers of the Western Church* (New York: Viking Press, 1951). For Jerome's biography, I am also indebted to: Stefan Rebenich, *Jerome* (New York: Routledge, 2002), pp. 87–137.

22 Payne, *Fathers of the Western Church*, p. 92 offers an English translation of Jerome's first-person account of these crypts.

character was one of violence; he was given to boastfulness and in controversies was vehement not to say scurrilous. He is often said to be the one saint canonized for his learning in spite of his character."[23]

You might think that quote describing Jerome as violent and of poor character to be a bit bold, but it might help to understand a little more about the man and his times to put that quote into context.

In the late fourth century, the Christian world was in turmoil as various sects sought to dominate.[24] What is relevant to our discussion is simply that during this period of religious turmoil, and before his Bible translation assignment, Jerome became an impassioned theological radical, aggressively insisting on a severely ascetic style of Christianity that chose deliberate self-injury as the true path to worshipping God. As Rebenich puts it, "[h]e had no companions but scorpions and wild beasts. He slept on the bare ground, drank only water, and spurned cooked foods as an unacceptable luxury. He mortified a body tormented by dancing girls. He subdued his rebellious flesh with weeks of fasting."[25] Or, as Rebenich adds, that's how Jerome liked to describe himself once he got on the ascetic sales circuit.

Let's hear how Jerome himself described this era.

> *Oh, how often, when I was living in the desert, in the vast solitude, scorched by the burning sun, which offers monks a savage dwelling place, how often did I imagine myself back among the pleasures of Rome. I used to sit alone because I was filled with bitterness. My unshapely limbs were covered in sackcloth and my skin from long neglect had become black as an Ethiopian's. Tears and groans were my every day portion; and if sleep chanced to overcome my struggles against it, I bruised my bare bones, which hardly held together, against the ground.*[26]

---

23   Clarke F. Ansley, ed., *The Columbia Encyclopedia in One Volume* (New York: Columbia University Press, 1940), p. 925.

24   See Rebenich's volume called simply *Jerome*, which describes these movements in detail, or any other quality church history that covers the fourth century.

25   Rebenich, *Jerome*, p. 19.

26   Rebenich, *Jerome*, p. 19.

If that sounds a little over-the-top to you, possibly even like the language of a huckster trying to snowball their audience, you've got a good ear. Truth be told, Jerome spent his desert years in a town with a rich patron, likely in a villa, for sure with a suite of rooms: a library; a staff of copyists engaged in manuscript production, sales, and trading; a regular correspondence with outsiders; and in an almost constant state of confrontation with local Christians. Rebenich's scholarship provides Jerome's personal correspondence from this time of his life, which reveals just how contrary his own accounts were. He lived an existence the opposite of solitude and deprivation.[27] Jerome didn't count on ancient manuscript preservation and modern scholarship to puncture his story. Like a shameful modern-day preacher railing against immorality while conducting a secret affair, Jerome was more show than reality, and modern scholarship found him out long before the internet was invented.

What does Jerome have to do with our study of Ecclesiastes? Unfortunately, he has everything to do with our study. We call Jerome's translation of the Bible the Latin Vulgate, which turned out to be one of the more influential sources used in preparing the far later King James Version (KJV) of the Bible that we're familiar with today. The KJV then became the standard that our modern translations often defer to.

So Jerome was a fake ascetic monk bent on whipping up as much self-loathing and guilt as he could inspire in his luxury-loving Roman audience. It seems that Jerome wanted a biblical text to support his mission. *Hevel* is the key word in Ecclesiastes. If Jerome could change the meaning of *hevel* from breath to something more suited to his purposes, he could reshape Ecclesiastes as his theme text.

Here is how Jerome translated Ecclesiastes 1:2.

Vanitas vanitatum, dixit Ecclesiastes; vanitas vanitatum, et omnia vanitas.[28]

---

27 Rebenich, *Jerome*, p. 13–17.

28 See *https://vulgate.org/ot/ecclesiastes_1.htm*, accessed July 2, 2023. See also "Overview: vanitas vanitatum," Oxford Reference (website), from *The Oxford Dictionary of Phrase and Fable*, 2nd ed. (Oxford: Oxford University Press, 2006), accessed July 2, 2023, https://www.oxfordreference.com/display/10.1093/oi/authority.20110803115204999;jsessionid=BCFA56FEE4E317CACBC333E76E73D035.

If that doesn't resonate with you, no worries! I can't read Latin either. But you don't need to be a Latin scholar to guess that "vanitas vanitatum" is Latin for precisely what the KJV has in English: "vanity of vanities." The ultimate vanity. The biggest vanity of them all. I don't believe Jerome thought breath was vain, useless, pointless, and so on. But the man needed a text to support his ascetic fixation (even if he wasn't that good at actually living the lifestyle himself), so *hevel* became vanity. Thanks to Jerome, "breath" or "vapor" was translated as "vanity."[29]

With the word *hevel* redefined, we will see that the rest of the message of Ecclesiastes was subsequently bent to conform to the idea that life is pointless, meaningless, and vain. The whole book was broken by that one translation crime.[30]

It all started with Jerome.

Subsequently, the KJV copied Jerome's mistranslation into English, and hardly any English translations since have been brave enough to break with that tradition. You can find this flaw pointed out over and over again in scholarly articles, in super dry commentaries, and sometimes even in the footnotes of study Bibles. Still, it seems no one has the guts to correct the original mistranslation.

Okay, what just happened here? I mean, besides blaming Jerome.

The key issue with Jerome's translation isn't that he was being creative. "Puff of air" is creative. "Drifting fog" is being creative while remaining roughly faithful to *hevel*'s actual meaning. "Vanity" is not being creative. "Vanity" is choosing not to translate the word at all but to interpret it instead.

Let me explain.

---

29 Jerome's abuse of his Hebrew translation responsibilities may have been influenced by more than just his passion for ascetic ideals. He also genuinely disliked the Hebrew language itself and believed that "it clattered along woefully" (Payne's translation, *Fathers of the Western Church*, p. 120). The man wanted Ecclesiastes not only to say what he needed it to say but to sound the way he wanted it to sound, neither of which were faithful to the original language.

30 Jerome's scholarly flaws went beyond just a mistranslation of Ecclesiastes. Even on simple matters of historical accuracy and honest quotation, he was notorious for "twist[ing] texts to suit his meaning" (Payne pp. 117–120 for this and further examples). For readers disturbed by this issue of Bible translation reliability, I would recommend digging in rather than running away. The Bible is a book that rewards effort. It's not always an easy read, but the fact that you're reading this book (and a footnote at that!) is a wonderful act of digging in. Well done!

If I wrote a poem and called my wife, Carolyn, a rose, you would understand that I didn't marry a plant. I mean that she's beautiful. Or maybe I mean she can be prickly or smells nice or something else that's plausibly related to the idea of a rose. It's a metaphor. The reader has to interpret the metaphor for themselves. That's part of the beauty of metaphors when used in poetry or other forms of literature.

"Breath" in Ecclesiastes is also a metaphor. Everything isn't actual literal breath. Instead, the breath metaphor points to how breath is essential but insubstantial, elusive, fleeting, temporary, impossible to pin down or grab hold of, or some other plausibly breath-like quality.

If a translator picked up my rose poem and, in another language, called my wife a pretty flower, we could debate how good a job the translator did in terms of poetic literary quality, but the basic idea is the same. However, if the translator said that she was beautiful or smelled nice, that's different. This translator isn't translating anymore but instead taking liberties and interpreting my meaning. Maybe I intended the ambiguity of multiple meanings: she's beautiful and smells nice, but she also has a few thorns you must be careful about.

Still, "Daryl's wife is beautiful" is a roughly accurate interpretation of what I probably meant.

If the translator instead took that rose poem about my wife and translated it as "Carolyn is a violinist," the only response I would have is, "What? Violinist? No, she's not. What does 'Carolyn is a rose' have to do with violins?"

And that's my issue with translating *hevel* to a word that means "pointless," which is an interpretation with no relationship to the original metaphor. If you're going to interpret the metaphor, at least make the interpretation plausible. A rose can mean "beautiful" or "smells nice," but a rose never means "violinist." Likewise, "breath" can mean essential to life, elusive, fleeting, or many other things, but it is never pointless, meaningless, or vain.

Let me repeat this: breath is never pointless, meaningless, or vain. On the contrary, breath is incredibly meaningful—it is essential to life. It just happens to also be elusive and fleeting—but still meaningful.

Okay, now that we understand that *hevel* is a metaphor and understand what it means, here are a couple of options for how this verse should have been translated.

Breath of breaths, says the Teacher, breath of breaths. Everything is breath.

Vapor of vapors, says the Teacher, absolute vapor. Everything is vapor.

If, on the other hand, we want to partake in the interpretative freedom that a poetic metaphor provides, we might say:

Important and fragile, says the Teacher, utterly important and fragile. Everything is important and fragile.

Mystical and fleeting, says the Teacher, absolutely mystical and fleeting. Everything is mystical and fleeting.

A rose can mean many things, but it's never a violin. *Hevel* can mean many things, but it's never pointless or meaningless or vain.

If this idea that you as a reader are responsible for interpreting scripture for yourself is a new and uncomfortable idea, my translator's handbook offers up two scholarly interpretation options you can rely on.[31]

Mysterious, says the Teacher, utterly mysterious. Everything is mysterious.

Enigmatic, says the Teacher, seriously enigmatic. Everything is enigmatic.

ECCLESIASTES 1:2

Hevel. Just like the difference between *lbs* and *tbs* on an old-school chocolate cake recipe, the translation of this one word is crucial to understanding Ecclesiastes. As with my preteen baking disaster, if you misunderstand *hevel*, you misunderstand the entire book. The cake is ruined by one repeated error.

Ecclesiastes will read differently to you now that you know everything is not pointless, meaningless, or vain. Let's be done with Jerome's weird personal agenda. Life is *hevel*. It is meaningful, temporary, fragile, life-giving, fleeting, enigmatic, and mysterious.

It is breath.

Hevel.

---

31   Ogden and Zogbo, *A Handbook on Ecclesiastes*, p. 4.

3

SEARCHING FOR LASTING BENEFIT

I LIKED ECCLESIASTES when I first discovered it as a kid, even though I found parts of it hard to understand. Its language was provocative, and as a teen, I grinned even when the verses didn't entirely add up to a reality that my juvenile self fully recognized.

I've still got a New American Standard (NASB) copy of the Bible that someone gave me when I was twelve. "Vanity of vanities" is the wording in the NASB. I don't think I knew what *vanity* meant, so I must have looked it up in a standard English dictionary. In the margin of that Bible, in ballpoint pen, I wrote "worthless, futile" beside verse two. I hadn't learned about commentaries and translator's handbooks yet, so I didn't know about *hevel*.

Ecclesiastes drew me in, but it also really bothered me over the years. Its pessimism at times had a cool vibe, but repeatedly, the author kept saying that everything was vain, pointless, or meaningless. My twelve-year-old clarification of "worthless, futile" didn't improve matters. I was willing to buy into the idea that sometimes things were pointless—but not everything, all the time. Surely being kind to people wasn't pointless. Loving someone wasn't meaningless. So Ecclesiastes attracted me, but it also repelled me, and somehow it managed to do both things simultaneously. I found it a strange, off-putting, yet captivating book.

The only times that Ecclesiastes one hundred percent resonated with me were when I was depressed or in some angry state in which I was willing to write off the entire universe. I might have blurted out "life sucks" or something equally juvenile. My point, however, aligned nicely with the NIV's "meaningless" translation of *hevel*. Teenage years can occasionally be like that, but a good funk is not unknown in adulthood either. I'm sure that at least some of you can relate.

When I first discovered that Solomon was saying not that everything was vain, pointless, or meaningless but that everything was breath, it was like a light switched on inside me. The writer of Ecclesiastes intentionally used a poetic metaphor with the expectation that I, as the reader, would be responsible for its interpretation. Not a professor or preacher. Not a translator, but me. We as readers are supposed to wrestle with the metaphor and find meaning that is true to the image, appropriate for the context of the book, and relevant to our own lives. With "breath" as the book's metaphorical theme, the rest of the book took on a whole kaleidoscope of new shades and meanings.

Solomon has a second thematic observation to add to his thesis that everything is *hevel*.

> [3] *What do people gain from all the hard work*
> *that they work so hard at under the sun?*
>
> ECCLESIASTES 1:3

Life is very fragile. A funeral for someone you love, or even someone you only casually knew, will shock you back to an intimate awareness of the temporary nature of our earthly existence. Life truly is like breath on a cold northern winter morning. You see it—breath on a winter's day, an acquaintance from work, a loved one—then it's gone, they're gone, and you don't know where. It seems as though the vapor, the loved one, or the acquaintance had never existed at all.

I mentioned previously that Ecclesiastes uses *hevel* and its derivatives thirty-eight times. Verse three here highlights another keyword that repeats many times in the book. That word is "gain." What do people gain in life?

"Gain" here is the Hebrew word *yithron*, and it appears ten times in Ecclesiastes.[32] More importantly, *yithron* appears at key junctures in the book's development. The word, strictly speaking, means profit or advantage, so "gain" is a good translation. In the literary context of Ecclesiastes, however,

---

32 Graham S. Ogden and Lynell Zogbo, *A Handbook on Ecclesiastes* (New York: United Bible Societies, 1998), p. 5–6.

the word always reaches for something more. We'll see this as we go deeper into the book. The translator's handbook I consulted recommended "lasting benefit" as the best translation choice.[33]

However, as I studied Ecclesiastes, I discovered that right here, at verse three, many modern sermons and books suddenly exit out of Ecclesiastes altogether and detour into the New Testament. I've listened to many sermons on Ecclesiastes that explain how Jesus provides many of the lasting benefits Solomon sought. It's as though, in answer to George's midlife crisis, I had told him to just hold on, trust in Jesus, and wait for heaven because the only lasting benefit to be found in life is that of getting to the next one.

That just wouldn't have been helpful for George, and it's not helpful for us either. Jumping straight to Jesus cheats us out of the wisdom embedded in Ecclesiastes. The book was written and preserved for a reason, and that reason wasn't to provide a shortcut to a different topic. George needed something more than heaven to look forward to. George needed to understand this life, his life, here and now, or he wouldn't hang on to his faith long enough to make it to heaven. Jackson deserved a real answer to his question and not pat religious lines. Real answers are what built his later adult faith, not dismissive shortcuts. And I needed to know how to do more than just survive long enough to catch heaven's train. I needed to know how to live well now, despite my circumstances.

In Ecclesiastes, Solomon is very focused on this world and this life. To make this focus very clear, he uses the phrase "under the sun" repeatedly. It is a phrase that does not appear in the rest of the Bible, but it (or a close equivalent) occurs seven times in this book.[34] The phrase means "on earth" or "in this world." Ecclesiastes is explicitly, insistently, and repetitively focused on dealing with earthly life, here and now.

So, what have we learned so far? Solomon's key thesis in Ecclesiastes is that all of life is *hevel* (breath), and as he unpacks the meaning of this metaphor, he intends to keep his focus narrowly fixed on seeking lasting benefit relevant to this mortal life. This is a book about how to live well, now, without giving heaven a great deal of attention.

Before we go on, I'd like to provide a bit more background on my state of

---

33   Ogden and Zogbo, *A Handbook on Ecclesiastes*, p. 5.

34   Ogden and Zogbo, *A Handbook on Ecclesiastes*, p. 24.

mind and life circumstances that prompted my focused study of Ecclesiastes. As I alluded to in the introduction, something was wrong.

Life for me had hit a crossroads. It was not the faith crossroads that had led to my study of Job and writing *Even the Monsters* but a satisfaction crossroads. I had learned to accept the medical and emotional challenges God had chosen for our lives, but I had lost the ability to enjoy life amid those challenges.

I needed the first step that Job offered—to learn to trust God even when monsters stalked my world. But once I learned to trust God, how could I enjoy life when it seemed to be an unending existence of compounding traumas and heartless situations that demand constant endurance? Trust and dissatisfaction had become tense copilots in my heart. I believed and so could endure—but was it possible, while enduring, to smile?

As we continue our study of Ecclesiastes, we're going to find how there are a myriad of meanings behind *hevel*, how they apply to the challenge of finding lasting benefit in this mortal life, and how this ancient wisdom applies to suffering hearts and troubled souls today.

The book of Job saved my life. *Even the Monsters* covers that.

Ecclesiastes saved my days. Let me explain.

4

THE PERSONAL NEED FOR SOMETHING MORE

"Daryl, I can't be your heaven."

I had asked my wife for something one day amid the seemingly unending grind that our entwined lives had become by that point. I was undoubtedly sleep deprived but also soul deprived, joy deprived, and consequently a bit depressed. I don't remember precisely what I asked of her, but I remember her answer very clearly.

"I can't be your heaven."

She wasn't wrong.

I was hurting badly, but so was she. I needed much, but so did she. More than a decade and a half of marriage had passed by that point, but those years hadn't changed the fact that neither of us could be each other's heaven. All the same, I was angry with her for saying the truth out loud. Still, she wasn't wrong. Only heaven can be heaven.

My wife and I, however, still had to live here and now.

I don't have a specific record of what project my son and I were shopping for when he asked me his "Why am I here?" question. Nor do I remember what I did for the rest of the day after George's visit, but I know roughly what both days contained. In the early days of the global COVID-19 pandemic when there were restrictions on gatherings, people mourned the lack of contact with others, the closed businesses, the inability to travel to favorite vacation destinations, and the loss of regular family outings and events with friends.

Jackson's tenth year and the summer of George's visit would have looked to our small family a lot like the globe's COVID summer of 2020. The year before would have looked the same. And the year after. And the one after that, and so on.

When COVID-19 hit the planet, the rest of the world started living like my family had been living for nearly two decades. My wife and I cannot travel together, go out to dinner together, or even go for a walk without someone to watch our daughter—and that someone must be a registered nurse, paramedic, or medical doctor. The life-saving medications and procedures she needs on a routine basis are not something you teach a well-meaning relative or neighbour. That is not a personal decision—that's the legal status of her fragile state. We have essentially run a palliative care unit out of our home for decades. According to the medical literature, our daughter is the only person on the planet with her combination of rare diseases, and we literally save her life three to five times a week. Medical trauma is Tuesday for us. And Wednesday. It might strike during the day or in the middle of the night, but it's a rare twenty-four-hour period without a medical emergency in our home. A therapist once declared, "You live in an emergency room," and she was right. Our normal has been over twenty years of focused medical care and marital lockdown. That's not how a health crisis is supposed to work. The trauma of palliative care is usually a season measured in weeks or months, not decades.

So the restaurants were open in 2012, but we couldn't go to them together at all. Ten times the restaurant bill amount would be committed to private nursing before we even left the driveway. As a one-income family, paying five hundred dollars or more for a casual dinner at Swiss Chalet or some other modest restaurant was impossible. So we didn't go out together and hadn't for over a decade.

Our son is now in university and has never had a family vacation because Carolyn and I cannot go away with him together. My wife and I had dinner at home for our tenth, twentieth, and twenty-fifth anniversaries because that was the only option available, as it had been for all of our anniversaries since Mackenzie was born. Anniversaries or other special occasions did not change the fact that we've had medical emergencies that day, that night, the next day, and so on for two decades and counting. As a result of our daughter's condition, we don't even attend church or weddings or funerals together—we trade off the privilege. My wife goes to one, and I go to another.

The doctors did not expect Mackenzie to live past age three. As I write this, she's twenty-three years old. It's a miracle that she is still alive, but she lost a lot getting here. She's in a wheelchair now, can no longer speak, and so on. Degenerative conditions degenerate. That's how it goes.

When I speak of toil and endurance, the lives we lived (and live) go beyond the complexities of COVID-19-style restrictions and having to forgo vacations or special dinners for two decades and counting. For example, the reality of our daughter's medical condition is such that we don't sleep at night. As a result, we struggle to function during the day on no more than two or three hours of uninterrupted rest (if things go well). If one spouse does sleep for five or six hours, it's at the expense of the other. Exhaustion sometimes makes one of us deaf, and the other carries the night burden alone through the darkest hours. Both my wife and I have tackled life-saving procedures at two in the morning solo while the other slept. That means straddling a badly seizing young woman and pinning her violence down with legs and one hand so the other can handle the syringe with its load of dangerous drugs. The whole procedure can take half an hour or more, from the seizure's start to its eventual resolution. When you bolt out of bed at two in the morning, save a life through a combination of fear, training, physical dominance, and careful adherence to all the necessary medical steps—well, the adrenalin rush of that experience doesn't go away in a few minutes. You lie awake for hours afterward with a heart that both pounds and breaks within you.

I don't share these details as a misery catalogue to make you feel sorry for us but rather to help explain why the message of Ecclesiastes was so important to me. This was a deeply personal study for me, not merely an academic exercise. When I began to study this book, I resolved to apply every tool and method I had used in my study of Job. I would leave no stone unturned.

If Ecclesiastes could teach me how to live and tell me how to gain a lasting benefit for all the toil at which I toil under the sun (Eccles. 1:3), maybe I could learn to smile again. And if it couldn't, why was this book in the Bible? I had become intimate with toil and endurance due to life circumstances and my study of Job. Enjoyment of life, however, was a foreign country and a seemingly impossible goal. Proverbs 13:12 says, "Hope delayed makes the heart sick; longing fulfilled is a tree of life." I needed some of that long-ing-fulfilled, tree-of-life business. My heart, though trusting, had grown sick.

At first glance, it may seem that within my context of long-term suffering and endurance, learning to enjoy life was a silly ambition. When executing life-saving procedures multiple times a week fills your calendar in addition to your regular day job, parenting, and general household tasks, enjoying life hardly ranks as a priority. And so it often happens that people who face a loved one's terminal illness or some other time-limiting crisis operate in this manner. They suffer for weeks, months, or even a few years, and then there's a funeral and a grieving period. And then life moves on. The grieving process continues, but there is change. For other trials, the job loss becomes a new job, the broken friendship gets replaced, the divorce is finally over, and old sorrows become memories or hurts to grieve. Compared to old hurts—even the ones that linger and struggle to heal—suffering a fresh wound day after day after day after day for decades on end is an entirely different creature. It's not PTSD (post-traumatic stress disorder) when you never get to the *P* part. You're never post. The trauma is refreshed daily and nightly.

The human heart cannot go on for decades with only trust and grim endurance to carry it. Life never blossoms if we merely survive. I began to study Ecclesiastes because I didn't want to just survive anymore—I wanted to live.

Like my friend George, I needed something more.

5

THE UNIVERSAL NEED FOR SOMETHING MORE

IMAGINE SOLOMON SITTING at his desk, having penned those first few lines about *hevel* and *yithron* and life under the sun, and then thinking about what to write next. Imagine him looking around. He's the king. It's a palace. Palaces are full of people. The palace is in Jerusalem, which is also full of people. He's an old man at this point. He's lived an amazing life. God granted him immense wisdom—the Bible declares him the wisest man ever. He spent seven years building the original Jewish temple. It would have been one of the wonders of the ancient world if the Babylonians hadn't destroyed it some generations later, well before Herodotus got around to recording the first of several lists of such architectural achievements. Solomon spent almost twice that amount of time building his palace on an even grander scale. Between the temple and palace flowed crowds of Jews and foreign traders, manual laborers, merchants, and even visiting dignitaries. In Solomon's day, Jerusalem was a kind of Paris or Rome—famed for its architecture, culture, and learning. Mining interests, international trade networks, and craft guilds populated by skilled woodworkers and stonemasons and many other trades contributed to making the city a hive of activity and wealth.

What does an old man, sitting at his desk, write about with that view?

> *⁴ A generation goes, and a generation comes,*
> *but the earth remains as it always has.*
>
> ECCLESIASTES 1:4

Interestingly, he says, "A generation goes, and a generation comes." That's not the natural way to say that phrase. It should be that a generation comes, then it goes. That's how generations work. Something can't go away before it's born to begin with. It must come, then it can go. But Solomon wrote this carefully and intentionally. He's not interested in a distant, academic, or objectively accurate view of reality. He is interested in his view. He's an old man. He's looking out the window, seeing old people and young people together on the streets, and his observation about the older people is that they are his people—a generation that is going. That's his starting point. While his generation fades away, another is replacing it. Meanwhile, the earth stays the same.

This opening line foreshadows thoughts about mortality that will come later in the book, but having touched on the impermanence of generations (with a focus on his own) and the comparative permanence of the earth, Solomon gives the topic of nature a bit more attention.

> *⁵ The sun rises, the sun sets;*
> *it returns panting to the place where it dawns.*

Generations go and come, and so does the sun. Then, after it sets, "it returns panting to the place where it dawns." Solomon makes the sun sound a bit exhausted here. That's not accidental, as we'll see in the coming verses.

> *⁶ The wind blows to the south,*
> *goes around to the north;*
> *around and around blows the wind;*
> *the wind returns to its rounds again.*
>
> ECCLESIASTES 1:6

There are some odd things about this verse in the original Hebrew that we don't see in our English translation.

First, the word "blows," found in our English translation, is the same word translated as "goes" in 1:4. That becomes important in a moment.

The second odd thing is the sentence structure, also known as syntax. For this part to make sense, you need to know that sentences are made of three core parts. Linguists call those three parts the subject, the verb, and the object, but you can think of them as the actor, the action, and the acted upon. Look at these simple sentences: the dog chases the bird, the bird flies in the air, the car honks at the dog. Each of them has those three parts: the dog (actor) chases (action) the bird (acted-upon object). All languages have these three core parts of a sentence, but in different languages, the order of these parts can change.

For Star Wars fans, that's what's weird about Yoda's speech. He often says things with the words out of order. "Decide you must how to serve them best," Yoda tells Luke at one point. A typical English speaker would say, "You must decide how best to serve them." In typical English statements, the actor (subject) always comes first, the action (verb) second, and the acted-upon (object) third. The same is true in Hebrew.

Take a look at the third line in Ecclesiastes 1:6: "around and around blows the wind." The subject—"wind"—appears at the end of the verse, not at the beginning, which makes the line sound odd to both English and Hebrew ears. Also, remember that the word "blows" is just the common Hebrew word for "goes," so the sentence gives us no hint about what is going around in various directions before we finally get to that word "wind" at the end.[35] Additionally, this "goes" verb is built into a phrase that in English would read as "goes round and round." That four-word verb phrase appears four times before we finally get to the subject and find out that it's the wind doing all of this circling. Here's how this might look in a more literal English translation:

---

35   For further details on this literary peculiarity, see Ogden and Zogbo, *A Handbook on Ecclesiastes*, pp. 29–30.

Goes round and round to the south, goes round and round to the north; goes round and round and goes round and round the wind.[36]

ECCLESIASTES 1:6

Wading through those repetitive verbs while waiting to find out what we're talking about can wear on a reader. That's Solomon trying to make you feel something. He's an old man, and his generation is going, and the sun is going but will come back, and the wind is going and will also come back. The whole world is moving, but nothing is materially changing besides swapping one generation out for another.

Solomon builds on this image of creation's repetitive nature by talking about the water cycle.

> [7] *All streams flow to the sea,*
> *but the sea is never full;*
> *to the place where the rivers flow,*
> *there they continue to flow.*

ECCLESIASTES 1:7

Unlike his father, David, who penned many expressive Psalms about the beauty of nature, Solomon seems to experience weariness rather than awe when viewing nature. Fleeting glimpses of beauty are insufficient when the mind struggles to find lasting benefit in this life. There has to be something more substantial to life than nice scenery. Solomon could also not be satisfied with just pretty words. Both poems and sunsets wearied him. His need was bigger than these trivialities. He needed something more. That's not just my opinion of this ancient king's state of mind. He says so himself in the following verses.

---

36 Author's own translation, adapted from: Ogden and Zogbo, *A Handbook on Ecclesiastes*, pp. 29–30; and Tremper Longman III, *The Book of Ecclesiastes*, The New International Commentary on the New Testament (Grand Rapids: William B. Eerdmans Publishing Company, 1998), pp. 69–70.

⁸ All words are tiring;
    no one is able to speak.
    The eye isn't satisfied with seeing,
    neither is the ear filled up by hearing.

⁹ Whatever has happened—that's what will happen again;
    whatever has occurred—that's what will occur again.
    There's nothing new under the sun. ¹⁰ People may say about
    something: "Look at this! It's new!" But it was already
    around for ages before us.
ECCLESIASTES 1:8–10

For Solomon, nature's wonders had become routine—a physical demonstration of the practical experience of human generations passing through their life stages.

That phrase "no one is able to speak" expresses the idea that various human senses and abilities had failed to provide satisfaction. In the previous verse, the rivers flowed, but the sea never filled. Similarly, a person can speak, but the words just tire that person out. You can't talk yourself to satisfaction any more than you can see enough to never want to see again or hear enough to never want to hear again. Speaking, seeing, and hearing are never done, just like the cyclical movements of nature: the sun is never done, the wind is never done, and the water is never done.

Everything is breath. Like the cycles of nature, your breathing is never done (until you die). You can't take one deep breath and then say, "Oh, that was an excellent breath. I think I'll stop breathing now." You will take about seven hundred million breaths in your life. It's a very repetitive habit we're all born with.

The bit about there being nothing new under the sun isn't Solomon making a grand statement about computers or space travel. Solomon is writing in roughly 1,000 BCE, and he himself had built new things. He was probably writing this book in a palace he designed and paid for, and it hadn't existed before he made it.

His point is not that there is literally nothing new in an absolute sense but that life is cyclical and endlessly repetitive. Like the confusing phrase "goes round and round the wind" that doesn't tell us what is going round and round until the end of the verse, life is also rather confusing, and we often don't find out what it's all about until it's over. Any given day, week, or year, there seems to be a lot of going round and round, and all that activity serves no apparent purpose. The most prosperous or interesting or beautiful person in the world—the most inventive person—will die like everyone else. There is nothing new.

Solomon follows up this observation by circling back to the idea of generations again.

> [11] *There's no remembrance of things in the past, nor of things to come in the future. Neither will there be any remembrance among those who come along in the future.*
>
> ECCLESIASTES 1:11

In other words, life is not only fleeting and fragile (*hevel*) but it is also quickly forgotten. In this context, where can lasting benefit be found? Where can it be found, especially considering the transitory nature of individual lives and entire generations? It's not just my life that is breath—briefly visible (if the weather is cold enough), repetitive, and then gone—but my entire generation is similarly temporary, and yours is too. Solomon's idea here is that you might get more vacation time and less medical stress than me (or the opposite might be true depending on your circumstances), but we're both equally gone at the end of our lives.

As I described in chapter four, my need for Ecclesiastes was very personal. Solomon's need, as described here, is universal.

As if to underscore both the universal and personal nature of this quest for meaning, Ecclesiastes provides us with a reminder regarding the book's authorship.

> [12] *I am the Teacher. I was king over Israel in Jerusalem.*
>
> [13] *I applied my mind to investigate and to explore by wisdom all that happens under heaven. It's an unhappy obsession that God has given to human beings.*
>
> [14] *When I observed all that happens under the sun, I realized that everything is pointless, a chasing after wind.*

¹⁵ What's crooked can't be straightened;
  what isn't there can't be counted.

¹⁶ I said to myself, Look here, I have grown much wiser than any who ruled over Jerusalem before me. My mind has absorbed great wisdom and knowledge. ¹⁷ But when I set my mind to understand wisdom, and also to understand madness and folly, I realized that this too was just wind chasing.

¹⁸ Remember:
  In much wisdom is much aggravation;
  the more knowledge, the more pain.

ECCLESIASTES 1:12–18

Only one man in history was a son of David and a king of Israel in Jerusalem. After Solomon's reign, Israel broke up into two separate and sometimes warring kingdoms. The northern kingdom kept the name of Israel and had its own line of kings. The southern kingdom, where Jerusalem was the capital, adopted the name Judea.

Nobody else in history was David's son and king over all of Israel in Jerusalem.

Okay, case settled. Whether Solomon literally wrote the text, spoke words that others wrote down, or inspired some other writing method, God's clear intention was to provide us with Ecclesiastes from Solomon's point of view.

So with Solomon's perspective as a bold and unflinching context, where can lasting benefit be found under the sun? That's what I and Jackson and George needed to know. I had learned to trust God and survive. Now I needed to learn how to do more—to thrive. And Solomon was the guy to show me the way.

6

THERE IS NO ONE-SIZE-FITS-ALL ANSWER TO LIFE'S COMPLEXITIES

WHEN JACKSON ASKED me his "What am I here for?" question, I'm pretty sure he wanted a short paragraph or a couple of bullets that concisely explained exactly what he personally was here for. When we simplify that big question into smaller ones, the internet is good at analyzing the larger population and giving us those quick summary answers. With a quick online search, you can find the top restaurants in your area, the best choice of a new dishwasher, or a new place to get your hair cut. The challenge, of course, is that five searches might yield five different results depending on which search engine you use, who is paying for sponsored content today, and a variety of other factors. Answers to existential questions are even harder to pin down.

My conversation with George was successful not because I gave him a complete answer in ten minutes. All I gave George were the keys to start his own work in Ecclesiastes. For that conversation, though, keys were enough.

Keys on their own, however, are completely useless if we don't know how to use them or can't find the door or the keyhole.

The book of Ecclesiastes is a book of keys, but it's also a book about learning how to recognize doors and keyholes and how to use those keys differently depending on the lock we're facing. I live with a history and ongoing experience of complex trauma—medical and other sorts. Your journey is likely different. Perhaps economic challenges dominate your life or political stresses, oppression, relationship dysfunction, or other concerns. Ecclesiastes describes all these doors and locks and shows us how to use the keys it provides to effectively deal with them sufficiently to find *yithron* (lasting benefit) under the sun.

The quest we're on here, however, is not an easy one. Solomon describes it this way:

> *¹² I am the Teacher. I was king over Israel in Jerusalem.*
>
> *¹³ I applied my mind to investigate and to explore by wisdom all that happens under heaven. It's an unhappy obsession that God has given to human beings.*
>
> ECCLESIASTES 1:12–13

As the king, Solomon set himself on a mission to understand everything that goes on under heaven, meaning on planet Earth. But once he states that as his mission, he gives us the odd second half of verse thirteen. "It's an unhappy obsession that God has given to human beings." What's an unhappy obsession? The NASB I grew up with translates this as a "grievous task," and the KJV says "sore travail." I like the NIV translation best. It renders this detail as a "heavy burden," which my translator's handbook supports, but none of that defines what exactly this heavy burden, sore travail, or unhappy obsession is.

This jump-cut, stream-of-consciousness, and topic-shifting writing style will characterize much of Ecclesiastes. Somewhat like Job, this book is a discovery book. Solomon wanders. He states a firm idea that he will contradict a few chapters later. Biblical wisdom literature is like that. For example, in one place, Proverbs says:

> *⁴ Don't answer fools according to their folly,*
> *   or you will become like them yourself.*
>
> PROVERBS 26:4

And then, in the very next verse, it says:

> *⁵ Answer fools according to their folly,*
> *   or they will deem themselves wise.*
>
> PROVERBS 26:5

Well, which is it? Do I answer or ignore? One clever soul told me I needed to read the rest of Proverbs to discover the answer to that riddle. That sounded wise until I read the rest of Proverbs and still didn't get a straight answer. "It depends" might be the best answer, but that's not a line you'll find anywhere in the Bible. Instead, you'll get Proverbs 26:4 followed by 26:5, and you, the reader, will be left to puzzle it out on your own.

That's not an editorial error. Wisdom literature is designed to make you think and often declines to hand you nicely packaged solutions. For the writers of wisdom literature, making readers and listeners think is what matters. The focus is on the thought process, not the facts. Getting the answers right on a divine quiz is not the point.

This is just one example of why *hevel* is the book's key word. Everything is breath, vapor. It's a metaphor. You figure out what it means in any given situation. Are things fleeting, insubstantial, precious, essential, temporary, vague, or mysterious? Which is it? Or is it a combination of these interpretations? Solomon's answer to a straightforward question like that would be "Yes," and then he would walk away.

The whole metaphor applies. Every interpretation of the metaphor doesn't apply in every situation, of course—the reader has to make that call on their own. That's how metaphors work. They require effort.

Wisdom literature requires effort. It is designed to make you think.

Okay, so we started Ecclesiastes 1:12–13 reminding ourselves about who the author was (king, scholar, generally capable wisdom explorer who grew up in a dysfunctional family and made a lot of mistakes of his own) and his mission (understand everything he can about life in this world). Then this bit about an unhappy obsession or heavy burden appears. What's that about?

Solomon's idea here is that the need to find meaning in life is itself a heavy burden. Why can't we be like dogs, bouncing around throughout our days and not worrying so much about the meaning of life?

Some modern-day gurus would suggest that this is exactly what we should do. "Turn on, tune in, drop out" was Timothy Leary's advice in the 1960s on an album that mixed psychedelic rock with narrated meditation. It was also the title of one of his books, the motto of his League for Spiritual Discovery—which was dedicated to legalizing LSD,—and so on. Leary got a lot of mileage out of that line.

Solomon's take on human existence, however, states that mature adults not overrun by Leary's drug addictions both want and need more. In fact, friends who have explored Leary's pharmaceutical life path describe those trips as just another way of searching for (or trying to escape) meaning in their lives. Their drug trips didn't resolve their need for *yithron*. Solomon was right. We're not Timothy Leary's escapists. We want something more. We want more meaning. We want our lives to be richer in a "lasting benefit" kind of way, but the journey from figuring out what we want to realizing it tangibly is not easy. It's hard. It's an "unhappy obsession," as the CEB puts it, or a "heavy burden," as the NIV phrases it.

The work Solomon describes here is a process. He is under no illusions that this burden is a once-and-done activity but instead is work that will require perseverance.

Maya Angelou's take on this idea of personal progress is helpful here: "Do the best you can until you know better. Then when you know better, do better."[37] Solomon's phrasing is a little rougher than Angelou's, but the lesson we can take from both of these teachers is that finding meaning— lasting benefit—in life requires sustained effort. There are no quick fixes or easy outs, but diligent progress is our calling.

So what is the meaning of life? Or as Jackson phrased it, "What am I here for?" The answer to both of those questions is "Well, that depends." Who you are, where you live, and what you're dealing with all shape the nature of your answer. Every door requires its own unique key. And not all doors and locks look the same.

To answer these questions for ourselves, we need access to the right keys and the training required to recognize different types of doors and locks. We've already started on that journey by acknowledging the *hevel* nature of life and the need for lasting benefit more immediate than escapist views of heaven. In other words, we've started looking for doors other than the one represented by death. Solomon warns us that this discovery is just the beginning. The work from here on is hard.

Let's get on with it.

---

37   The quote is ascribed to Maya Angelou by Oprah Winfrey in a *Washington Post* article in 1995. See "You Did What You Knew How to Do, and When You Knew Better, You Did Better," Quote Investigator, published November 30, 2022, accessed October 10, 2023, *https://quoteinvestigator.com/2022/11/30/did-better/*.

7

WE MUST LET GO OF WHAT WE CAN'T HAVE

I'VE LIVED IN thirty different places so far in life, seventeen of them before I exited my teen years. As a result, I can very clearly date memories based on where I was living at the time.

One of my earliest memories—possibly my first memory—is that of being in my maternal grandmother's kitchen and listening to Lynn Anderson's version of "(I Never Promised You a) Rose Garden" on the radio. With the song's release date as the early date bookend and moving from Ontario to British Columbia as the latest date, I know that I was between two and four years old when this memory was formed.

Another memory competes as potentially the first thing I can remember from my earliest days. This memory is one of me transplanting trees in our undeveloped front yard. Looking back, they were probably tall weeds, but as I was four years old or younger at the time, I can be forgiven for misclassifying the plants I felt were important to relocate.

Trees remain a lifelong fascination for me. This comes out in my bonsai hobby and even persuading the book designers we work with to sneak trees onto the covers of a few of my books, including this one.

Music has likewise been a lifelong obsession. I joke sometimes that I dislike German polkas and Chinese atonal music, but otherwise, I've got just about everything on my playlists: rock, country, flamenco, classical, Latin, folk, heavy metal, rap, R & B, jazz, reggae, gospel, techno, and even some very odd experimental productions that barely count as music at all. I can hear music in my head that hasn't even been made yet—improvements to existing arrangements or completely new creations—but no matter how hard I try, I can't make music myself. I've tried.

I've taken drum, piano, and guitar lessons to no avail. I took up the cornet in elementary school, played in a junior high school band for a few years, practiced faithfully for over a decade, and was never able to take the music in my head and produce it with my own horn. I was a slave to sheet music. Playing by ear and understanding music theory completely eluded me. In middle age, I tried again. I rented a guitar and tried to teach myself with YouTube videos. I was determined to make this work. At the time flamenco was my passion. I eventually stopped renting my guitar and bought a specialty flamenco model and worked hard at learning some basic songs. Eventually, I could reproduce the notes in the right order, but the sound was dead. I had no gift for music production. No matter how hard or long I try, I can't produce music. If I could have one wish, aside from wishing for world peace or my daughter's healing or something equally profound—just one fun, passionate wish—it would be the gift of music. It's not an accident that the main character in my first published novel was a gifted musician—she had the magic I wanted.

Solomon speaks about things more serious than an inability to play a flamenco guitar, but he has a similar point in the next two verses.

> [14] *When I observed all that happens under the sun, I realized that everything is pointless, a chasing after wind.*
>
> [15] *What's crooked can't be straightened;*
> *what isn't there can't be counted.*
>
> ECCLESIASTES 1:14–15

Everything is *hevel* (breath), and it's all like chasing the wind. Solomon's poetic connection between the images of breath and wind is a nice literary flourish. You can imagine *hevel* in the vapor version of its definition—it slowly drifts away on a cold day. Imagine trying to catch it. It is not really there and so it eludes you. Then the image shifts to the wind—it comes with more volume, it's faster, you can hear it now, but it's less visible and even more hopeless to try to chase.

But what is that bit about crooked things not being able to be straightened? Solomon's idea is clearer in the second half of the line: "What isn't there can't be counted." Well, that's obvious. And that's the point of the first half of the line as well. If you straighten something crooked, it's not crooked anymore, so you can no longer call it crooked. The Hebrew idea of "crooked" doesn't carry a negative meaning the way it does in English. To grasp the Hebrew word's mood, think of a crooked vein of mineral in a rock or the interesting shape found in a twisted tree. You can't straighten it. You wouldn't want to straighten it. Crooked things are crooked. They just are. In the case of bonsai trees, sometimes crooked is the point.

Likewise, you can't count something that isn't there. You just can't. It's not there.

I want to be a gifted musician, but I'm not, and no amount of practicing has changed that reality. I can't get the magic to spark even a little. Some things are not the way I want them to be.

Solomon explains this further in the following three verses.

> [16] *I said to myself, Look here, I have grown much wiser than any who ruled over Jerusalem before me. My mind has absorbed great wisdom and knowledge.* [17] *But when I set my mind to understand wisdom, and also to understand madness and folly, I realized that this too was just wind chasing.*
>
> [18] *Remember:*
>> *In much wisdom is much aggravation;*
>> *the more knowledge, the more pain.*
>
> ECCLESIASTES 1:16–18

Oh, that doesn't sound very good. The more knowledge, the more pain? What is Solomon saying here?

His point is not to discourage us from our quest for *yithron* (lasting benefit) but rather to let us know up front that not every answer we find is going to make us happy. Crooked things stay crooked. Missing things cannot be counted. I'm never going to wow an audience, or even myself, with my original compositions performed on any instrument of any kind. Likewise, you will discover limitations in your life, and that's a reality we all need to accept. Life is *hevel* enough without stubbornly pursuing dead ends. Wisdom sometimes requires acceptance and moving on.

It was with great sadness that I eventually put that flamenco guitar up for sale and let it go to a new and more worthy owner. Having it take up space in my office and knowing I'd never come even remotely close to satisfying myself made its presence a source of unhappiness. Music production is a crooked and missing thing for me—in my fifties, I finally accepted that reality. Maybe in heaven I'll get to play the way I dream about, but in the meantime, I need to live here. Accepting my non-musician reality is part of finding the *yithron* my soul craves in this life. I can't get what I need if I keep chasing what I can't have. Accepting that some things are crooked is an early lesson we need for our quest to succeed.

What's your flamenco guitar? What waits to replace it?

PART TWO:

THE EXPERIMENTAL STAGE OF THE SEARCH

8

YOU WON'T FIND DEEP MEANING AT A PARTY

I REMEMBER WHEN I was ten, thinking, *Life cannot get any better than this.* We lived in Fort St. John at the time, an oil town in northern British Columbia. I was a free-spirited boy with great friends at an age when nothing but fun surrounded me. Locals would joke that there were ten months of winter in Fort St. John and two months of poor sledding.

In Fort St. John's brief but glorious summers, many of us shared a unique hobby that I've never encountered elsewhere. Businesses in that northern oil town were fond of stocking stickers that advertised their company's logo and services. I suppose they were meant to be stuck on pickup truck bumpers, toolboxes, and snowmobiles, but we boys liked to collect them. They weren't the sorts of things you'd find at retail stores, but trucking companies, oil rig maintenance firms, welding shops, and similar businesses reliably stocked them. Tow truck companies had the flashiest and best stickers of all.

On any given Saturday during the summers of 1979 and 1980, I tore around Fort St. John's gravel streets on an old one-speed bicycle with a huge purple banana seat, popping into businesses in the industrial sections of town—which was basically the whole town—asking, "Do you have any stickers?"

I have no idea why they gave them away to kids. We didn't have trucks or toolboxes to stick them to. But give them they did, and I wound up with an entire photo album full of stickers.

That was life at ten years of age.

When I turned eleven, I thought, *Man, eleven is even better than ten!* If life works right, eleven is a fantastic age for a boy. Friends are still non-judgmental and not terribly competitive yet, hormones haven't fully kicked in, the level of freedom is nicely balanced by a general lack of responsibility relative to later years, and romantic rivalries haven't started. Consequences—of school, personal responsibility, and life decisions—are not real yet. When I was eleven, I didn't understand why; I just understood and clearly articulated to myself that eleven was fantastic.

Then I turned twelve. That happened six weeks after we moved to California, and I remember that first California summer, thinking, *Oh man, twelve is even better than eleven*. I really loved turning twelve. However, later that year, a sexual assault occurred that I've written about elsewhere.[38] That was an unexpected shattering of my progression from boyhood high to boyhood high. Six months later came the trial with its humiliations. Another six months passed, and when I was thirteen, my father moved me out of the house to that four-year night nurse job. Upon reading that last bit, one of my editors asked me, "Who was there to look after you?" and the answer to that question was me. Thirteen-year-old me looked after me. Later in life, I interpreted that sequence of events as the cause for an overly serious quality that entered my personality.

Solomon and I both needed to find meaning in our lives. My approach to life switched from that of a rambunctious boy racing around town on a beat-up bicycle with his friends to that of an isolated and still traumatized thirteen-year-old learning to handle a night shift packed with nursing duties. Real nurses at least got vacations and weekends. I'd always been a reader, but at this stage of my life, reading became more than a pastime. It became a lifeline as I tried to figure out how to live in a world I suddenly no longer liked.

Solomon's next step in his own *hevel* investigation and *yithron* quest was not to read. Instead he embarked on a phase of intense experimentation. He set theory aside in favor of exploration, and his first experiment in this new phase was one I found very surprising. It was not a deep dive into philosophy, religion, or ethics but a focus on fun. While I read books to try to understand why I was alive, Solomon literally partied to find his purpose in life.

---

38 Potter, *Even the Monsters*.

Solomon was, to say the least, an interesting man. Don't take my word for it. Here's how the Queen of Sheba put it after she visited Solomon herself:

> *6 "The report I heard about your deeds and wisdom when I was still at home is true," she said to the king. 7 "I didn't believe it until I came and saw it with my own eyes. In fact, the half of it wasn't even told to me! You have far more wisdom and wealth than I was told. 8 Your people and these servants who continually serve you and get to listen to your wisdom are truly happy! 9 Bless the Lord your God because he was pleased to place you on Israel's throne. Because the Lord loved Israel with an eternal love, the Lord made you king to uphold justice and righteousness."*
>
> *10 The queen gave the king one hundred twenty kikkars of gold, a great quantity of spice, and precious stones. Never again has so much spice come to Israel as when the queen of Sheba gave this gift to King Solomon.*
>
> 1 KINGS 10:6–10

One hundred twenty kikkars of gold equals four imperial tons. That's at least forty camel loads of gold. In volume, that's two hundred liters or a block measuring roughly seven cubic feet. As of early 2022, that's worth about two hundred million US dollars.

She gave Solomon a gold mine, already mined, packaged, transported, and delivered to his doorstep. She was impressed.

The recipient of this queen's extravagant gift is our tour guide to the meaning of life, and he starts his quest with a party.

Solomon and I both needed to find meaning in our lives. If I could have traded night-shift nursing responsibilities for that beat-up bicycle with its cracked purple banana seat and that same group of ten-year-old friends— dropping into dirty, steel-walled, industrial shops and asking unshaven guys in hard hats "Got any stickers?" and wildly celebrating the latest score—I would have done it in a second. Instead, at this stage of our respective searches, I turned to books and Solomon turned to fun.

Here's how Solomon described the beginning of his experiments.

¹ I said to myself, Come, I will make you experience pleasure; enjoy what is good! But this too was pointless! ² Merriment, I thought, is madness; pleasure, of no use at all.

ECCLESIASTES 2: 1–2

Solomon says here that he planned to enjoy the good life. However, his quest seemed to stall immediately. "[T]his too was pointless! Merriment, I thought, is madness; pleasure, of no use at all." He starts saying this before verse one is even complete.

But remember, this search for a good life was not pointless, as our translation keeps tricking us into believing. His quest was *hevel*. It is breath. *Hevel* is a metaphor, and the reader should decide what it means. I hope by now you are solid on the concept that breath is not pointless—it keeps you alive.

So this quest is . . . what?

Here are some legitimate options.

But this too was fleeting and fragile! ² Merriment, I thought, is madness; pleasure, of no use at all.

But this too was enigmatic and mysterious! ² Merriment, I thought, is madness; pleasure, of no use at all. ³⁹

Hmm. But doesn't verse two say the same thing as the "pointless" word I'm trying to teach us to reexamine? If merriment is madness and pleasure is of no use at all, then that seems fairly pointless, doesn't it?

As I have argued, something important is damaged when a keyword is mistranslated. When *hevel* is distorted to become "pointless," it seems that all of the following translation choices are bent to support that original misstated thesis.

Everything is not pointless. It is breath. It is fleeting and fragile.

So what does the Hebrew say merriment is if not madness?

The Hebrew isn't talking about some mental illness or moral evil, as our English word "madness" implies. My translator's handbook offers two plain

---

39   These are the author's own versions as he plays with interpreting the metaphor. You are free to try out other ideas. Just remember, a rose is never a violin. Your interpretation needs to remain faithful to the original metaphor. We don't need modern day Jeromes distorting the meaning of Ecclesiastes!

English translations that are not artful, but they convey the Hebrew point much more clearly.

> *Failure to take life seriously is dangerous.*
> *If we are too lighthearted, we are being stupid.*[40]

Well, that's not as judgmental as our more common English translation, and the conclusion isn't controversial. Being lighthearted isn't bad. But being too lighthearted—well, we probably all know people who haven't taken life seriously enough and have suffered for it.

What about the bit regarding pleasure being of no use at all?

Here, my translator's handbook comes to the rescue again and points out that the Hebrew isn't a statement (i.e., a judgment) but rather a question. Instead of stating that pleasure is useless, the Hebrew asks, "What use is it?" or "What does it accomplish?"[41]

Do you see a pattern here? First, *hevel* was distorted to mean "pointless"—a metaphor replaced with a judgment. Second, "dangerous" was replaced with "madness," and fair enough, madness can be dangerous. But "madness" leaves no room for good whereas "dangerous" is a much kinder and more qualified assessment. We need to be on guard with danger, not despise it. And lastly, a reasonable question ("What does it accomplish?") is replaced with another harsh judgment that pleasure is of no use at all. Remember, this whole pattern of negativity and judgment by translators goes back to Jerome, who was no language scholar and had an agenda to sell a radical ascetic lifestyle he wanted everyone else to practice while he avoided doing so himself.

What we observe here is similar to the problem of one lie requiring additional lies to cover the first one. In this case, one bad translation choice requires other distorted translation decisions to back up the original mistake or dishonesty.

Let's get back to Solomon and his question regarding the practical value of pleasure. Pleasure is actually of some use. Even if the only thing pleasure

---

40   Graham S. Ogden and Lynell Zogbo, *A Handbook on Ecclesiastes* (New York: United Bible Societies, 1998), p. 52.

41   Ogden and Zogbo, *A Handbook on Ecclesiastes*, p. 53.

accomplishes is temporary enjoyment, that's a result. That is an accomplishment. So our English distortion ("of no use at all") is demonstrably wrong in life and, fortunately, isn't what Solomon said. He *asked* what use it was. He didn't judge it as useless. Sometimes questions are just that: questions. Not rhetorical devices but an honest search for an answer.

Next up, Solomon wondered if adding alcohol might improve his partying results. Here he is in his own words.

> *3 I tried cheering myself with wine and by embracing folly—with wisdom still guiding me—until I might see what is really worth doing in the few days that human beings have under heaven.*
>
> ECCLESIASTES 2:3

Some commentators try to package this up to be a little more sanitized than we might believe and suggest that Solomon was a wine connoisseur, searching out an excellent variety and vintage.[42] That might be true, but the second half of that phrase, "and by embracing folly," makes it clear that he didn't just sample and spit—he got drunk.[43] Moreover, he did so "with wisdom still guiding" him.

Putting this in plain language, it appears that Solomon kept his head in the game as long as he could, measuring the distance between a buzz to being drunk and experimenting with a full-on blackout drunk, after which other people would have to update him on the previous night's proceedings. Perhaps his method was slightly different than I describe, but however we picture the details, the verse just isn't amenable to the kind of sanitization that characterizes many commentaries.[44] Our wise man here, especially loved

---

42   For example, in *The Book of Ecclesiastes*, p. 89, Longman quotes Leupold's *Exposition of Ecclesiastes*, p. 60.

43   Some commentators struggle with the idea of Solomon committing actual sin and deny that he got drunk. They make this argument despite God himself pointing out Solomon's sins in 1 Kings 11:4–11. For example, see Fox, *JPS Bible Commentary*, p. 12. Most, however, are clear on what Solomon was up to. For example, see John Phillips and Jim Hastings, *Exploring Ecclesiastes: An Expository Commentary* (Grand Rapids: Kregel Publications, 2019), pp. 73–75.

44   Even my translator's handbook, concerned primarily with the meaning of the

by God, crossed all kinds of lines to see if something of lasting benefit could be found in the land of intoxication.

As I mentioned earlier, Solomon will come around later to a positive view of wine and celebrations. Unfortunately, that apparent reversal of his position causes many commentaries to pile on with criticism of the overall value of Ecclesiastes. According to this school of thought, the Teacher couldn't make up his mind about what was true and said all manner of nonsense.[45] The problem, however, is with the commentaries and not Ecclesiastes. God knew what he was doing. He chose Solomon (or the Solomonic point of view), and he didn't have nonsense to present; he had wisdom.

So Solomon tried adding alcohol to find satisfaction in life and that didn't work.

Even more interestingly, Solomon will return to this topic of pleasure later in Ecclesiastes and present it positively, commending its good qualities. But remember, his mission right now in chapter two is a search for *yithron*—for lasting benefit—and in the context of lasting benefit, merriment and pleasure and intoxication are not delivering the goods. There is no deep meaning to be derived from partying.

To spend a day again as that ten-year-old on my old bicycle might be a blast, but if I could make such a magical event occur, I wouldn't find any *yithron* in it either. Fun is fun. For *yithron,* though, we need something more than fun.

---

words and translation complexities versus practical application, clearly understood the nature of Solomon's drunkenness (Ogden and Zogbo, pp. 53–54).

45   For example, see Fox, *JPS Bible Commentary*, p. 12.

9

MORE PRODUCTIVE DOESN'T EQUAL MORE MEANING

IN MY LATER teen years, there was a retired contractor in California who grew bored with idle hours. His name was Ed. He decided to buy a lot in a nearby town that had a hundred-year-old house on it, tear the old house down, and build a new house in its place.

I had graduated high school a year early and finally, at seventeen, shed that night nurse job. I started paying rent to sleep at home again at seventeen, so now I needed a new full-time job. Ed offered to take me under his wing and teach me the construction business. My first task was to mow the waist-high grass so we could see what we were dealing with.

Once I finished levelling the lawn, Ed showed up with a massive construction forklift, a maul, a heavy tow chain, and an enormous demolition debris bin. My job that week was to tear down the one-hundred-year-old house and put it in the bin. Seriously. Ed gave me the keys to the forklift, jumped in his brown Chevy El Camino, and left me on my own with my lunch bag, my water jug, and a mission. No instructions. Just a mission.

The forklift in question was the only power tool Ed provided. It was not a small warehouse machine. This was a construction-grade forklift with a thirty-foot boom. Still, it was a forklift, not a demolition machine.

I wandered through the house with the maul and tentatively smashed it through several walls. It turns out they were lath and plaster walls. I'd never seen a lath and plaster wall before. I went up to the second storey and kicked a door, but it stayed solidly attached to its hinges. The house was old and very solid. I pulled up the linoleum in the floor and found World War II *San Francisco Chronicle* newspapers used as an underlay and wasted a few hours salvaging them. I still have them today.

Then it came time to look at the rest of the house that still needed to go into the construction bin.

You would think that any sensible person would go home at this point. Put an entire two-storey house into what amounted to an oversized trash can? By myself? Without any proper tools or equipment? I didn't even have a hard hat. I'd brought my gloves and probably wore a baseball cap because the California summers could get over a hundred degrees Fahrenheit. Gloves, a baseball cap, no experience, and no one around to give me any clever ideas were not the right start to this kind of job.

But I was seventeen. I didn't know this was a ridiculous assignment. I had the keys to the biggest forklift I'd ever seen and would get paid to wreck a house with it. That was awesome.

I started off teaching myself how to drive the machine. Once I figured out how to work all the levers, I maneuvered the lift's forks between the cement foundation and the wooden walls, raised the house a few feet on one corner, and then dropped it. That was cool. That did nothing to dismantle the house, though. I tried lifting the house higher and higher—after all, this thing had a thirty-foot boom. Surely if I raised it high enough, it would come crashing down hard enough to shatter into tiny pieces that I could then toss into the bin.

Remember, I was seventeen. If I'd got one side of the house up thirty feet in the air, I'd have ripped the whole thing off its foundations and tipped it into the neighbor's yard. That would have been a memorable disaster. You shouldn't give a seventeen-year-old boy a construction-grade forklift, no safety equipment, no directions, no supervisor, and no help at all and leave him on his own for a week. Later, in my early twenties, with the benefit of a fully developed frontal cortex, I looked back and shook my head at how stupid I'd been. Now, in my fifties, I look back and wonder if maybe Ed was suffering from a judgment-impairing medical condition.

Anyway, I did try to lift the house thirty feet in the air. What happened was completely unexpected. Having the weight of a good portion of the house on my forks caused the entire machine to tilt forward into the house and pin itself against the building. The forklift was now balanced on its two front wheels and leaning onto the house. That pinned position only lasted briefly. As I tried in vain to lift the house higher, my front wheels began to roll away from the house, which caused the house to slip off the forks and pull the tilted forklift farther forward until the house slammed back to the ground and the forklift bounced off its face. It bounced off its face because it had a big engine and cantilevered weight on its back end to keep it from falling forward to begin with. It didn't bounce back upright and onto it's wheels, though. Instead, the machine bounced upright and then kept going over, flipping itself back onto its rear engine compartment, where it briefly balanced and then rolled back onto its wheels again. If it had landed on its side, I'd have been in a real pickle. We'd have had to rent a second piece of heavy equipment to stand the original forklift back up onto its wheels.

The machine landed on its wheels, though, and despite not having any safety harness, I somehow stayed in the seat the whole time. The forklift was fine. I was fine. I think I lost my hat somewhere along the way. Ed would not have been happy with me if I had damaged his forklift on the second day on the job, so I decided that repeatedly lifting and dropping the house wouldn't work.

Plan B was a much cleverer plan. I took the massive lengths of tow chain Ed had provided, crawled in one window, and walked through the house, crawling out a window on the far side. I then went along the back side of the house, into another window, back through the house toward the forklift, and out a fourth window. The house had a lot of windows. I really ought to have done this routine through doorways. Did I mention that I was seventeen?

With both ends of the chain in my hands at the forklift, I now had one central wall lassoed. The rear of the forklift had a trailer hitch. I attached the wicked-looking hooks on the ends of the chain to the trailer hitch, saddled up behind the wheel, and hit the gas. The first exploding two-by-four stud was music to my ears. Then the next cracked. And the next. And so I drove across the freshly mown yard, snapping one two-by-four after another with the heavy chain cutting an entire central wall clean through at about waist height.

At no point did it occur to me that Ed might have left me a saw to do any of this work. This was an era before battery-powered tools and we didn't have a generator on site and there was no way I'd have agreed to take a house down with a handsaw.

My idea with the stud-cutting heavy chain worked brilliantly except for one problem. Despite now missing one interior wall, the house hadn't fallen. It was a big two-storey house with many interior walls. One broken ground-level wall would not collapse the whole place. A technique, however, had been tried and proven useful. That was a success.

The next step in this plan was to crawl through another set of windows and do the same thing to another interior supporting wall. If a part of you is thinking, "Wait a minute, you've just destroyed the central supporting wall in this house. This is a job for a wrecking ball, not a kid with a pair of work gloves, a baseball cap, a length of chain, an oversized forklift, and apparently no sense at all," well, you're not seventeen. Head trauma can make you stupid. So can testosterone in excess supply and a frontal cortex still in development. I was having the best time of my life and getting paid for it.

I never told Ed about bouncing his rented forklift off its face and then its rear engine compartment. It was a tough machine. No one noticed. At the end of that week, he drove up in his dirt-brown El Camino, and the entire house, including its sturdy doors, was nicely loaded into the massive demolition bin. I was ready for the next phase of the construction business where we would start building something.

Ed taught me surveying next and then foundation preparation and cement pouring. I have no memory at all of what happened to the original foundation. I remember it being there when I tried to forklift the house into the air, and I remember shaping the forms for the new foundation. How we got the original cement and stone out, though, I don't recall.

For the new pour, Ed hired a few other guys to help us because it gets hot in California, and you don't want that cement curing before you're ready. When it was time for framing, Ed hired a professional framer. Ed drove off in his El Camino again, and the new guy taught me how to frame. We inspected the blueprints each morning, and he showed me how to handle a framing hammer with its cheese-grater head. If I couldn't drop a four-inch sixpenny nail through my joint with one swing, he would shoot me a disapproving look, and I got the message. You held the nail and swung. You let go of the nail at the last second, and that serrated hammerhead caught the yellow-coated nail before it toppled and slammed it through four inches of wood in one go. One swing, one nail, then on to the next. Anything less efficient was unsatisfactory.

When we laid the second floor, I walked on top of the first-storey walls with a hammer and nails in my belt and heavy sheets of plywood on my back. When we framed the roof, we walked on top of the second-storey walls and carried roof trusses. It was all work that today would give a modern occupational health and safety representative a heart attack. I wound up going to university later in life because I figured out while working for Ed that I wouldn't be able to keep doing this in my sixties. I loved the job, but the toll on my body was a bit much. I needed to find a different line of work, or I would wind up dead.

Once we'd framed the roof, either Ed or a hired specialist taught me everything else to know about building houses. I laid shingles with the roofers, pulled wire for the electricians, drilled holes for the plumbers, used a finer grade hammer with the flooring guys, sanded with the drywallers (for the record, I hate drywalling), got messy with the painters, and used an even finer grade of hammer with the finish carpenters, tacking the last baseboards into place and checking the lock on the front door before we closed it. The last thing I did for Ed was mow the lawn again. Then he sold the house and went back into retirement. I was disappointed to lose access to the construction business, but I quickly recovered and got a new job wearing a tuxedo as a waiter in the most expensive fine dining restaurant in our town. That wasn't my weirdest job transition, but it was up there.

Solomon also had an itch to build, to create, to do something more than just be entertained. Or maybe, said differently, his entertainment moved on to a different and more productive path than simply drinking and partying.

> *4 I took on great projects: I built houses for myself, planted vineyards for myself. 5 I made gardens and parks for myself, planting every kind of fruit tree in them. 6 I made reservoirs for myself to water my lush groves.*
>
> ECCLESIASTES 2:4–6

These projects that Solomon took on were not Ed's single-family house built on spec for the local market. Solomon's landscaping and gardening creations were not my later adult fascination with the art of bonsai either.

First Kings gives us a detailed rundown of the scale of projects Solomon got up to during this phase of his life. The temple he built wasn't a seventeen-year-old's summer job. Solomon's temple was an entire nation's seven-year construction project.[46] Work on his palace followed, taking thirteen years of hard labor to perfect.[47] He made another palace for his wife, Pharaoh's daughter.[48] We'll talk more about her shortly.

When it came to gardening, Solomon built parks, not vegetable patches, and planted forests and orchards. Southern Israel is a dry place, so he made this magic in the desert happen by creating reservoirs and piping water from distant places to his new Garden of Eden.[49]

Garden of Eden. That's a good reminder. Solomon wasn't doing all this for pride, as a summer job, or because it's what kings were expected to do. His father, David, certainly never got into landscaping and gardening. Solomon did this for pleasure. This phase of his experiment had more to show for it and was certainly more socially commendable than mere partying. But remember his preface to this quest where he told us the conclusion before telling us the steps. Decades spent on creating buildings, parks, gardens, and water features did not provide lasting benefit either. They were okay. But not great. Once you've built one of the world's seven wonders, then what? The existential crisis that completion exposed was exactly Solomon's problem, but he'll tell us that in his own words later.

The key thing to note here is that even though his building projects were more commendable than his partying, from a *yithron* perspective, they were equally empty. A party is a party, a garden is a garden, and a building is a building, and none of them will fill an empty heart.

In the meantime, Solomon still had a pleasure quest to finish. He's tried parties and projects. How about exploring a completely different category of pleasure?

---

46   See 1 Kings 6 for a detailed description.

47   1 Kings 7.

48   1 Kings 9:24.

49   For an extensive overview of Solomon's building projects, see William Whiston, trans., *The New Complete Works of Josephus: Revised and Expanded Edition*, commentary by Paul L. Maier (Grand Rapids: Kregel Publications, 1990), pp. 272–282.

10

SEX AND MUSIC ARE NOT ENOUGH

I WENT THROUGH a decade-long season where I was fascinated by rock band documentaries. I was less interested in the solo artist exposés. The formation of a band, the interplay between its members, the arc of their personal and collective journeys, and how together they made the magic we call music is what captured my attention. The inevitable tales of drug use and sexual misadventures had no appeal to me.

Recent lawsuits from aging fans suddenly realizing that encounters from decades ago were not rock and roll naughtiness but assaults further underscore the lies of at least some of these stories. But the evolution of the music and the relationships among the band members were what drew me.

The next stop in Solomon's pleasure quest took him in a very rock and roll direction. He'd done the alcohol part already. The next phase focused purely on music and sex.

Here's how he puts it:

> *I acquired male and female singers for myself, along with every human luxury, treasure chests galore!*
>
> ECCLESIASTES 2:8B

There were no record collections or streaming services in Solomon's day. All music was live music, and as one humorous preacher I heard put it, when Solomon liked what he heard, he bought the band.

The second part of that sentence is, however, a lot more problematic for many readers, whether they are Christians or Jews or just not crazy. The CEB says that in addition to music, he acquired "every human luxury, treasure chests galore!" This is either the most prudish translation of plain Hebrew in the Bible or the "treasure chests galore" line is taking a simple statement and wrapping it up in a surprisingly crude image. I think the crude image angle is probably unintentional and the translators were going for prudery. Or maybe the translation committee was divided, and some subversive translation committee members slipped one past the more conservative scholars who didn't realize what they were approving.

Okay, what am I talking about?

"Treasure chests galore" is most definitely not what the original language says.

Here is a sampling of the more common English translations:

> I acquired male and female singers, and a harem as well—the delights of a man's heart. (NIV)

> I provided for myself male and female singers, and the pleasures of the sons of mankind: many concubines. (NASB)

> I got singers, both men and women, and many concubines, man's delight. (Revised Standard Version (RSV)

I wonder if the CEB's "treasure chests galore" is influenced by the startlingly candid translation found in The Message Bible (MSG):

> I gathered a chorus of singers to entertain me with song,
> and—most exquisite of all pleasures—
> voluptuous maidens for my bed.

Oh boy. We're pretty clear now on what Solomon was talking about here. For the record, this self-report barely hints at what Solomon got up to in the bedroom. First Kings gives us a proper history with plenty of data to further flesh out the idea. As with everything else Solomon did, when he investigated something, his sense of scale often beggared the imagination and any semblance of reason.

¹ In addition to Pharaoh's daughter, King Solomon loved many foreign women, including Moabites, Ammonites, Edomites, Sidonians, and Hittites. ² These came from the nations that the Lord had commanded the Israelites about: "Don't intermarry with them. They will definitely turn your heart toward their gods." Solomon clung to these women in love. ³ He had seven hundred royal wives and three hundred secondary wives. They turned his heart.

1 KINGS 11:1–3

Secondary wives? What's a secondary wife? The CEB is being modest again. These were concubines. Mistresses. Women who did not serve a political or heir-creating purpose in that day and age but were there just for sex.

If Solomon is starting to creep you out a bit, then you probably grew up reasonably well, or at least in adulthood, you have adopted a sense of human decency that finds this man's behavior repellent. I want to remind us again that God chose to present this quest through a Solomonic lens for a very good reason. Solomon's case is an extreme case. Extreme wealth, extreme wisdom (misused but nevertheless present), extreme power, and let's face it, even for his era, extreme sexism. Solomon didn't need pornography. He had real women at his beck and call, women of every size, shape, color, and accent. He was the king. He ordered from a menu.

If you find that idea gross, you're not alone. Solomon was not a guy I would have wanted in my home. But he wrote this book, or at least God presented this material through a Solomonic lens, and it can be compelling to hear stories of people who dived off decency's dock into a cesspool of iniquity, whatever its flavor. It's like a car wreck. You can learn a lot from a car wreck, though they sometimes hold a lurid fascination that may be unhealthy.

In the case of Solomon, he didn't just leap off decency's dock into one cesspool. He leaped into them all. I visualize him climbing out of a slime pit, getting back up on the dock, taking notes on how that latest swim went, then flinging himself off in another direction. Though he doesn't cover it in Ecclesiastes, as previously discussed, we know that even murder was in his repertoire.[50]

---

50   1 Kings 2:25, 29–34, 46.

Okay, so a guy, this guy, went nuts and did everything a man might want to do with no self-restraint, financial restraint, political restraint, or any other kind of restraint. From decent things, like building orchards and irrigation systems and a grand temple, to indecent things, like engaging in drunken debauchery, a maniacal sex life, and murder, this guy did it all.

How did this insane lifestyle work out? Here is Solomon's conclusion regarding his multidecade pleasure quest.

> *⁹ So I became far greater than all who preceded me in Jerusalem. Moreover, my wisdom stood by me. ¹⁰ I refrained from nothing that my eyes desired. I refused my heart no pleasure. Indeed, my heart found pleasure from the results of my hard work; that was the reward from all my hard work. ¹¹ But when I surveyed all that my hands had done, and what I had worked so hard to achieve, I realized that it was pointless—a chasing after wind. Nothing is to be gained under the sun.*
>
> ECCLESIASTES 2:9–11

Just because Solomon's wisdom "stood by" him, it doesn't mean that he acted on it. You can know what is right and still do the wrong thing. This dynamic comes out in daily life, even in small things like choosing fries over a salad. Solomon was wise enough to know that the stuff he embarked on in this pleasure quest would not result in genuine satisfaction, but the man was like an early scientist, happy to prove a thesis wrong with negative test results. Thought experiments were not his cup of tea. He "refrained from nothing" that he desired and "refused [his] heart no pleasure."

And here's a fascinating and honest thing that he records: he admits that, on a certain level, it worked out.

> *Indeed, my heart found pleasure from the results of my hard work; that was the reward from all my hard work.*
>
> ECCLESIASTES 2:10B

I don't know about you, but that's not the conclusion I expect to find in the middle of the Bible. Things worked out? He was a sex maniac and employed forced labor gangs to construct his buildings, landscaping, and irrigation projects and got drunk and collected human slaves. The result of all this was that his heart "found pleasure from the results of [his] hard work"?

I appreciate his honesty, even if a part of me doesn't like his conclusion. He enjoyed it. It was fun.

As I watched rock documentary after rock documentary, their stories started coalescing into a pattern resembling a genre with standard plot arcs and tropes. The band would begin as a group of unlikely nobodies who shot to fame (fast or slow, each story had its variation), which then led to a middle period that was usually a mix of out-of-control hedonism of a Solomonic flavor combined with some management or record label corruption and abuse. Usually, by the end of the documentary, the surviving band members or the lead singer were older and soberer, and they were relatively regretful of their youthful excesses, mistakes, and outright crimes. But then there would come a point near the end when the interviewer (or narrator or editor or the documentary subject themselves) would ask a question along the lines of "Was it all bad?" and the cinematographer would capture that wry addict's smile and there would be an acknowledgement—either through words or merely body language—that no, it wasn't all bad. They got some pleasure from it.

Sin wouldn't be attractive if it didn't have something to offer. Those trapped by heroin aren't there because their first shot was terrible and every shot after that was also awful. They struggle because it gave them something that felt good (or took away pain), and they went back for more, not seeing—or ignoring—the claws that slowly stole the pleasure and left them with a relentless, soul-consuming addiction. Sin is like a strange cancer that feels good at first and then later consumes its host. It's a sweet poison. It's an attractive and comfortable captivity before the torture begins.[51] Even healthy things can become unhealthy when they're used as permanent coping mechanisms. Coping mechanisms are supposed to be short-term crutches, not permanent solutions to real problems.

But we're getting way ahead of ourselves. For now, in the second half of

51   I've read a great deal of medical literature on addiction and listened to stories from friends who've escaped such traps, but the story that made this topic most real for me was a novel: Gregory David Roberts' book *Shantaram* (New York: St. Martin's Griffin, 2003). I found it to be a powerful inoculation against chemical temptations. It seems that—if properly translated and absorbed—parts of Solomon's Ecclesiastes can serve a similar preventative function.

verse ten, Solomon admits that he enjoyed his decades of excess. This isn't Sunday school. This is a worldly giant of a man looking life right in the eye and investigating every corner of it to find lasting benefit from anything that goes on under the sun. But in the end, though Solomon admits he found a bit of pleasure there, he cannot stop on that note because a bit of fun was not his goal.

> *¹¹ But when I surveyed all that my hands had done, and what I had worked so hard to achieve, I realized that it was pointless—a chasing after wind. Nothing is to be gained under the sun.*
>
> ECCLESIASTES 2:11

Remember, not pointless. It wasn't pointless, although, from a conservative religious perspective, we might prefer that as the moral of the story. It wasn't pointless. It was *hevel*. Breath. It was temporary, insubstantial, elusive, fleeting, important, life-giving, or transitory. Take your pick of interpretations, but breath is never pointless.

Pleasure—positive pleasure, like the satisfaction from building a glorious temple, or sinful pleasure, from his objectification and abuse of women—was temporary, fleeting, and transitory. He got that pleasure but found that it did not satisfy him. He breathed once and then found that he immediately needed another breath. That's how he wound up with a thousand women between in-house mistresses and official wives. Ten was not enough. One hundred was not enough. Five hundred was not enough. How did he even keep track of their names? Enough was never enough.

Everything he did was *hevel*. Chasing after the wind is a truly apt expression. In verse ten, he said pleasure was the reward for his hard work, and in the next verse, he said nothing was gained. There was no lasting benefit from his labor. Pleasure counted as nothing. His heart needed more than that. He needed something more than a transitory pleasure to satisfy him.

Of course, he did. God is our heart's maker; he built it for more than fun. Oh, but I'm sneaking ahead again here. Solomon is not only thorough but also methodical. He's not going to wrap up this quest so quickly. He was smart enough to get off this endless pleasure treadmill, but the lasting benefit quest was still on. He just needed a new focus.

PART THREE:

THE SEARCH REVEALS PRELIMINARY CONCLUSIONS

11

CHOOSING WISDOM OVER FOOLISHNESS REQUIRES FAITH

I'VE BEEN CARRYING a sealed box around with me for over thirty years, which I recently opened. Inside were journals I'd written in from age twelve to twenty-one. Reading them in my fifties, I was shocked to discover people and events I had no memory of. Even more startling, there were some events I remembered with nostalgic fondness that I had not recorded positively in the moment. This turned out not to be an issue of my teenage self refusing to recognize how good I'd had it but my adult self selectively forgetting terrible details. Discovering a first-person account of your own childhood in your own handwriting is a wild experience.

I started the journals when I was twelve, shortly after moving to California. The first entry is the police statement after my assault. The second entry is a pasted-in copy of the court summons to the trial. Then my own handwriting starts.

I remember details of that night nurse job because I recorded what happened, day by day, for the entire four years. I told myself from the opening pages of the journal that I was going to keep a record of my childhood because adults obviously forgot what kids were like, and we mattered. It was a deliberate message to me in the future. That's not my adult interpretation of the work four decades later but my explicit intention that I recorded when I was thirteen years old.

There were times when I wrote absolute nonsense, and a day or two later, I'd report on Thursday that I now believed Tuesday's opinions to be total stupidity.

But then I would write that Tuesday's writings were a record of Tuesday, and so on Thursday, I was not going to cross out what I had written or tear out the page. Let the record of Tuesday's stupidity and Thursday's better reflection both stand.

Those accounts now, in my fifties, are a treasure. I stopped writing at twenty-one. I closed out the last entries of the journals stating that I'd completed the assignment. I could get on with living my life now.

That Maya Angelou quote comes to mind again. "Do the best you can until you know better. Then when you know better, do better."[52] I'd never heard of Angelou when writing those journals, but I agreed with the sentiment, and the journals were my attempt to help myself know better so I could do better when I had my own children. To write the journal to my future self required faith that I would preserve them and act on them in my own adulthood. Self-parenting isn't perfect, but it is progress.

Solomon also sometimes tried to think his way through things in the same way that I tried to think my way through my childhood by journalling. Here is what he writes next.

> [12] *My reflections then turned to wisdom, madness, and folly.*
> *What can the king's heir do but what has already been done?*
> [13] *I saw that wisdom is more beneficial than folly, as light is*
> *more beneficial than darkness.*
>
> [14] *The wise have eyes in their head,*
>   *but fools walk around in darkness.*
>
> *But I also realized that the same fate happens to both of them.*
> [15] *So I thought to myself, What happens to the fool will also*
> *happen to me. So why have I been so very wise? I said to myself,*
> *This too is pointless.*
>
> ECCLESIASTES 2:12–15

This collection of verses is a bit of a mess. Some commentaries go to great lengths to point out the awkward prose and ascribe bad editing as proof of their various theories of authorship.[53] The criticism goes something like this:

---

52   See chapter 6, footnote 1.

53   See Longman, *The Book of Ecclesiastes*, pp. 95–99 for a sample survey of the conflicting literature on these verses.

- In verse twelve, Solomon starts a new topic: an intellectual quest. Then he switches to despairing about what his son might do once he is king.

- In verse thirteen, Solomon praises wisdom as better than foolishness. That's an innocuous observation that has nothing to do with the previous comment about his son and hardly bears stating.

- Then, in the next verse, Solomon goes negative, pointing out that everyone dies, both the wise man and the fool. His point seems to be that wisdom isn't so great after all if you're just as dead in the end. This is the opposite of an innocuous comment and risks making wisdom look pointless.

- And then, in verse fifteen, Solomon confirms this fear and sums it all up by saying in plain language that it's all pointless.

Ah, but wait a minute. You're on to the pattern now, aren't you? It's not pointless. It's all *hevel*. It's all breath. It's all repetitive, fragile, enigmatic, mysterious, temporary, and elusive.

But what is all repetitive, fragile, enigmatic, mysterious, temporary, and elusive?

Fate. "What happens to the fool will also happen to me. So why have I been so very wise?" (2:15). If wisdom or foolishness ultimately don't matter—wise person or fool, they all wind up dead—then what does it all mean? How does it all matter?

Solomon is not judging the difference between wisdom and foolishness as pointless; he simply states that trying to understand why wisdom is better, given that everyone winds up dead in the end, is frustrating, intangible, and super important (breath is life-giving) but fleeting and elusive. This is Solomon crying out that when he applies his mind to the meaning of life, he just does not understand.

So let's unpack these four verses again, but we'll read his words this time, understanding where he's going with this discussion.

- In verse twelve, he starts a new plan: to take an intellectual approach to understanding life. It's not as though he's left other stones unturned that his son needs to explore one day to finish the job. Solomon has done it all. Twice. There are no unexplored avenues for unpacking reality. Thought experiments are all he has left.

- In verse thirteen, he states a truism: wisdom is good.

- In verse fourteen, the point is that the wise at least know where they are going. Good or bad, they can see what's going on around them. But then he wraps up the verse with the observation that the wise can see far ahead, and death is what is ahead.

- This leads us to verse fifteen and Solomon's unhappiness with seeing his own death coming, and he's suddenly not so sure that wisdom is so great after all. He doesn't abandon wisdom here, but he asks, What was I wise for if the result of wisdom is simply knowing that darkness is coming?

This whole business was really *hevel* for Solomon. He had to pursue it, but remember, in 1:3, he referred to this quest as an "unhappy obsession," one he couldn't put down. This unhappy obsession was given not just to him but to all of humanity by God. Once again, I like how the NIV phrases this verse.

What a heavy burden God has laid on mankind!
Ecclesiastes 1:13b (NIV)

We will encounter this idea that God has given humans something almost unbearable as part of their everyday existence again later on. For now, though, where does this conclusion leave Solomon the Seeker?

Remember, this isn't Solomon coming to a conclusion one weekend after a few days or months of effort. This is Solomon after a lifetime of labor, building projects, and seven hundred weddings, plus affairs. In his gray years, this is a man sitting at his desk overlooking the city he built, seeing his generation going and another coming, and realizing that he doesn't know what it all means and where to find lasting benefit in life.

Where does this leave him?

We don't have to guess. Solomon tells us his state of mind in such plain, angsty language that you would think it was a modern confessional piece in *The New Yorker*. The way he expresses himself reads to me like a lifetime therapy patient with solid self-awareness and a gift for personal expression describing his general unhappiness with the world.

> *17 So I hated life, because the things that happen under the sun were troublesome to me. Definitely, everything is pointless—just wind chasing.*
>
> *18 I hated the things I worked so hard for here under the sun, because I will have to leave them to someone who comes after me. 19 And who knows whether that one will be wise or foolish? Either way, that person will have control over the results of all my hard work and wisdom here under the sun. That too is pointless.*
>
> ECCLESIASTES 2:17–19

Reading my journals last summer and reading Solomon's cry of despair here, I found the similarities between the two voices startling. I was a California teenager from farming country working a night-shift job, and Solomon was an aging king in the Middle East, but we both were torn up by the reality we observed around us. There seemed to be no solution to the frustrations in life. There was very little difference between the heart of a searching teenager and a hungry old man. Existential despair does not discriminate.

Ecclesiastes is the record of a man exposing his heart three thousand years ago. So little has changed below the skin.

"Definitely, everything is pointless—just wind chasing," he says (2:17b). Pointless is, of course, that word *hevel* again.

Solomon is despairing because of the fragility of life and its repetitive, temporary, and ultimately unfulfilling nature. This realization made him hate life because of the angst that brooded within him, the heavy burden he couldn't put down, the unhappy obsession he couldn't get rid of, and all the avenues he'd explored and found empty. He longed for lasting benefit. Instead, he had found a life of labor without control, certainty, or clear purpose. The more he accomplished, the more aware he became that he was running out of hopeful solutions to his problem.

There's a subtle biographical note embedded in these words as well. Solomon's son and eventual heir was an enormously foolish individual. Apparently, Solomon had learned his father David's parenting patterns, and his kids were a mess. This isn't me laying my reading of Jewish history over Solomon's words or even Solomon's own wisdom forecasting the future. In 1 Kings 11, God visited Solomon and personally showed him what a wreck Solomon had made of things and how the next generation would break up the entire country as a result. Solomon knew, directly from God, what would come after his lifetime.

Regardless of whether his son stayed the course and became the disaster God had predicted (for the record, God predicted accurately; he's God, after all), the fact remained that Solomon had no control over what would happen after his death. He spent thirteen years building the palace he penned these lines in, and somebody else, good or bad, wise person or fool, would inherit it all.

For a guy with a lot of power, he had no control over what mattered most to him. Solomon didn't even live to old age. He died at about sixty.[54] Billionaire or pauper, we all go out the same way and at the same time: when and how God chooses.

That, to Solomon, was just a whole lot of *hevel*. All of existence was essential and meaningful but oh-so temporary, fragile, and fleeting. For the king, this was almost unbelievable. You would think a wise king would get a reality that was more than just *hevel*. But no. Even wise kings live lives that are just a breath. Here today, then gone, with very little control over the coming and the going.

Solomon did not dismiss wisdom here. He called the distinction between wisdom and foolishness *hevel*. The distinction was real but rarely clear. It was like breath, a wisp of fog on a cold winter's day. That breath is beautiful in the air and so very clearly there. Then gone.

Hevel.

---

54 "Ancient Jewish History: The Kings of Ancient Israel," The Jewish Virtual Library, The American-Israeli Cooperative Enterprise, accessed July 3, 2023, *https:// www.jewishvirtuallibrary.org/the-kings-of-ancient-israel.*

12

THE HUNGRY SOUL NEEDS MORE THAN A BETTER JOB

THE FANCIEST RESTAURANT in the small California town I moved to when I turned eighteen was a place people flew to from San Francisco on private planes for Sunday brunch.

After I wrapped things up with Ed, I applied to be a waiter there.

"We need a dishwasher to start tonight," the manager countered.

"But I want to be a waiter," I said in my jeans and white T-shirt, watching one of the tuxedo-clad servers pass by.

"How old are you?" the manager asked.

"Eighteen," I said.

"Kid, the drinking age is twenty-one. You can't serve alcohol for three more years, so you can't be a waiter here."

"But you need a dishwasher," I said.

"Tonight," the manager said with a more hopeful expression.

I was now unemployed, living with a roommate, and needed to eat and pay rent.

"I'll make you a deal," I said. "I'll start as a dishwasher tonight if you promise to train me as a waiter within two weeks."

He took the deal. Two weeks later, I donned a tuxedo and started learning the waitering business even though my peers had to serve the beverages for my tables.

Serving in that place wasn't just regular waiting on tables. A few special meals were cooked tableside. Steak Diane was one of those everyday menu items that the kitchen team prepped while the waiter handled the final touches tableside. These touches included flambéing the finished dish with a mixture of ninety-two-proof vodka cut with brandy and lit by a fancy lighter on a silver stick. Baked Alaska was a dessert similarly set on fire tableside as part of the presentation. I extolled their reported virtues to folks spending more on their dinner than I was going to make all week. I was amazed by the whole rich-person subculture on display before me.

"Our chef's variation on steak Diane was originally developed," I started one night while prepping the dish for a beautiful young couple. I never got to the end of that spiel. I fumbled the small silver container and flambéed myself instead of the main course.

"This vintage was originally bottled," I began another night before firing the cork through the arboretum in the middle of the room where it landed somewhere unknown to me. This couple was less entertained by my error. Looking back, I realize that we must have been a bit liberal with the alcohol rules since both the champagne and the ninety-two-proof vodka were alcohol, and I was not supposed to serve them.

I eventually got fired. Apparently, twice, tables assigned to me were never served. I didn't find out about this until the exit interview. I was pretty sure at the time the maître d' didn't tell me they were my tables. The flambé fumble and champagne explosion were the only two errors I was consciously aware of. Nearly four decades later and with a better understanding of late teenagers' attention to detail, I'm more open to the idea that I deserved dismissal.

It is the only time in my life I've been fired, and in the end, they couldn't bring themselves to finish the job. After taking my tuxedo back, the owner offered me the night-shift janitor job. That's a pretty extreme fall from glory, but I had rent to pay, so I took the job. I showed up around midnight the next night as the folks I used to work with wrapped up their evening. I set to work cleaning the place from top to bottom, starting with the bathrooms. I was the only member of the night staff. I locked the door when the last person left for the night and let the morning crew back in the next day.

Cleaning everything from the kitchen to the bar to the restaurant was my nightly task and silent domain. I scrubbed, vacuumed, and polished everything. Once a week, I partially stripped the hardwood floor in the bar, rewaxed it, and buffed it to a mirror-like shine with a large ornery buffing machine.

Once, I sampled Glenfiddich single malt Scotch on my own at about three in the morning. I made some of the best sandwiches in the kitchen before the morning crew came in—the finest meats, sauces, cheeses, and peppers. The whiskey and the meals weren't part of the deal, but I had the run of the place through the night's darkest hours, and sitting alone in the beautiful bar with its atmospheric lighting and bottles and mirrors, carrying on conversations with myself in the mirror behind the bar, sipping Scotch, and eating a sandwich were my only forms of satisfaction when everything outside the tall windows was black and still. Later, reading Stephen King's *The Shining*, I counted myself lucky that as a budding writer flying solo and sampling rare whiskeys through those long nights, I didn't go a bit bonkers.

Eventually, the owner asked me to stay behind after the place opened in the mornings for a new opportunity. In this way, I began a second part-time job in the accounting office. We were somehow affiliated with an adjacent hotel, and so occasionally, I also did room service runs, travelling from the kitchen, through the empty and freshly polished bar, out the back door, and across a luxuriously maintained garden of trees and plants with leaves larger than me to the hotel to deliver eggs Benedict or an egg-white omelet with freshly squeezed orange juice and a couple of hot coffees to yet more people living a life I could only imagine.

Many months later, the owner announced that he wanted to make me the restaurant's buyer. This job paid well in that small town and would put me in charge of managing contracts, communicating with vendors, and even sourcing new suppliers for our needs. By then, however, I'd decided to move to Canada. I declined the offer, packed up my little Italian mid-engine, two-seater convertible (an early 1970s Fiat X1/9), and drove to Canada.

I wasn't just moving. I was hunting. I needed something that California and nursing and construction and waitering were not giving me. I was hungry.

Solomon was hungry too, but as he worked through his experiments and observations, he kept coming up empty. He was approaching one of his positive conclusions in Ecclesiastes, but before he got there, he slipped into this bit of sorrow.

> ^{20} *I then gave myself up to despair, as I thought about all my laborious hard work under the sun, ^{21} because sometimes those who have worked hard with wisdom, knowledge, and skill must leave the results of their hard work as a possession to those who haven't worked hard for it. This too is pointless—it's a terrible wrong. ^{22} I mean, What do people get for all their hard work and struggles under the sun? ^{23} All their days are pain, and their work is aggravation; even at night, their hearts don't find rest. This too is pointless.*

ECCLESIASTES 2:20–23

Hevel. It was all *hevel.* Waitering and royalty were both *hevel.* Solomon had more prestigious work to consume him than my gigs, but he was no happier.

At nineteen, I didn't have Solomon's full angst yet, but it was coming. I settled into life as a Canadian. I shopped my résumé around immediately and started work at 4 p.m. the day after my arrival at a place called Michael's Rib and Omelet House.

I started as a line cook despite never having been a real cook before. The business could only afford one cook per shift. The menu ranged from burgers and fish and chips to liver and onions or steak and potatoes. Many patrons came into the place wearing thigh-high dairy farmers' boots.

A few days later, the owner sat me down. "You don't know how to cook," he said.

"I'm learning," I replied.

"Yes, you are," he said. "So here's the deal. I like you. If you do everything I say, I'll teach you how to cook."

Thus began my cooking apprenticeship. I made a lot of omelets at that place and can't ever recall anyone ordering ribs.

One night, I was cleaning the grill, which involved cranking the temperature to its maximum, pouring hydrochloric acid over the metal, scraping it down with a flat scraper, and then pouring water all over the now shiny metal to clean off the last steaming bits. The mess of oil, burnt scraps, hydrochloric acid, and steaming water emptied into a long metal container. I then picked that container up with insulated rubber gloves and dumped it into a waste barrel designated for this toxic stew.

That night, the gloves slipped on the oily metal. The tray dropped from my hand, bounced off the grill, and splashed me in the face. I don't remember what happened after that, but someone must have seen or heard and got me to a sink because I don't have any permanent scarring on my face from the accident. Still, I couldn't see, and the pain in my eyes was unbelievable. Someone drove me to the hospital, where my eyes were frozen and washed, which I've got to tell you is an utterly surreal experience. I could see everything they were doing to my eyeballs but not feel it.

I was able to witness the cleaning of my eyes, but then I stopped being able to see at all for a day. Then I could see, but only blurry shapes. Three days later, I was back on shift at the restaurant, but I had to wear sunglasses indoors until my eyes could deal with light again.

A short while after that, Michael sold the restaurant to a chef from Spain. The new owner replaced ribs with a dish called Chicken Mediterranean. This creation required making a roux from scratch so that you could make the white sauce from scratch, and only then could you start making the actual dish from scratch. Next, he replaced liver and onions with escargot and various fish dishes. Burgers were off the menu altogether.

This new chef watched me for a day, then took me aside and informed me that I didn't know how to cook.

My answer was, as before, that I was learning fast.

His response was similar to Michael's before him. "If you do everything I tell you, I'll teach you how to cook." That was the nicest he ever was to anyone in that place. This chef from Spain perfectly foreshadowed later cooking show histrionics once things like the Food Network became a thing. After a few months, I'd had enough of the drama.

I saw an ad in the paper: "Chicken catchers wanted—$9.99 per hour." Chicken catching? I didn't even know that was a job, but apparently, it was a job that paid a lot more than cooking. The job also advertised "transportation provided." How great was that?

They picked me up at 10 p.m. in a 7-Eleven parking lot in a windowless panel van. When the silent and frowning driver opened the rear doors, it was filled with haggard-looking men who spoke little to no English. There was no light in the van when the door closed. We drove for an hour or more, crowded shoulder-to-shoulder on the benches, and then when the van stopped, we got out. Our handlers led us into long low barns filled with thousands of sleeping chickens. The job was to bend down and—with one hand—grab one chicken's leg, then another's, and then a third's until you had three stirring chickens in one hand. Then you'd do the same with your other hand and suddenly hoist six chickens in the air and hurry out of the barn with these flapping birds before they woke up the other ten or twenty thousand birds to be collected that night.

We would walk through the barn to a massive semi-truck trailer filled with small cages and lift the birds to a man on a ladder who would stuff them into the cages.

It wasn't really chicken *catching* because the chickens weren't running. They were sleeping. They kept the lighting dim, and the technique minimized the disruption to the other sleeping chickens. Chicken lifting and chicken carrying would have been more accurate job descriptions. Perhaps also chicken bench-pressing—lifting six chickens above your head repeatedly for ten hours straight is one fantastic workout. These were not just dead-weight reps. By this point, the "caught" chickens were flapping and squawking and often attacking with their free leg, which has a wicked hook specifically designed to draw an opponent's blood. To save myself from unnecessary blood loss, I learned to turn a pair of jeans into gauntlets by cutting thumbholes in the legs to anchor one on each arm. I've never read a kinesiology assessment of the micro-muscle benefits of bench-pressing weights that moved independently and aggressively attacked you with sharp hooks, but surely this workout has some fine motor skill benefits.

The experienced guys wore masks and goggles because all that flapping raised a haze of dried manure and chicken dandruff dust that got in your eyes and lungs. Of course, the goggles fogged up and the lighting was low, and so were the crossbeams in the low ceiling (the barns were designed for chickens, not people). So I had to walk bent over with six flapping chickens and low visibility. As a result, I walked into a lot of vertical support posts with my head bent down. That couldn't have been healthy for my noggin. When I stood up in frustration, a different part of my hurting head would connect with a horizontal crossbeam. Right about then, a chicken would find my legs with its fighting claw, and so the only thing to do would be to bend over again, holding six chickens as far away from my legs as possible, and try to remember where the vertical support posts were in the dark barn. Thus, bent-over reverse-fly curls were added to the challenge of bench-pressing attacking chickens.

If the barn was particularly low or dark, or you felt like you'd had enough, you couldn't quit this kind of job in disgust. We had no idea where in the province we were. It was dark; we had travelled here in a windowless panel van. Nobody had cell phones yet. Commercial GPS was still years away. The only way out was to finish the job and hope that the ride was home and not to another farm.

At the end of each shift, when I returned to the lovely suburban home where I now rented a room, I had to strip naked in the basement and shower before going upstairs. My clothes, hair, face—everything—was ghostly white as though I'd been dumped into a bin of super finely ground white flour.

Each morning, freshly showered after chicken catching, I went to bed and slept until around three in the afternoon. When I woke, I invariably found that, despite wearing goggles in the barns, my eyes were glued shut. I would feel my way to the bathroom and soak my face in warm water to clean and open them again, trying not to lose too many eyelashes in the process.

After a week, my finger joints began making a strange clicking noise. Somehow the strain of clutching six angry chickens for ten hours straight was swelling and altering my knuckles. All this for $9.99 an hour.

They mailed us our cheques after two weeks of work. The pay turned out to be $4.50 an hour. I called the office to protest, and they informed me that $9.99 was the rate for full time. I'd been working ten hours or more a night, seven nights a week for several weeks by then. Full time, it turned out, meant that you'd been working for six months.

After the pay fraud, I couldn't continue bench-pressing attack chickens for a living. Six months of this would wreck my back, lungs, and eyes for life.

At this stage, I moved houses, looking for cheaper rent, and wound up sleeping for an extended period on a hardwood floor with only a blanket for a mattress. At one point, I had a quarter to my name when I went to the grocery store. I searched the store for something to eat and found a bunch of greens priced for exactly twenty-five cents. I was ravenous. I bought it and ate it in the parking lot. It turned out to be parsley. Parsley hadn't figured heavily into the menu with Michael or the Spanish chef. Parsley is not a main course or a side dish. I ate the whole bunch anyway. I couldn't return it for a refund, and I had nothing else to eat. If my digestive system could talk, it would have had questions for management about the new dietary regime: extended fasting punctuated by herbs and water was not meeting my needs. I lost weight I couldn't afford to misplace.

I began to better understand what Solomon was saying when he complained that people work hard and struggle to make a living and "All their days are pain, and their work is aggravation; even at night, their hearts don't find rest" (Eccles. 2:23a). It was as true for the king as for me, but at nineteen years old, I still had enough life left in front of me to believe that a better job, more money in the bank, and a more reliable car would fix my troubles. I didn't have Solomon's wisdom yet. I wanted something more, and then I would start to become happy. I just knew it.

But I was wrong.

> [23] *All their days are pain, and their work is aggravation; even at night, their hearts don't find rest. This too is pointless.*
> ECCLESIASTES 2:23

A better job wouldn't erase the *hevelness* of life. But I was only nineteen, and it's the only idea I had at the time on how to do better.

13

THE BEST CAREER IN THE WORLD IS ONLY TEMPORARY

AFTER THE CHICKEN-CATCHING pay fraud, I walked back to the 7-Eleven but didn't get into the panelled van. Instead, I went into the store and got an application. Working solo night shifts at what amounted to a combination of a convenience store, VHS rental hub, local video game emporium, and gas station was heaven compared to the chicken barns.

The pay was basically the same as the chicken catcher's actual (versus advertised) rate, though. As a result, despite working full time, this financial reality still meant that I couldn't both pay rent and eat. I had to pick one.

I solved this problem as best I could. I started by salvaging all the expired 7-Eleven hoagies and other premade sandwiches I was responsible for throwing away during my shift. I took the expired subs out back as required but put them beside the garbage bin instead of in it. Then, after my shift, I snuck around back and collected them to take home. This was technically stealing, but since I was stealing from what otherwise would have gone in the garbage, it was easy to rationalize. Even so, I continued to lose badly needed weight during this period. I remember someone offering me a free coffee with cream or milk, and I jumped on the chance for cream. I was not too fond of coffee at the time, but I craved the calories, specifically the fat, to keep me going—definitely cream over milk.

I also studied ballet during this period, which didn't help my finances nor my drift toward becoming involuntarily underweight. I'd started dancing before chicken catching after I'd read a ballet dancer's autobiography.[55] Her story of a life focused on art ignited my creative imagination. I enrolled in every dance school in town, in some cases by negotiating for discounted rates to stretch my few dimes and dollars. I was probably the only forklift operator/framer/cook/chicken catcher in Canada with serious ballet training.

The various schools opened at 4 p.m. each day, which was why I had to be up by 3 p.m. after catching chickens all night. I danced five to six hours a day for six days a week (none of the schools were open on Sunday) and took private lessons as well. One school taught Royal and one taught Cecchetti, which for non dancers translates to English and Italian ballet schools. It was a constant mental challenge to remember which school I was in so I could perform the various moves according to either the Royal or the Cecchetti standard. Later in life, I became friends with a staff member and former dancer at Canada's National Ballet and learned that the various dance schools are not as rigidly differentiated anymore. However, back then, Royal versus Cecchetti was still a big deal. I would work out at the various studios until nine or ten at night, then hurry home and get changed for my night shift. When I caught chickens, I just went to work sweaty from the studio workouts. Once I got the job at 7-Eleven, I had to shower before work instead of afterward. My life became an endless cycle of working, working out, sleeping, and surviving on expired sandwiches.

Ballet didn't work out. I was a creative soul but a terrible dancer, probably better suited to country line dancing than classical ballet. Dancing, it turned out, was like music for me. I could feel it, imagine it, and enjoy it but not do it with any kind of real talent. Before quitting, I talked to my teachers about my chances of making a career in Canada's dance world. One of my teachers had previously danced with the National Ballet of Canada as well as the San Francisco Ballet; another had been with the Royal Winnipeg Ballet. They both offered the same advice: my career would be over at about thirty, even if I was a superstar. Age, injury, or both would leave me unemployed early in life. Follow-up career prospects were limited. I was already in my twenties. Training for another few years for a one percent chance of being barely employed for five years and then landing back on the street in my thirties, trying to find food-and-rent money, didn't seem like a good plan.

---

55   I read a lot of ballet literature during this period, but the book that started it for me was Gelsey Kirkland's *Dancing on My Grave* (Doubleday: 1986).

7-Eleven was not the new long-term plan either. In addition to minimum-wage pay, I got robbed at knifepoint, swordpoint, and at various times, gunpoint. There's not much to do when you're on the night shift with a gun or a Samurai short sword in your face but to hand over the till.

I have copies of my various police reports from that period of my life in my journals. In some cases, the officers that came in weren't responding to my call. They'd come in for coffee and discover that dispatch hadn't passed on my 911 call, so they'd end up taking over the case by accident. That kind of dispatch disinterest or disorganization is not comforting to a store clerk at two or three in the morning.

After the police left, I would continue my shift solo. On a few nights, a second robbery occurred, and I had the problem of a largely empty till while facing an unhappy gunman or knife-wielding masked stranger. When calling the police a second time, I felt like I was bothering people who had other priorities in those dark hours.

In the morning, I would hand over the till to the incoming morning manager.

"Anything interesting?" the manager would ask.

"Another robbery," I'd say. "A knife this time."

"Okay, how much?"

I'd tell him.

"You've got all the police paperwork?"

I'd hand that over to him, and that would be the end of the conversation. Without the police reports, I would have had a till short of cash and no way to explain it until the manager reviewed the videotapes later in the day. Looking back, I find it so strange that I had no one to call at 3 a.m. after the police left. The store stayed open and I looked after it alone. I helped the next customer. Once my shift was over, I'd leave as sunlight brightened the day, collect my expired hoagies from around the back, and walk home. I ate hoagies every day. I didn't need variety. I just needed calories.

My nearest friend lived twelve hundred kilometers north of me. My closest relative was thirteen hundred kilometers to the south. Email hadn't arrived for the general public yet. Social media wasn't even an idea. So I was happy for the illicit sandwiches. The people who knew me either did not know about the night's violence or did not care. At the time, it did not occur to me that this situation was a problem.

Later in life, when I was robbed as a bank teller for the first time, the bank brought in trauma counsellors to talk the staff through their distress. I was more traumatized by the trauma counsellors than the robbery. Being forced to talk about my feelings wasn't helpful when I had a volcano bottled inside and the conversation was to be just a thirty-minute debrief and we're done. When the bank was robbed again, I dodged the trauma counsellors to avoid stirring that volcano.

Avoiding thoughts about distress isn't a healthy long-term coping mechanism—trauma comes out later in other ways, as I talk about in *Even the Monsters*—but it worked for me for a time. I was a single man alone in the country who just needed to eat. Therapy and healing came much later.

However, it wasn't just low-paying and unsafe jobs that wore me down and made me start to understand Solomon's existential angst. As I write this, I work for a major Canadian bank on Bay Street (my US readers can think of it as the Canadian equivalent of Wall Street) and have been with the company for over thirty years. My pay, benefits, working conditions, and prospects are far from where things stood in my early days in California and British Columbia. But something interesting occurs when you've worked for a major international corporation for three decades. You wind up living and working long enough to spend years launching a major project that took late nights, long weekends, and cancelled vacations to achieve, only to see that very same thing dismantled and discarded a decade later. The world and its underlying technical infrastructure move on to new products, technologies, and client expectations.

Solomon despaired that he was going to leave his work to someone undeserving. I gradually realized that I wouldn't leave my work to anyone at all. I would outlive my work. Everything I "built," whether in my pre-university retail jobs or banking career, would be discarded or burned down (so to speak) within a few years of the party celebrating its launch.

As Solomon puts it,

> [22] *I mean, What do people get for all their hard work and struggles under the sun?* [23] *All their days are pain, and their work is aggravation; even at night, their hearts don't find rest. This too is pointless.*
>
> ECCLESIASTES 2:22–23

This verse is even more true for me now than it was as a laborer or retail clerk. What does a person get for all their hard work, whether catching chickens or navigating through System Integration Testing, Business Acceptance Testing, User Acceptance Testing, Production Acceptance Testing, and production deployment? Younger readers with IT backgrounds will laugh at my outdated waterfall[56] technical language in an age of Agile methodologies with their new processes and vocabulary, but I can assure you that in a decade or two, someone will laugh at your outdated Agile methodology language as well. Agile development with its features, epics, stories, and scrum huddles will be subject to a future generation's mockery when something new takes their place.

A different career isn't the answer either. You could be the world's best surgeon, saving lives every day. That would be amazing and meaningful work. But every one of your patients will eventually die anyway. I only state that to illustrate the truth of Solomon's realism. All our work is temporary, and what do we really get from it?

On rough days, I tell my wife and son, "That's why they pay me and call it a job." And they pay me well. I'd rather do what I do now than go back to bench pressing chickens again for $4.50 an hour, but Solomon's complaint isn't about the quality of the job—he was king, after all. His complaint was about where to find *yithron*—lasting benefit.

People work hard, and "even at night, their hearts don't find rest" (2:23). That is truer for me now than it was as a chicken catcher. Solomon will point out the likelihood of this dynamic in a later chapter, which we'll see when we get to it.

The bottom line here is that all work is *hevel*. Retail clerk, banker, IT manager, or surgeon, it's all breath. It's important—if you don't work, you don't pay your rent and you don't eat—but it is also repetitive, temporarily helpful, and then must be repeated and then repeated again. People will never be completely satisfied. After that first good breath, we will need another one—and a paycheck to go with it. Another customer will need to be served. The IT job will need an upgrade. The patient will one day need another doctor and eventually a mortician. The need for something more is relentless.

---

56   For non-technical readers, "waterfall" in this context is a project delivery methodology developed in the 1970s and popular even to the present day even as it's slowly being replaced by variations of a new methodology called "Agile".

Ultimately, what does a person gain from their work that offers lasting benefit? What is that "something more" that offers worth greater than just keeping ourselves alive for a while longer? Nothing. It's all *hevel*.

You can see from this discussion how Jerome and so many English translations turned *hevel* into pointlessness or meaninglessness, but remember, that's not Solomon's message. Everything is not pointless. It is breath. Temporary. Required. Life-giving. But frustratingly demanding, fleeting, and insubstantial. Life is need on repeat.

As a follow-up to this existential crisis, the next thing Solomon does is take a surprising and seemingly contradictory turn as he offers up a positive observation.

14

FLOW IS NOT JUST FOR ARTISTS

I USED TO manage an operations center for the bank near the Lake Ontario shoreline. Queen's Quay is located a few blocks away, and it contains collective space for artists in various disciplines. The public can view the artists at work from behind railings or glass walls.

I discovered the space during a lunch break when I needed to clear my head after dealing with an HR-related management problem. Stress had churned within me. My mind felt fogged. The air along the lakeshore was not the saltwater of my West Coast youth, but if I squinted and ignored the lack of saltiness, I could pretend. After a few minutes of walking, I entered one of the buildings and crossed into a little slice of heaven that I would come back to again and again.

The craftspeople in that place seemed oblivious to my presence. I would stand awhile and watch them and feel a rare peace come over me. I'd watch the potters, then move on. Next came the papermakers, then I'd move on. I found the glass-blowers particularly mesmerizing. Even from my distant vantage point, the heat from their ovens was intense. The men and women I watched stood before their oven's glowing maw, handling long iron poles tipped with melting blobs of brightly flowing glass, turning, burning, and shaping. Sweat poured from the artists as they gave their craft their total concentration. I found it beautiful to watch. Even now, writing in my home office or a café, I can feel the heat of those ovens and recover the particular joy I absorbed from watching that day.

Solomon understood the distinction between soulless labor and what I witnessed with the craftspeople and artists on Queen's Quay. Here are his thoughts on this distinction.

> *²⁴ There's nothing better for human beings than to eat, drink, and experience pleasure in their hard work. I also saw that this is from God's hand— ²⁵ Who can eat and find enjoyment otherwise?— ²⁶ because God gives wisdom, knowledge, and joy to those who please God.*
>
> ECCLESIASTES 2:24–26A

Wait a minute, Solomon just finished a multi-decade pleasure quest that brought him no ultimate fulfillment or lasting benefit. Yet here he is advocating for the very thing that failed him?

Well, no. Not exactly. As we saw, his pleasure quest was over-the-top in at least three ways.

First, the scale of his dive into pleasure was ludicrous. A thousand women? National parks? We didn't even discuss the scale of his eating, but since we didn't, let's do that now by taking another peek at the background in 1 Kings.

> *²² Solomon's food requirements for a single day included thirty kors of refined flour; sixty kors of flour; ²³ ten head of grain-fattened cattle; twenty head of pastured cattle; one hundred sheep; as well as deer, gazelles, roebucks, and the best of fowl.*
>
> 1 KINGS 4:22–23

You know where I'm going to go with this by now. How much is a "kor"? A kor is equal to a homer. Okay, that doesn't help. In metric, a kor is about 230 liters. That's a little over six bushels or around sixty gallons for my American friends.

So thirty kors of refined flour translates to just shy of 7,000 liters or around 1,800 gallons. That is a lot of refined flour. The daily ration of regular flour was double that. The cattle, deer, and fowl are straightforward, although I'm pretty sure you can't conceive of cooking a day's worth of meals that demanded a combination of 230 sheep and cattle "as well as deer, gazelles, roebucks," and, of course, birds. Notice how these extras are not enumerated, but they are plural.

That's all for one day. Obviously, Solomon fed a lot of people besides himself, but the point is clear that he overdid things in the food department to the same degree as his weddings and other activities.

So, Solomon's scale in his pleasure quest was over-the-top to a bizarre level.

The second over-the-top aspect of Solomon's pleasure quest was its righteousness, or rather, its unrighteousness. Said differently, he didn't just walk up to the line of sin or cross into a few gray areas. He blew through the guardrails. He got drunk. He married idol-worshipping women that the law forbade him to engage with. Do the math on a thousand relationships and a sixty-year lifespan, and you get roughly one wedding or new mistress added to his harem per month. That's disturbing. As he put it, he denied himself nothing.

The last excessive aspect of his pleasure quest worth noting is how much he sought to get from it. He wasn't just looking for a good time. He was seeking an existential answer to his heart's deepest need. He wanted more than pleasure. He wanted lasting benefit and could not find it. All of life was breath: take one and you immediately need another. One good breath would never satisfy.

So that was his pleasure quest, and it came up dry: he says, "I hated life" (2:17) and "gave myself up to despair" (2:20).

So what happened? How did Solomon go from despair and hating life because of the ultimate emptiness of pleasure to suddenly advocating for pleasure again? He even uses the same kinds of words: "There's nothing better" (2:24).

It is early in our study, so I want to avoid importing too much of what Solomon reveals later into this current conversation, but by looking just at these verses, what can we glean?

The first thing that stands out is that Solomon has dramatically reduced the scale. We've gone from national concerns and personal excesses to talking about lunch and the ability to enjoy our work. It is essential to notice that Solomon is now discussing the pleasure of the work itself, not of the work's result.

I've had moments over the years where work produced something inside me that matched what I observed in those men and women before their magical ovens at Queen's Quay. Woodworking was one such activity. I didn't just watch woodworkers, but I engaged in the craft itself. I have found pleasure in hearing the sliding scrape of a plane and smelling the difference between oak, mahogany, and bubinga woods. I've watched the beautiful curls appear from my hand tool and felt joy in my heart in direct response.

I once had an electric planer, but I traded it to another woodworker in exchange for a canoe. My day job had enough automation. I needed to hear the scrape of a blade I had sharpened myself and see the shavings accumulate in human time and not amid an overwhelming roar of powdered sawdust that filled the air and darkened my heart.

Working on my bonsai trees does something similar for me. It is a nearly silent activity except for the snick-snick of scissors, the rustle of leaves, and the whisper of breath. Psychologists and artists both call the state I'm describing "flow." It's a beautiful experience, an out-of-body joy, a true pleasure. My wife seems to enjoy a similar state when sewing. Others find flow in creating music, painting, skiing, sailing, and a variety of other activities.

Do these activities provide a lasting benefit? No. I can't hand plane a precious piece to perfection and then call it a day and never do it again and expect that experience to satisfy me forever after. Woodworking doesn't work that way. I must repeat it to rekindle the benefit, and even then, the reward is not guaranteed. The flow state is not available on demand. And even perfect flow gives you no lasting satisfaction—just pleasure in the moment and a later desire to recreate the experience.

Humans need lasting benefit from their work—Solomon will continue his quest to find it. But humans also need temporal pleasures. Yes, temporal pleasure is temporary—it should never be confused with an answer to our existential need for eternal benefit—but we should not dismiss it on that account.

Enjoy your lunch. Enjoy your work. I gradually began to understand that if everything I did at the bank could be hidden in a spreadsheet and tossed out within a decade, then I needed work that at least gave me some of that temporal pleasure Solomon was talking about. Hence my woodworking and bonsai and my wife's sewing.

In some ways, this is one of the gifts our daughter has given us. As a result of her health challenges, we have been confined to something like marital house arrest for over two decades. With one income, no vacations, and maybe one date night a year—not even the simple break of an afternoon at a park since there are no facilities for changing a teenager or grown woman on a beach, nor are these places conducive to regular emergency medical interventions—we've been forced to find forms of stress relief and pleasure within the boundaries of our suburban property. It turns out that almost all the things we've found involve flow.

Hobbies didn't immediately transform our lives, but like starting to work out, the benefits accumulated as the years passed.

Are hobbies really that important? Well, Solomon did say that "there's nothing better for human beings than to eat, drink, and experience pleasure in their hard work" (2:24a).

"Nothing better" sounds important. Ideally, our day job supplies that pleasure. If it doesn't, we either need to change careers or find something else for our off-hours that provides it. A hobby might just fit the bill.

By the way, TV doesn't count. TV isn't inherently evil, but the Bible states that we need to experience pleasure in our *hard work*. It doesn't say that we should find happiness from passive consumption. Don't get me wrong, rest is important. Solomon will even touch on the importance of rest later, but right now, in chapter two, the thing that is of such vital importance that it's identified in the "nothing better" category is pleasure from hard work. Solomon identifies an engaged joy that comes to us only when working hard *and* enjoying our labor. Flow is not just for artists.

15

JOY IS FOUND IN THE PROCESS, NOT THE RESULT

As I WATCHED those glass-blowers at Queen's Quay and felt some of their intensity and joy, I wondered about my own life, the choices I'd made, and the opportunities that had presented themselves as well as the doors that had been closed to me. I thought about the work situation that had led me to go on that lunchtime walk and wondered why I didn't have a career that had less friction and more flow to it.

That last verse we looked at in the previous chapter also bothered me. Let's look at it again.

> [26] *because God gives wisdom, knowledge, and joy to those who please God.*
>
> ECCLESIASTES 2:26A

I did not—that day or week, perhaps even for that entire year—have joy in my work. So was I not pleasing to God? Were those artists all pleasing to God and I was somehow cursed?

The second half of verse twenty-six made me question my place in life even more.

But to those who are offensive, God gives the task of hoarding and accumulating, but only so as to give it all to those who do please God. This too is pointless and a chasing after wind.

ECCLESIASTES 2:26B

If you didn't grow up with a strict religious background, or you're just not the introspective type, then that verse may not fuss you too much. But for me, it was deeply upsetting. I was unhappy at that particular stage of my career, and this verse implies a harsh explanation: God somehow found me offensive. God, after all, is the one who gives gifts, including pleasure in our work, but he only does so, though, "to those who do please God."

Wait a minute. Is Solomon saying that only Christians get wisdom and joy from our work? No, it doesn't say that. Christ's arrival was still a thousand years in the future.

Okay, so reworded, is Solomon saying that only followers of God get this gift and no one else experiences it? Well, no, it doesn't say that either. It says that God gives gifts to those who please him, not to those who believe in him.

That nuance was not helpful for me as I walked away from Queen's Quay back to the office. Religious readers might also wonder where I'm coming from with that kind of observation. I would argue that God loves everyone. Doesn't John 3:16, probably the most famous verse in the Bible, say it quite plainly? Other passages teach that he brings rain to bless everyone so that everyone will experience gifts from his hand, even those who don't respect him or believe in him. Scriptures teach that God is love, not that God only loves people who join his club.

Don't get me wrong. I'm not talking about salvation or heaven or any of that here. What I'm describing here does not discount the seriousness of sin or warnings about judgment, which the Bible also speaks about. But those hard truths don't erase other aspects of God's character.

Those glass-blowers, who were mesmerized by their hard work and mes- merizing to watch, exuded the wisdom of the glass-blower's craft and radiated joy in their work. Their flow state was visible and even absorbable as I took a lunch break and watched them. What they experienced, regardless of whether they believed in God or loved God or even thought about him at all, was still a gift from God. The babies of those who never think about God are born and breathe God-given air. Atheist farmers still get rain. Atheist artists still experience flow. These are all gentle gifts from our Creator, whether we acknowledge him or not.

That's all Solomon is saying here, but the statement in and of itself is profound. It teaches that not only does God love everybody and provide this rich blessing throughout the world but also that this gift of finding joy in our labor is one of the highest things for people to experience. "There's nothing better," Solomon says. I can think of many things equal to these kinds of experiences, but he's right—there's nothing better. For an artist to be lost in their art, for an artisan to flawlessly execute a project at the peak of their powers, for a bricklayer to find that groove where their every fiber is engaged and in the moment and working as they could and should—those are beautiful things. I once had a university calculus teacher dive into a mathematical proof so enthusiastically I could barely follow him. What I could follow quite clearly, though, was what I saw in him. He was in flow. He loved what he was doing. He demonstrated passion and talent for advanced math, and joy radiated from him as he did so. He made me interested in calculus just by watching him at the chalkboard. We're not all cellists or painters or mathematicians, but we're something. My wife is wise and experiences joy in baking and also sewing bespoke handbags. We're all different, but that thing we all experience in that hard work is both joy and a gift from God.

But if you try to find lasting benefit in flow, that flow will escape you, and something evil will take its place. That is why Solomon says,

> But to those who are offensive, God gives the task of hoarding and accumulating, but only so as to give it all to those who do please God. This too is pointless and a chasing after wind.
> ECCLESIASTES 2:26B

At what point do we move from being pleasing to God to being offensive? That's not a question that Ecclesiastes covers specifically, so I won't get distracted by trying to parse those details here. Suffice it to say that we can land ourselves in a situation where we become displeasing to God, and God interferes by making our pleasure in our work evaporate as a result. Solomon isn't proposing a mathematical cause-and-effect formula here. It's a dangerous—and judgmental—business to try to draw a conclusion along the lines of "losing your possessions means you're displeasing to God." The book of

Job refutes that kind of simplistic analysis. Similarly, you can't say "if you've lost your joy in work, it's because God is mad at you." As a general principle, however, Solomon is pointing out that we can lose even the simple joys of life if we're not careful.

Many commentaries I consulted describe Solomon as a character who had displeased God and, as a result, lost his ability to enjoy life. I agree with their conclusion on this point. First Kings articulates God's displeasure in plain language, so we don't have to guess regarding that detail. And what Solomon describes here as the curse for such a person is, in fact, how his life played out. He hoarded everything—gold, land, buildings, slaves, musicians, women, anything he could get his hands on. He denied himself nothing, and the result was that he learned to hate life instead of enjoying it. If we lose that gift of God, the ability to enjoy the simple things, then of what use is an exotic car, a tropical holiday, a lover, or any other pleasure in life? Any of my readers who work in hospitality have probably seen wealthy patrons who seem incapable of appreciating the most basic pleasures in life. Some seem to have traded the fundamental joy of a nice meal for a focus on fighting with their relatives, criticizing the chef, servers, and decor, and generally being dissatisfied with reality. Hollywood's elite don't burn through marriages, stints in rehab, and other stereotypes of that industry because things are going well.

The lesson I needed to take as I left Queen's Quay wasn't to question whether God liked me or not (John 3:16 and thousands of other verses make it clear that he loves me). The lesson I needed to take was that soulless materialism (or social status or income level or industry award or promotion or whatever other marker of success I choose to strive for) is not only an empty pursuit but achieving it might also even be a curse from God as a result of the distraction it provides. At the very least, real joy is not found there. Healthy joy is found in blessed processes—flow—not milestone achievements whose value and award is often dependent on others. The path to joy through materialism is a dead end, one that makes you subservient to the whims or opinions or regard of others, and like anything else in life, this path must be mercilessly repeated to maintain its mirage of lasting meaning.

If the translucent curl of a wood shaving rising in front of your slow-moving plane—or whatever work brings you joy—is lost to you, then you're truly lost. It's time to find your way again.

PART FOUR:

EXPANDING THE SEARCH WITH A BRIEF SURVEY OF TIME

16

DOUBLE HEPTADS, THE BYRDS, AND TIME

NEARLY A DECADE before my first memory of music, a California band merged the popular Beatles style with folk music and dubbed themselves the Byrds. They helped create folk-rock before going on to pioneer psychedelic rock and then two years later helped to create country rock. One of their first members was David Crosby of later Crosby, Stills, Nash, and Young fame. The Byrds were nothing if not innovative and talented. In 2004, when Tom Petty put together *Rolling Stone* magazine's list, "The 100 Greatest Artists of All Time," he placed the Byrds at number 45.[57]

During their folk-rock phase in the early 1960s, they remade Pete Seeger's 1959 song "Turn! Turn! Turn!" and took it to number one on the *Billboard* Hot 100 chart. I don't know how many number one songs have Bible verses as their lyrical base, but the lyrics of "Turn! Turn! Turn!" are lifted straight out of Ecclesiastes chapter three.

> *¹ There's a season for everything*
> *and a time for every matter under the heavens:*

---

57   Tom Petty, "100 Greatest Artists: 45; The Byrds," *Rolling Stone* (website), published December 3, 2010, accessed November 7, 2023, https://www.rollingstone. com/music/music-lists/100-greatest-artists-147446/the-byrds-89183/.

² a time for giving birth and a time for dying,
    a time for planting and a time for uprooting what
    was planted,

³ a time for killing and a time for healing,
    a time for tearing down and a time for building up,

⁴ a time for crying and a time for laughing,
    a time for mourning and a time for dancing,

⁵ a time for throwing stones and a time for gathering stones,
    a time for embracing and a time for avoiding embraces,

⁶ a time for searching and a time for losing,
    a time for keeping and a time for throwing away,

⁷ a time for tearing and a time for repairing,
    a time for keeping silent and a time for speaking,

⁸ a time for loving and a time for hating,
    a time for war and a time for peace.

ECCLESIASTES 3:1–8

In previous chapters, we've seen how excesses can lead to a terrible life state. The excesses we discussed were more than just good things taken too far: a pleasant meal leading to gluttony, the joy of marriage leading to Solomon's thousand women, and so on. Those excesses also included an excess of expectation. If someone looks for a wedding, job, hobby, or meal to fulfill their soul's most profound need, they will be disappointed. This is where hungry-to-be-married singles can warp their expectations and set themselves up for a post-honeymoon disaster. The same applies to job seekers and others who think the prize they're pursuing will bring them *yithron*. Without a course correction, the seeker risks entering Solomon's world of hoarding and hungering to the point where life becomes something hated. Solomon got there. It's not a good place to end up.

Solomon's point appears to be that everything needs to have its place and be limited to its proper proportions. But just in case we're the sort who need things really spelled out for us, Solomon elaborates even more on this theme with his now-famous lyrical poem.

The famous nature of this poem is a problem for many Western readers of a certain generation because musical familiarity divorces us from its context. My generation and older readers might think of the Byrds or Pete Seeger and not Ecclesiastes. There were no chapter breaks in the original, and this poem was not the start of something new but just the continuation of Solomon's previous points regarding excess and its cursed consequences.

This connection between the passages is not just visual, as the verses flowed from one to another, but also stylistic. For example, when Solomon says that there is "a time for every matter under the heavens," the Hebrew word he's using for "matter" shares the same root as the Hebrew word he kept using for "pleasure" in the previous chapter. In other words, in chapter two, Solomon names pleasure as a multi-decade pursuit that ultimately led to emptiness and even hatred of life. But, at the end of chapter two, he said that pleasure in its place is good. Pleasure is just not the ultimate good. It is not something that provides the lasting benefit he wants. Still, there's nothing better than those simple moments, and they should be viewed as gifts from God, even if the receiver doesn't even know God. Solomon ends chapter two then with a warning that those who fail to accept these pleasures with God's blessing (i.e., those who displease God) wind up driving themselves into a greedy, hoarding state of mind just like Solomon at the end of his personal pleasure quest.

Now, in the next paragraph (which modern Bibles label as the start of chapter three), Solomon continues this argument. He tells us that not only should the pleasures of life be accepted for what they are—and nothing more than that—but that these pleasures themselves are limited to their timing or seasons. Not every moment is a moment for partying, woodworking, making love, or enjoying a fine meal. Every matter, each pleasure under heaven, has its appropriate time and place.

If you've had bad experiences with religious dogma, this might sound like the dreaded beginning of a bunch of Christian rules. No sex before marriage, no drunkenness, no this, no that—the whole catalogue of religious *don'ts* could get trotted out here, but that's not Solomon's intent. Remember, he's approaching this entire book from an incredibly experimental perspective. If I'm correct in positioning the author of this book as Solomon, then he's an old man, reflecting on a life gone miserably wrong and offering wisdom for the next generation, one that is already beginning to replace his own. If I'm wrong, then God—through some other author—is using Solomon's persona as a lens through which to evaluate these matters. Either way, the result is the same. Solomon isn't interested in divinely given rules. He's interested in practically discovered truths. Today we might classify this as experimental psychology, though that might be putting too much of a twenty-first-century spin on what Solomon was up to. Perhaps philosophy is a better term.

One of Solomon's first bits of practical wisdom is the message that we should enjoy the simple things in life. A second bit of practical wisdom is the lesson that this pleasure should never become central to the meaning of our lives. Other places in the Bible will identify such a focus as idolatry and become quite polemical against this sin, but Solomon isn't approaching things that way. He doesn't use the word idolatry. He simply shows that things go wrong when you engage in behavior that we think of today as idolatry: putting anything in place of God or trying to find ultimate meaning in life without God.

Notice that this is wrong not because of divine punishments. Solomon simply discovers that things go wrong because of the reality of basic human wiring. Pursuing pleasure as an end in and of itself will fail. To satisfy us, we need something more than gourmet food, a better vacation, more money, or a more beguiling lover. Solomon knows. He tried all these things. He tried these things to levels you and I could never hope to approach, and it didn't work. A thousand women, gold measured in tons, and musicians and singers collected like you and I might compile playlists all made him hate life.

There's a right time for the things we experience in life.

Solomon could have just ended his argument at 3:1, but he's a thorough teacher who wants to ensure we understand his point. He's not just talking about dinner or money or marriage. He wants it to be clear that he's talking about everything. To do this, he created a list of fourteen things that there was a time for. This is not a random list. A list of fourteen things was a big deal in ancient Hebrew culture.

Before getting to his specific fourteen things, we must understand this ancient Hebrew concept. Numbers meant a lot to the ancient Hebrews. I won't bore you with all the symbolism, but one detail is essential for our purposes: a heptad.

A heptad is a list of seven things. Seven was considered a complete number in ancient Hebrew. A modern-day analogy in Western societies is a top ten list. If I published a book on the top nine reasons for something or other, any self-respecting publisher would tell me to come up with one more. You need ten or the list is not complete. The number one hundred is similar in English. Ninety-seven great vacation ideas are short three.

Similarly, in Hebrew, a list of seven was a complete list—a perfect list.

In English, we also have the somewhat random idea that one hundred and one is even better. One hundred and one is fantastic. Suppose I wrote a book on the top eleven reasons to do something. That would be odd. It's one more than ten, but eleven isn't a good idea. Yet one hundred and one is one more than a hundred, which is fantastic. That's a perfect list and then some. Why are ten and one hundred considered complete, and one hundred and one even better, while eleven is just weird? I have no idea. That's just how Western culture looks at numbers.

The ancient Hebrew equivalent of one hundred and one was to double the list of seven. In other words, what made a perfect list of seven things better was doubling it to a list of fourteen. Scholars call a list of fourteen things a double heptad.

So after his bitter experience, Solomon wants to assure us that taking pleasure in life's simple things is good but needs to be taken in stride and not made central in our lives. He underscores this point by showing us how all the stuff of life has its limited time and place. Then he backs up and illustrates that claim with a double heptad list. The double heptad list then doubles again as it pairs fourteen positive experiences with fourteen negative ones, all of which have their time and place.

Pete Seeger and the Byrds latched on to these verses in Ecclesiastes for a good reason. There is something timeless about this poem about time, so let's get into it.

17

THERE ARE TIMES FOR BEGINNINGS, RESTARTS, AND ALSO ENDINGS

MY RELATIONSHIP WITH time has changed as I've got older. It's not a surprise to my peers that my days, months, and years seem to go startlingly fast in my fifties when they dragged along at an unbearable pace in my younger years. I understand from the generations that have gone before me that this experience is not unique to my Generation X but is a universal phenomenon. Nevertheless, this aspect of aging somehow escaped my awareness in my younger years. I knew that later in life my eyesight might deteriorate and my hair would gray, but I did not expect my internal clock to tick faster. Younger readers, take note.

Perhaps because of his age and increasing awareness of his own mortality, Solomon starts his poem about time with the bookends of human existence.

> *¹ There's a season for everything*
> *and a time for every matter under the heavens:*
> *² a time for giving birth and a time for dying,*

ECCLESIASTES 3:1–2A

Barring suicide or a medically assisted death, you don't get to choose either of those things for yourself. If there's any doubt about how not-in-control-of-our-lives we are, our powerlessness over our births and deaths should clear things up. The bookends of our lives are in God's hands. However, one of the problems with humans is we block out the significance of this fundamental lack of control. This willful blindness seems normal for people, but Solomon starts his double heptad with these exact two points—birth and death. Everything else he's going to touch on happens in between.

The next two items on Solomon's list draw upon farming imagery. As the owner of orchards and vineyards and the king of a nation whose economy is dependent on agriculture, this example meant a lot to him.

> *a time for planting and a time for uprooting what was planted,*
> ECCLESIASTES 3:2B

An alternative translation could be "a time for planting and a time for harvesting." You can't harvest if you haven't planted already. You also can't harvest at any random time after planting—there is a particular season when crops are ready for harvesting. In fact, you can't plant most crops whenever you want either—there is a specific annual season for that activity too.

Next on his list is a startling pair.

> *³ a time for killing and a time for healing,*
> ECCLESIASTES 3:3A

Pacifists and vegans might take offence at the first of these two points and hope there's an alternative translation that takes the sting out of the word "killing." Alas, there is no such relief except to state that the word is "kill," not "murder." Despite this, I think even vegans would agree that if some must eat meat, the time to do the butchery is not while you're trying to serve dessert.

Likewise, there is a time for healing. You don't want a physiotherapist running out onto a hockey rink, football field, or a sprinter's track mid-game or mid-heat with a massage table. There's a proper time for a massage, and the middle of the match isn't the time.

We can take these two points beyond their literal meaning and understand them figuratively as well. There's a time to end a relationship—with a person, company, or social group—and a time to heal one. In Christian and other circles, a lot of damage can happen when people insist that the only proper course of action is to heal the relationship rather than end it. In some circumstances, ending things is the right thing to do. Ecclesiastes doesn't deeply explore these side topics, but *Necessary Endings* by Dr. Henry Cloud is one book I found helpful during a challenging career stage. I had a necessary ending to execute, and the book was a useful guide to ensure I did not go overboard with my departure but managed the situation as wisely as possible. Likewise, Lysa Terkeurst's book *Good Boundaries and Goodbyes* is a powerful tool for those trying to navigate more emotionally fraught situations. I highly recommend both texts.

There is a time to kill and a time to heal. Each has its place.

At a first read, it sounds like Solomon is repeating himself in the next line.

> *a time for tearing down and a time for building up,*
> ECCLESIASTES 3:3B

What is Solomon up to here? Aren't tearing down and building up just another way of saying killing and healing? Is Solomon duplicating and rephrasing a previous line simply to fill out the double heptad?

Killing and healing involve living beings. Even metaphorical killing and healing is all about the relationships between living beings. When we kill or heal a relationship with a company or organization, it is really the people in that company or organization that we're leaving or making amends with.

In contrast, tearing down and building up speak to *things*. These things can be literal physical objects, such as the hundred-year-old house Ed had me tear down and the new three-bedroom home we built in its place.

These things can also be figurative. Some philosophies, political movements, and trends within religious denominations or family traditions serve their purpose for a while—perhaps even for generations. But those same philosophies, movements, trends, and traditions can calcify and become irrelevant, maybe even a hindrance when times and circumstances change. Then it is time to tear down.

For example, parenting is a process of transitioning from having nearly complete control over your child as an infant to relinquishing that control over your child as an adult. This process involves many stages of tearing down old parent-child interaction models and replacing them with reimagined age- and maturity-appropriate practices. Companies do this as well when they mature past the wilder start-up phase of their lifecycle and have to adopt more advanced management, operations, customer service, and other practices.

On a larger scale, this can be a hard lesson for older generations who may see the work of their hands dismantled within their lifetime. Conservatism has its value, by which I don't mean a specific political party but merely the human desire to maintain an established order. Innovations are not always improvements. Sometimes the old ways are better.

But Solomon here reminds us that there are also times for tearing down. Not everything should stay the same forever. You can open up Seneca from the first century BCE and find his contempt for the recent invention of glass windows.[58] Likewise, you can find folks in the sixteenth century ridiculing Queen Elizabeth I's godson for inventing the water closet—an early form of our modern indoor toilet. On the back of this abuse, only the queen and her godson used his invention, and the idea died for another two-hundred years before its revival.[59] Both Seneca and the anti-indoor plumbing crowd may have had a few valid concerns, but on balance, I'll keep my windows, running water, and working toilets.

Nevertheless, change can be tough on older citizens. Solomon told us earlier that if we're looking for ultimate benefit or lasting satisfaction from anything in this life, we're in for disappointment. Hanging on to ideas that need to be retired isn't helpful. This is in small part what the New Testament is getting at more directly when it attacks our love for the world. John says it most succinctly.

> [15] *Don't love the world or the things in the world. If anyone loves the world, the love of the Father is not in them.*
>
> 1 JOHN 2:15

John's point isn't to be a killjoy and ensure that we don't like anything about life or where we live. John's letter doesn't erase Ecclesiastes or all the

---

58   Robin Campbell, trans., *Seneca: Letters from a Stoic* (London: Penguin Classics, 2004), p. 170.

59   An easily digestible source of the water closet backstory can be found at: "The Men that Made the Water Closet," Plumbing & Mechanical (website), accessed July 19, 2023, *https://www.pmmag.com/articles/91499-the-men-that-made-the-water-closet*.

other places in the Bible that speak to the wonders, beauties, and pleasures of this planet and life on it. John's point is a more religiously phrased version of what Solomon said a thousand years earlier in Ecclesiastes. If you love something in excess, it will ruin you. Everything has its time and place. There's a time for the things you enjoy and make you comfortable, and there's a time to get rid of them. None of the things of this world are ultimately satisfying in the end, and if you try to make them so, life will likely turn out quite badly for you.

John phrases the point more directly, applying his lesson to Christians who must let go of distractions that lead a soul away from a holy life. In his formulation, you either love God, in which case you find ultimate satisfaction and lasting benefit in him, or you love the world. It's one or the other.

Solomon keeps things less religious and, for now, avoids the eternal. He stays focused on life in this world, but his conclusion aligns very nicely with John's point. There's a time to build things up and also a time to tear them down. Enjoy things, but don't get so attached to them that you can't let go of them when the time for change arrives. The older I get, the more meaningful this point becomes to me.

I wonder sometimes if time goes faster as I get older to help me remember more clearly the ephemeral nature of this life and force me to focus on what matters. If we think we have forever, we might take forever to do what we ought to do right now. There's a right time for everything. What time is it for you now?

18

EACH PLACE ON THE SPECTRUM OF HUMAN EMOTION HAS ITS RIGHT TIME

I DESCRIBED IN *Even the Monsters* how it took me months after our daughter's birth and the onset of her medical problems before I learned to cry. Long before she came along, however, medical and other crises had been a mainstay of life. I'd dealt with each one by stuffing it down and soldiering on, as I'd been doing since childhood. My experience is, of course, not unique. Each of us deals with our hurts differently, but everyone has something that causes pain.

As I described earlier, after a particularly violent bank robbery, the bank's trauma counsellors did more damage than the robbery itself, not because there was a flaw in their function but because, by my mid-twenties, I'd already buried too much within. The bank's counsellors weren't there to unpack a lifetime, just the one event. Opening the lid, however, to only deal with part of what was bottled inside wasn't helpful.

Crying isn't stereotypically guy territory. Once I realized how painful the bank's crisis counselling process was going to be, I got the team off my case as quickly as possible. Growing up the way I did created a hardness that shut down tears. People struggling for survival often feel they don't have the luxury of tears, but that doesn't mean trauma or distress doesn't occur. Unacknowledged and suppressed suffering lingers in the human heart and comes out later, sometimes in distorted forms that bear little surface-level resemblance to the original hurt. To aid healing, inexpensive self-serve resources can be found in plenty of psychology books on post-traumatic stress disorder, grief, and similar subjects,[60] and while they may not substitute for the aid of a good counsellor, they are far superior to my original bottling process. In my case, an unexpected and very positive family discovery as well as a good therapist in later life were both immeasurably helpful. I'll talk more about these personal discoveries later.

In the meantime, long before technical language for grief recovery had entered human discourse, Solomon understood these topics and soberly taught there is a time to cry.

> [4] *a time for crying and a time for laughing,*
>
> ECCLESIASTES 3:4A

Solomon is quick to point out that there is also a time for laughing. This is, frankly, something I was also terrible at. Crying was a stunted emotional response, but so was laughing. I've written elsewhere about how I became much more careful after an assault when I was twelve years old.[61] That carefulness made me distrust nearly everything, including fun. I perceived danger—social and otherwise—everywhere. My exit from my home at thirteen to work that night nurse job compounded the shutdown that occurred within. Years later, it took a close group of friends in Vancouver to teach me once again to laugh. I was a young university student when that process started, and that same group of friends, after our daughter's birth, had to reteach me that it was still okay, sometimes, to laugh. Even if your child is in the hospital and your wife is going through her own medical challenges and money is tight and work is hard—it is okay, even then, in the right moment,

---

60   One of our daughter's nurses shared the best online resource I've found on this topic with my wife and me. It is a fourteen-part lecture series on YouTube by Tim Fletcher called *Understanding Trauma*. For readers interested in an academically dense yet incredibly helpful digest of this topic, the series can be accessed at *https://www.youtube.com/watch?v=HCa-dTuwOBM&list=PLpvbEN3KkqoL81XgB4Pfl7pMhddi9nkXp* or by simply googling "Tim Fletcher Understanding Trauma YouTube." A book that helped me understand the concept of complicated grief and how that grief can unexpectedly resurface decades later was Marilyn Kriete's book, *The Box Must Be Empty*. Other helpful volumes were Lois Lavallee's *Eloise: Letters to a Lost Child*, C.S. Lewis's *A Grief Observed*, and John W. James's *The Grief Recovery Handbook*.

61   Potter, *Even the Monsters*.

to laugh. In our case, the right group of friends occasionally circled up our minivans in a Dairy Queen parking lot like middle-aged has-been rebels, enjoying indefensibly sweet desserts in the dark and laughing while we forgot about parenting and finances and medical concerns for just an hour—those were moments when it was time to laugh. I would cry again later, but with those friends, in those moments, it was time for laughing.[62]

The heart needs both. Life in this world requires laughter and tears. There are times for both.

> *a time for mourning and a time for dancing,*
> ECCLESIASTES 3:4B

Mourning and dancing. If there's any confusion about the Bible's take on dancing, this verse should clear it up. Crying and laughing are opposites. Life and death are opposites. Mourning and dancing are opposites. The dancing Solomon is talking about is dancing for joy.

This is not just Solomon's idea. This is what Miriam's followers were doing after the Israelites escaped Egypt through the miracle at the Red Sea.

> [20] *Then the prophet Miriam, Aaron's sister, took a tambourine in her hand. All the women followed her playing tambourines and dancing.*
> EXODUS 15:20

The book of Lamentations is essentially the exact opposite of Exodus chapter fifteen. As its title suggests, the entire book is a sequence of sorrowful laments. In Exodus, the nation had been freed from captivity and thus dancing for joy was called for. Lamentations covers a period much later when the nation was conquered by the Babylonians and deported into a period of multi-generational captivity. The writer of Lamentations felt as though none of the surrounding nations cared at all about the horror his country had endured. As a result, he writes,

---

62   A heartfelt thank you to Eli and Liane, Carl and Sharon, Jeff and Yvonne, Colin and Melissa, and many others who were part of those late-night sugar-therapy sessions.

¹⁵ Joy has left our heart;
our dancing has changed into lamentation.

LAMENTATIONS 5:15

Dancing and mourning are opposites. How much of Solomon's insight here relates to his personal biography and how much of it is a wise reflection on both his nation's history and human psychology, I don't know. What I do know, from Solomon and personal experience, is that there are times for mourning and times for dancing, and they never occur together. When God allows trouble into your life, that's a good time for mourning. When he saves you from trouble or provides a joy-filled blessing, dancing is the right idea. You don't dance at funerals.

But what is this next bit about?

⁵ a time for throwing stones and a time for gathering stones,
a time for embracing and a time for avoiding embraces,

ECCLESIASTES 3:5

The careful reader will notice that I'm covering four things this time, not the usual pattern of one opposing pair. That's because these four items are related.

At first glance, the first pair only half makes sense. Farmers will gather stones together to build a fieldstone wall or, at a minimum, to get them out of the field where they will interfere with plowing, but when is the right time for scattering stones? Why bring this up? How is scattering stones—or, for that matter, gathering them—relevant to our study?

It turns out that, while the Hebrew text does talk about scattering and gathering stones, that was not the point. The phrasing here is an ancient Jewish euphemism for sex.[63] You might think it's a terrible euphemism if there is no relationship between the figure of speech and the actual action referenced, but that is sometimes how euphemisms work. We talk about two people sleeping together to describe something that most definitely does not involve sleep and might not even involve a bed.

---

63 See: Robert Alter, *The Hebrew Bible: A Translation with Commentary*, vol. 3 (New York: W.W. Norton and Company, 2019), p. 68; and Ogden and Zogbo, *A Handbook on Ecclesiastes*, p. 94.

In plain language, Solomon says there is a time for having sex and a time for not having it. Unfortunately, this lesson took him a lifetime and a thousand women to learn.

The second half of this verse doesn't drift euphemistic but instead speaks in plain language about the non-sexual expression of physical affection. Hugging also has its place and time. Shortly after our wedding, I began to realize that a touch was not always the right thing. While expressing deep pain about some matter or other, my wife sometimes needed a hug, but just as often, a hug was deadly to the conversation, and she reacted negatively. I found it very confusing to interpret. It was clear to me that neither she nor I interpreted my hug attempt as a sexual advance—but still, my efforts sometimes created a rift in the middle of a conversation that was already unhappy, and the increased negativity confused me.

Decades into our marriage, I read an off-hand comment in a grief counsellor's guide that noted that physical touch amid an expression of pain signals the end of that expression. It is as if physical touch short circuits the heart's flow and rebottles it. The advice in the guide was to never touch someone expressing grief but rather let the grieving soul sit and speak without interrupting them with words or touch. Let them talk. I wish I had known that decades earlier. It would have prevented many communication misfires with my young bride.

But of course, there are times when that pain does need to be short-circuited, when leaving a soul suffering and weeping and untouched, not held, would be cruelty itself. How are you supposed to know when to touch and when not to? Well, that's not what Ecclesiastes is about. My personal advice on this topic, going beyond what Ecclesiastes is trying to communicate, would be "If you're ever unsure, just ask." One of my editors (Amelia) offered this sample line as a way of communicating in these kinds of situations: "I love you and I want to help, but I'm not sure how best to do that. What do you need right now? Would you like a hug?" Brilliant advice. Too often I hesitate because I want to do the perfect thing, but after nearly three decades of marriage I still can't read my wife's mind. Asking is a lot simpler than failed attempts at mind reading.

Getting back to Ecclesiastes, Solomon is just pointing out that sometimes a couple should strip down and make love, and sometimes not. There are times when the relationship requires a different focus than sex. And sometimes, people need to be touched non-sexually—just a hug between friends—and sometimes, that same touch can be damaging. There's a suitable time for everything. Each heart, culture, and situation is different, but knowing that there are times to hug and times not to is the start of learning to read our own times and relationships and act accordingly. At the very least, this knowledge should make us more aware of the need to ask what a loved one needs in uncertain situations.

Living life well requires paying deep attention to the times and seasons. The ways I've learned over the decades to read my wife's needs are likely to fall flat with another woman. Every soul is different. The signals are different. Every heart is born different, shaped by different life experiences and as a result understands things differently. After twenty-seven-plus years of marriage, I sometimes joke with my wife that she's stuck with me forever. Given the years we have left, it would be too much work for her to train a new husband. But, of course, that works the same way in reverse. She reads me now the way no one else can. My unconscious signals would be a foreign language to any other woman.

I'm pretty sure Solomon, with the thousand women he cycled through in his life, probably never deeply understood any woman, whether she was his wife or concubine. Just keeping their names straight likely required the assistance of palace staff. The same holds true outside the romantic realm. After moving from Vancouver to Toronto in my thirties, I discovered the unhappy truth that it takes ten years to build a ten-year friendship. Likewise, it takes twenty-seven years to build a twenty-seven-year marriage. There are no shortcuts.

I wonder how much of these two verses is Solomon kicking himself as an old man, realizing how badly he handled relationships throughout his life, as opposed to any kind of wisdom he had personally practiced. Sometimes, we're wise enough to have a healthy diet and exercise regularly before health concerns arise, but sometimes we only admit to that reality after a heart attack. I suspect the latter was Solomon's case when it came to interpersonal relationships. We'll see more evidence of his relational regret later in Ecclesiastes.

What I take away from this grouping of times is that understanding the full range of human emotions and desires—and customizing that learning to your specific culture, personal relationships, and life history—is part of healthy maturity. You may need the aid of online resources, books, courses, a counsellor, or at minimum a patient partner or circle of close friends, but there is a time for all the myriad of things that humans feel. If you don't have the wisdom or maturity to automatically know the right time and place for these expressions, then seek help to learn. It's life changing—in work, in marriage, in parenting, in friendship, in every imaginable social interaction, including the ones you may have with that voice in your own head.[64] A failure to accept a necessary human emotion doesn't just impoverish a soul. In addition to fuelling psychological and relationship issues, repressing your emotions can also lead to physical health concerns. Modern medicine knows it.[65] So did Solomon. It's wisdom old and new and important to learn to grow a healthy heart and mind.

---

64   For exceptionally curious readers interested in exploring this idea of internal conversations as more than just a personality peculiarity, the school of psychotherapy called "Internal Family Systems" might be of interest. An introduction to this topic that I found personally useful was *No Bad Parts: Healing Trauma and Restoring Wholeness with the Internal Family Systems Model* by Richard Schwartz, Ph.D.

65   For example, see Dr. Bessel van der Kolk's book *The Body Keeps the Score* (Penguin Random House, 2015) for a medical doctor's take on this topic. Another volume I found helpful on this topic was *When the Body Says No: The Hidden Cost of Stress* by Gabor Mate, MD.

19

THERE IS EVEN A TIME FOR UNPLEASANT THINGS

ONE OF THE annoyances in life that carries more weight in my psyche than it should is the irritation I feel when I misplace something like my glasses, keys, or phone.

Solomon, on the other hand, seems to think that losing things is a good idea.

> [6] *a time for searching and a time for losing,*
>
> ECCLESIASTES 3:6A

Searching I get, but losing seems odd. Why would you want to have a time for misplacing things?

In Hebrew, the word translated here as "losing" conveys the idea of giving up. There is a time to push on, to search, to seek what is lost, and there is a time to give up on something.

The Hebrew here can also convey the idea of searching for something you've never had to begin with. In other words, there is a time for pursuing a goal, and there is a time to surrender that goal as unachievable.[66]

That's a tough-love bit of wisdom that is uncomfortable to accept in a capitalist society that prides itself on the idea that you can achieve anything

---

66   Ogden and Zogbo, *A Handbook on Ecclesiastes*, p. 95.

you want in life with sufficient effort. However, Solomon is right—it is good to have prospects and know that hard work can be well rewarded, but it is important to understand that there are also times to surrender some goals as unachievable. That surrender may come after we recognize that there is a gap in our talents, that the timing is wrong, that the odds stacked against us are too high, that the cost of achieving a given goal is something we should be unwilling to pay (ethical costs, relationship costs, and so on), or simply that God is trying to direct us somewhere else.

In more familiar twenty-first-century language, there is a time to pursue dreams and a time to let go of dreams.

What passions did Solomon chase? What dreams should he have lost? Clearly his pleasure quest was one focus he should have abandoned far earlier in life. The man knew a few things about obsessions run amok.

Okay, on to Solomon's next pair of ideas.

a time for keeping and a time for throwing away,
ECCLESIASTES 3:6B

This bit seems related to the second half of 3:3 with its discussion of tearing down and building up. I described earlier the resistance to tearing down that many of us feel as a natural conservatism that can grow as we age. The second half of verse six seems to be saying the same thing.

The difference here is the nature of the activity. In verse three, Solomon spoke about building and tearing down as active enterprises. In modern terms, we might think of it as deliberately creating or dismantling traditions or practices within a company, a family, a society, or a nation.

In verse six, the activity is less about creation versus demolition and is instead more focused on retention versus dismissal. Hanging on to memories is an example. There is a time for keeping a precious memory, but there is also a time not just for letting that memory go but for actively throwing it away.

If we look for case studies on this teaching in Solomon's biography, 1 Kings 2:8–9 provides one such example. In that story, a man named Shimei is sentenced to death for insulting Solomon's father years before. This seems to have been, in part, a case of not appropriately dealing with a problem in the moment and then that problem growing within the extended family's psyche over the years until murder seemed like an appropriate response. This incubated drive for revenge should have been thrown away by the previous generation and not brought into Solomon's adulthood.

To use a less extreme and more modern example with less emotional charge, imagine you've had a lousy boss and moved on from that workplace. There is a time to remember that experience, such as when you're evaluating a new workplace opportunity. "Once bitten, twice shy" is an old expression that applies here. But there is also a time to put aside your memory of that bad boss and not let it consume your interactions with a new manager. Some of us nurse hurts long after rumination has drifted into something psychologists refer to as a cognitive distortion. There is a time to throw away.

> [7] *a time for tearing and a time for repairing,*
> ECCLESIASTES 3:7A

When is a good time to tear something? That seems like an odd action to do deliberately, and it might be tempting for the casual reader just to skim over this part of verse seven and not learn anything.

Some readers, however, will recognize that tearing clothes was, in Solomon's day, one of the traditional and common ways of demonstrating deep pain. Solomon tells us here that there is a time for conveying deep hurts. If we understand tearing, then, as a reference to ancient mourning practices, then the word "repairing" is referencing the end of mourning. There is time to put your clothes back together and reintegrate with life again.

But we already covered mourning, didn't we? Verse four already contrasted mourning and dancing, so why bring mourning up again? As some commentators have suggested, is this an editorial error, a clunky duplication just to fill out the poem?

No. Solomon was a better writer than that and the Holy Spirit a more gifted source of inspiration. Ecclesiastes 3:4 and 3:7 are not duplicate ideas but different ideas set in similar contexts.

Verse four teaches us that two contrasting life events are valid parts of life. Both mourning and dancing—that is, grief and celebration—have their time and place.

Verse seven, on the other hand, does not address the contrasting states of grief versus celebration but instead speaks about opposite ends of the same experience. There is a time to tear your clothes and repair those torn clothes:

there is a time to start mourning and to finish mourning. Solomon doesn't dictate the timing of that beginning and conclusion. As rich as the Bible is with God-revealed truths, God never lays out mandatory mourning periods or even guidelines for various stages and types of grief. Each circumstance and heart and perhaps even culture has its schedule. But there is a time for that schedule to begin and a time for it to end. Never learning to live again after a loss is not a romantic ideal—it is a sign that someone is stuck and needs help. There is a time to repair. When to repair will vary by individual, but repair should come at some point.

a time for keeping silent and a time for speaking,
ECCLESIASTES 3:7B

Wouldn't it be great to have a smartphone app that lets you know, in all social circumstances, whether it is time to speak or not?

This verse has been helpful to me as a father. As my son has grown over the years, I've needed to exert conscious effort to selectively silence unsolicited input in order to respect his maturing independence.

A verse in the Bible that describes a very different set of circumstances also strikes me as relevant here. The verse occurs in Amos. After discussing a period of national oppression and social injustice, the passage goes on to say,

13 Therefore the prudent keep quiet in such times,
  for the times are evil.
AMOS 5:13 (NIV)

In context, Amos's point appears to be that one symptom of a society gone wrong is that people stop talking—the careful clam up. I know the truth of this as a manager of teams in a corporate environment. If the people I work with stop pushing back when I head off in a direction they disagree with, I'm in trouble. I need people to speak. Once a decision is made, gossip and grumbling don't help a project team succeed, but during the planning and later review stages, I need people to speak up to help us all be collectively successful.

There is a related idea in the Gospels where Jesus talks about not giving pearls to pigs. We've already discussed the problem of Proverbs 26:4–5 and how you sometimes need to respond to a fool's nonsense and sometimes you don't. I love how Solomon here aligns with Proverbs and Jesus as well. There is a time to speak up and a time to be quiet.

Solomon's final two pairs might make some readers uncomfortable. Here is the first of these two pairs.

> *⁸ a time for loving and a time for hating,*
>
> ECCLESIASTES 3:8A

Loving I get, but hating? Why is there a time for hating? A good example of positive hating is found in Exodus.

> *²¹ But select capable men from all the people—men who fear God, trustworthy men who hate dishonest gain—and appoint them as officials over thousands, hundreds, fifties and tens.*
>
> EXODUS 18:21 (NIV)

In context, these directions were to help set up the Jewish nation's first bureaucracy while they were still nomads en route from Egypt to the Promised Land. These new government agents were to be honest and not susceptible to favoritism or bribery. In fact, they should hate dishonest gain the way a sailor hates a fire below deck.

Solomon should have learned to hate his appetite for excess decades prior to writing Ecclesiastes. It would have saved him and the nation much pain.

Right. So it turns out there is a time for both loving and hating. That makes perfect sense.

The next one, though, is tougher to swallow.

> *a time for war and a time for peace.*
>
> ECCLESIASTES 3:8B

Why isn't the time for peace all the time? Why is there a time for both?

First Samuel tells a story that illustrates why there is sometimes a time for war.

Picture this: an eleventh century BCE town called Ziklag where David, before he became king, lived with his men and all their families. As the scene opens, David and his men are busy with a complicated series of political maneuvres out of town. His business eventually wraps up, and David begins his journey home to Ziklag.

> [1] *Three days later, David and his soldiers reached Ziklag. The Amalekites had raided the arid southern plain and Ziklag. They had attacked Ziklag and burned it down, taking the women and everyone in the city prisoner, whether young or old. They hadn't killed anyone but carried them off and went on their way.* [3] *When David and his soldiers got to the town and found it burned down, and their wives, their sons, and their daughters taken prisoner,* [4] *David and the troops with him broke into tears and cried until they could cry no more.*
>
> 1 SAMUEL 30: 1–4

Let's be clear: this wasn't a game. Rape, slavery, or delayed ritual murder—some would face all three—were on the agenda for these captives. This was a time for action.[67] I hope, whatever your political persuasion, if your spouse and children had been taken captive in this manner, you would understand that this was a time for war. Somebody needed to rescue these kidnapped souls.

In a modern context, we'd call 911 (112 in the EU, 999 in the UK, and so on). There were no phones and no one to call in David's day. To save their families, they had to do the job themselves.

Solomon is not advocating for war as a regular good thing any more

---

67 To any Christian readers who think that Jesus's command to turn the other cheek in Matthew 5:39 might apply here, please refer to *Engaging the Powers: Discernment and Resistance in a World of Domination* by Walter Wink as well as the works of other scholars. These help us understand that, surprisingly, Jesus was not teaching pacifism. Space does not permit a thorough discussion here, but suffice to say, Jesus's words had a very specific context in Roman law. In that context, "turning the other cheek" was an act of political protest that put a supposedly superior Roman perpetrator on awkward legal footing. The same applies to the tunic and extra mile bits in this Matthew 5 sermon. It's a fascinating study but a serious digression from our Ecclesiastes work, so I'll leave you to the work of Wink and others on this topic. In short, know that Jesus was not a weakling. He was personally, purposely sacrificial, but he offered subversively bold counsel to his followers.

than he's advocating that it would be good to make a habit of tearing clothes (mourning), giving up on ambitions, or even dying. War shouldn't be anyone's first choice. But I hope there's someone in your life that you love enough that you'd make time for action if they needed rescue.

There is a time for everything. And here is the thing casual readers can miss when they read this poem about time in isolation from the rest of Ecclesiastes: Solomon is making the point that, whatever approach to life we take, it has got to deal with all the times that human beings experience. If, for example, your approach has no time for mourning or dancing or any other pair of opposite times that Solomon espouses, we may be living lives that are, at best, missing key parts.

What do you need to make time for?

PART FIVE:

THE SEARCH UNCOVERS CRITICAL COMPASS POINTS

20

THE HEART OF ECCLESIASTES

IN THE WINTER of my first year at the University of British Columbia (UBC), I made my way down from the university grounds to the rough Pacific Ocean beach. Rain fell lightly. A cold breeze bit my cheeks and crept through my jacket. I tasted ocean salt and smelled the Gulf Islands' evergreens that filtered the air before it crossed the Strait of Georgia to my solitary stretch of shoreline.

I had recently begun planning to immigrate to England. Why England? I don't know. I was hungry. Hunger isn't a force that makes you good at thinking, and England seemed like a good idea. Nothing came of the immigration plan. On that beach, I was self-aware enough to know that if neither California nor Vancouver satisfied me, then my location was not the problem. I walked on slightly lost, both literally and in other more personal ways. I was hungry and searching.

Solomon had the same feeling in old age that I did walking Wreck Beach that cold December.

> *⁹ What do workers gain from all their hard work? ¹⁰ I have observed the task that God has given human beings. ¹¹ God has made everything fitting in its time, but has also placed eternity in their hearts, without enabling them to discover what God has done from beginning to end*
>
> ECCLESIASTES 3:9–11

There's that word "gain" again. *Yithron.* Lasting benefit. Solomon wanted an ultimate answer, and so did I. A UBC degree, new friends, England— none of these prizes offered anything of existential value. They were potential steps, but steps to where?

Solomon uses that word "task" again as well. God gave humans a task. In the original Hebrew, "given" means that the task was both a gift and an assignment. The word is translated as a "burden" by the Good News Translation, the NIV, and other translations, which captures the assignment part well but misses the gift aspect.

In chapter one, Solomon already covered this combined idea of a gift and assignment.

> *It's an unhappy obsession that God has given to human beings.*
> ECCLESIASTES 1:13B

These are the same words in a different order. A heavy burden is assigned to humans. An arduous task is given as a gift. But what is that unhappy obsession, task, or burden?

> *[11] God has made everything fitting in its time, but has also placed eternity in their hearts, without enabling them to discover what God has done from beginning to end.*
> ECCLESIASTES 3:11

That word "fitting" is often translated as "beautiful" (see RSV and NIV for examples). Everything is beautiful in its time, but that beauty is not absolute or complete. In addition to that beauty, God "has also placed eternity" in our hearts and has gone one step further—God deliberately prevents humanity from discovering everything he has done.

Solomon describes a three-part burden here. Externally, everything is achingly beautiful. Internally, eternity lives within us. And these two poles live in tension with one another because God has deliberately created both realities and then prevents us from truly understanding and experiencing it all. It's like being able to smell a banquet that you can't quite locate and therefore never taste.

That is the heart of Ecclesiastes. That is Solomon's explanation for the hunger embedded in the soul of every man and woman who has ever lived.

In his book *Surprised by Joy*, C.S. Lewis talks about this same idea. In that book, Lewis articulates the intangible wonder of absolute joy, which correlates nicely with Solomon's idea of beauty. Lewis also shows how each experience of joy in life is necessarily temporary and rarely re-creatable. He describes these moments as fleeting glimpses of eternity and cautions that they are merely signposts pointing the way forward to what we truly crave.

To place Lewis in my current geography, I'll reference Algonquin Park. That nearly 7,700-square-kilometer wilderness is a wonderland for campers, backwoods canoeists, nature lovers, photographers, and poets. Its southern edge is about three hours north of where I now live in Ontario. There is a sign on the highway some hours before you reach the borders of the park that advertises how many kilometers are left before you reach your destination. That sign always brings me a spark of joy. But it's just a sign. To pull over on the side of the road and have a picnic under the Algonquin sign—or crazier yet, to spend the entire vacation camped out under the sign—would be foolish. It's just a sign.

That was C.S. Lewis's point at the end of *Surprised by Joy*. He spent an entire book recording his experiences of joy and his realization later in life that they had all just been signs pointing him toward God, the one who had placed eternity in his heart to begin with and then left that heart frustratingly incapable of consummating the experience.

But why? Why would God do such a thing?

Before answering this question, Solomon pauses for a moment to ground us again in the practical. He will answer the question, but remember, Solomon is not writing a theology here. His objective is to discover how to live well in this life while dealing with his insatiable hunger. That is his narrow mission.

With that in mind, Solomon prescribes how to live in the face of life's beauty versus the soul's unsatisfiable desires.

¹² I know that there's nothing better for them but to enjoy themselves and do what's good while they live. ¹³ Moreover, this is the gift of God: that all people should eat, drink, and enjoy the results of their hard work.

ECCLESIASTES 3:12–13

So there's this bit again. Solomon's advice is to enjoy the simple things in life.

Ah, but he doesn't say "enjoy yourselves" period. He says "enjoy [your] selves and do what's good." There's a catch, right? Have fun, but perform good deeds as well. There's always a catch with this religion stuff.

No. The Bible does talk about good deeds, but that's not what Solomon is saying here. I'll spare you the complicated Hebrew grammar and give you the punchline: the good we're supposed to do are the good acts that bring enjoyment. Seriously. That's in the Bible.

Here are a few translations that make this point more clearly.

¹² I know that there is nothing better for them than to rejoice and enjoy the good life. (Holman Christian Standard Bible)

¹² I know that there is nothing better for them than to be happy and enjoy themselves as long as they live; (RSV)

¹² So I concluded there is nothing better than to be happy and enjoy ourselves as long as we can. (NLT)

My translator's handbook agrees that the emphasis in the Hebrew is on enjoying life, not a call to ethics or good deeds.[68] We are called to enjoy our lives as much as we can.

I grew up with a religion of criticism, judgment, and exclusion. Love did not factor into its message. Enjoyment of life was swamped by a sex, drugs, and rock-and-roll hysteria that seemed to make even smiling a violation of some commandment or other. I smiled—teenage rebellion being what it is—just not at home or church. Then I abandoned Christianity with

---

68   Ogden and Zogbo, *A Handbook on Ecclesiastes*, p. 102.

its rules and frowns when I moved to Canada. The idea that God intended for me to enjoy life never crossed my mind. The God of enjoyment was no God I'd ever met.

I didn't notice verses twelve and thirteen in my younger years. And verse thirteen really drives the point home. Not only is there "nothing better" than to enjoy our lives—that being a divinely endorsed focus for our lives—but another zinger follows on its heels.

> *13 Moreover, this is the gift of God: that all people should eat, drink, and enjoy the results of their hard work.*
> ECCLESIASTES 3:13

That is about as blunt as things can get. God's gift to all people is enjoyment. That word "enjoy" is alternatively translated as "take pleasure in."[69] God's gift is for us to eat, drink, and take pleasure in the results of our hard work. That's so contrary to everything I'd originally understood about God that my childhood experiences bordered on a religious conspiracy to mask God's true nature. God was a killjoy as far as I'd ever known, not a giver of pleasure. But no, the God I'd understood is not the one that is. Smiling was not supposed to be a clandestine activity but a natural response to the Creator's gifts. He said so right in his book. This is one of those examples where, if you grew up like me, you need to ignore God's followers and just read what God himself said.

Eternity's hunger can be born from negative experiences. That was my state on Wreck Beach that day. Solomon got to the same state through his failed pleasure quest and eventual hatred of life. But that same spark can be ignited in other, more positive ways. In his book *The Way of the Wild Heart*, John Eldredge advocates for igniting our pleasure through the joy of art and appreciation of nature, and he describes seeing his sons come to life in that context.[70] Here, in Ecclesiastes chapter three, Solomon also advocates for a healthy route to that spark rather than his own failed path. He prescribes

---

69   See the RSV translation as well as Ogden and Zogbo, *A Handbook on Ecclesiastes*, p. 103.

70   John Eldredge, *The Way of the Wild Heart: A Map for the Masculine Journey* (Nashville: Thomas Nelson Inc., 2006), pp. 198–206.

enjoyment of the simple things in life while cautioning his readers to not misunderstand them as a source of lasting benefit.

But why has God set life up in this way?

Well, now Solomon finally answers the question.

> [14] *I know that whatever God does will last forever; it's impossible to add to it or take away from it. God has done this so that people are reverent before him.*

ECCLESIASTES 3:14

My translator's handbook provides a more accurate version of that last sentence.

> *God has done this in order that people may honor him.*[71]

C.S. Lewis was right. His sparks of joy and Solomon's observations of beauty are simply signposts pointing us toward God. External beauty and internal eternity are twin poles of a tension that should make a hungry soul seek God. That's not a by-product or accident of human experience but part of our deliberate design.

As I walked that cold winter beach, Solomon's words accurately captured my state of heart and mind. Eternity was an irrevocable resident within me—a hunger completely unsatisfiable by earthly pleasures of any kind, in any quantity. England or grades or girlfriends were never going to fill what I hungered for.

I looked around me, at the beach, at the foggy gray ocean, at the bordering cliffs and high forest. I thought about my new life on campus, and I could clearly see the truth in what Solomon said. Some of my university peers pursued relationships. Others strove for academic excellence. Others chased artistic fulfillment or social or political causes. Others chased intoxicants, a partying lifestyle, and similar distractions. Regardless of what people pursued, however, the hunger never faded.

Shortly after that beach walk, I broke up with the girlfriend I'd started seeing before university. I felt my hunger might be connected to God, and I wanted to explore not just Christianity but all the world's religions in a

---

71   Ogden and Zogbo, *A Handbook on Ecclesiastes*, p. 106.

quest to find meaning beyond materialism or sex or success. She found this offensive for various reasons, and it led to the end of the relationship.

My noble quest for spiritual meaning, however, didn't last long. An attractive first-year student in my residence had been interested in me for a while, and we started dating before I'd got anywhere in my search for God or spiritual fulfillment. What followed were several months of an emotionally conflicted new romance. I wasn't entirely convinced then that celibacy and spirituality had to be corequisites. Even as the dating relationship started, however, I was aware that another girlfriend wasn't what my heart craved. I wanted something more than what romance could offer, but I couldn't name what my soul wanted, so how was I ever supposed to find it?

Most of Christianity and many of the world's other religions draw clear lines between sex before marriage (bad) and sex after marriage (okay). A serious spiritual quest suggested that celibacy was a good idea, but it interfered with that twenty-year-old's desires and thus the new relationship.

I think that continuum from bad to just okay, when discussing sex in a religious context, is part of the problem with how most religions relate to the topic. God created joy in life on purpose and wanted us to experience joy and seek it out. Sex is part of the joy that God created. In the future, God willing, I'll tackle this topic in more detail by sharing my study of Song of Songs. That is another work Solomon possibly authored, and it is uniquely focused on romantic and physical love. Song of Songs clearly shows that, when discussing sex, the opposite of bad is not supposed to be simply okay. Great, fantastic, and glorious are better descriptors of the Song of Song's position on sex (after all, God invented it), but that's a book for another day.

In the meantime, I got off Wreck Beach, and winter drifted into spring. I traded one girlfriend for another, and my spiritual quest stalled. After I gave this second romance a go for a few months, it fizzled out. My heart was pointed elsewhere. After that freshman spring, I stayed celibate for the next half of a decade. I was determined to find my own *yithron* in this *hevel* of a life.

21

ENJOY PLEASURE IN ITS PLACE BUT PURSUE YITHRON

I HAD A real "aha" moment during my long period of celibacy. Having shed all romantic entanglements, I wandered somewhat aimlessly for a while, seeking across various religions and then Christian denominations, before my eventual church home found me. I noticed during this period how something like calluses began to fall off my heart. I didn't know what to make of it, but it was similar to when I quit farming and construction work and my hands eventually began to soften and peel. Over time, I developed a waiter's hands and then a student's. Similarly, my heart changed with celibacy. I became softer but not in a weak way. If anything, I became stronger, more purposeful, but also more tender. I didn't understand what was happening, and I didn't know how to ask anyone about it, so I observed but said nothing.

After Solomon exposed God's trail of breadcrumbs from pleasure and enjoyment to beauty to a dawning awareness of the existential hunger built into every woman's and man's soul, he went on to describe something that I had also experienced. My own journey had left a similar mark on me, but I didn't understand what the mark meant or what to do with it or who to ask about it.

15 Whatever happens has already happened, and whatever will happen has already happened before. And God looks after what is driven away.

ECCLESIASTES 3:15

One of the challenges with unpacking this odd verse is that the ancient Hebrew itself is a bit obscure. The grammatical and translation complexities are enormous.[72] The verse, however, remained caught in my imagination. Like the calluses falling off my heart, this verse meant something, but I didn't know what. I didn't know who to ask about this kind of thing, but I did know how to research. I opened a pile of dry commentaries and translation guides, determined to make sense of verse fifteen's enigma.

My translator's handbook provided the greatest clarity and offered an alternative translation that made the passage's point easier for me to understand.

> *Whatever happened in the past is happening now. Whatever will happen in the future has already happened in the past. God requests that we pursue what is hidden.[73]*

This alternative translation is what the CEB and other translations seemed to be driving at. When the CEB posits that "God looks after what is driven away," it does not mean that he acts as the missing item's caretaker but rather that he literally looks at it after it has passed, and by inference, we're to follow his gaze. My translator's handbook simply takes the subtleties of the ancient Hebrew poetry and presents the image in more plainspoken language. God's looking at what's lost or hidden to draw our attention to it.

Poetry is awesome. But if it gets too delicate with its presentation, and you try to translate it into another culture and language three thousand years later, the magic sometimes gets lost. So, in plain language without the magic but with a bit of Lewis's signpost imagery, here is what Solomon is saying.

God created pleasure for us as a series of signposts that points us to eternity and to him. This is how things were done in the past. This is how things

---

72   See Ogden and Zogbo, *A Handbook on Ecclesiastes*, pp. 107–108 for a thorough treatment.

73   Ogden and Zogbo, *A Handbook on Ecclesiastes*, pp. 107–108.

are done now. This is how life will work in the future. As a result, he wants us to pursue the hidden mystery of eternity in our hearts while understanding that we'll never ultimately satisfy that hunger here in this life. So enjoy the little things, but don't worship them. Keep signposts as just signposts and not the destination. Keep *yithron*—lasting benefit—as your ultimate goal.

If I had understood this as a teenager, I would have been more into Christianity. God wasn't some frowning rule maker in the sky saying "no" to every fun thing. God was more like an aware parent, not allowing their kids to run mindlessly into the street. Running is fun. Running mindlessly into the street, though, can get you maimed or killed. Good parents set guidelines so that a child can run with bliss but not get run over while they're at it.

All the Christian "rules" around sex, ethics, character, use of alcohol and related substances, financial responsibility, respect for God and neighbors, and so on are simply the explanations that the maker of human hearts is telling us about how we work best. God is no different in that respect than a good parent. From the point of view of the child, parents can seem like real killjoys at times. But parents know better. And God knows better.

I remember when my first sexual relationship ended; it nearly destroyed me. The second breakup was painful as well but easier. And as I looked around at my friends who measured their number of partners in the double-digits and beyond, I saw that breakups became increasingly more manageable for them as the breakup count climbed. The pain lessened. Calluses grew. The people I observed appeared to get good at goodbyes. The most "advanced" in the breakup art had moved into one-night-stand territory where there wasn't even a breakup after the union. It seemed that separation from a sexual partner was a skill in the same way that violence, theft, or deceit could become a skill. This generation uses the term "situationship" to describe how relationship statuses have become so ambiguous that some people having sex together don't even know what they mean to one another.

In my case, even though I was a relative amateur in the romantic arena, it took about five years for the calluses to entirely melt away. Relative to some of my peers, my experiences were few, and I left the game while I still remembered the innocence of that first time. But how long does it take a heart to heal after a person has used casual sex for short-term entertainment or as a coping mechanism to deal with other troubles.? How long does it take before they no longer even know that their heart needs healing?

The "save sex for marriage" implications of these observations are ridiculous in the context of common morality in the modern West, but so is "don't run in traffic" when spoken to a four-year-old. Parents know. God knows.

God is all for pleasure. But camping under the Algonquin sign is missing the point, and I hope that we can all agree that living under it will eventually get you run over.

22

HOW TO DEAL WITH INJUSTICE

When I moved to Canada, I crossed the border in a Fiat X1/9—a slick Italian convertible mid-engine, two-seater sports car that stood on shiny mag wheels. It had been designed by the great Marcello Gandini of Alfa Romeo, Maserati, Ferrari, and Lamborghini fame. Unlike the designer's high-ticket assignments, the X1/9 was a poor man's sports car, but it looked cool and was a joy to drive. I use my wife's MINI Cooper now as much as I can because it reminds me of that Fiat.

When an accident put the Fiat beyond repair, I bought another one. When the engine went on that second Fiat, I couldn't afford to replace it or the car again, so I wound up with an old 1970s Plymouth Duster—a semi-fastback two-door coupe with muscle car aspirations. The car had been painted fire-engine red with a roller, and its cracked dash had been repaired with several rolls of black electrical tape applied in even rows to hide the underlying dashboard foam. I paid three hundred dollars for the car because it had a $300 stereo in the falling-apart dash I thought I could sell. This was in my financially and nutritionally precarious months between Michael's Rib and Omelet House and chicken catching, so mobility was all I was buying. Once I sold the stereo, I'd have a free car.

I came outside the next morning after purchasing the Duster to find the car neatly unlocked and the stereo gone. A few months later, when travelling down the Trans-Canada Highway, there came the loudest bang I'd ever heard in my life, and the car immediately died. I drifted over to the side of the highway and stopped in a safe place between the pavement and the adjacent ravine. I got out, wondering what craziness awaited me, and popped the hood. A hole the size of my fist had punctured the side of the engine block like a shiny-rimmed crater. I'd thrown a rod. If you're not a car person, let me paraphrase Monty Python to say this was an engine that was no more, had ceased to be, and was now an ex-engine.

I hitchhiked the rest of the way home, and due to work commitments, two days passed before I could arrange for a tow truck to bring the Duster back into town. The Duster's engine would have been cheaper to replace than the Fiat's, but I knew I couldn't afford that either. However, the manual transmission came with a Hurst shifter, the frame was solid, and other parts had value. At least I could sell the car for scrap.

I travelled with the tow truck driver to help him locate the car, and when we found it, it wasn't where I'd left it. Someone, presumably for kicks, had tipped the car onto its side and then onto its roof and probably onto its side one more time to get it over the ravine's edge, where it had tumbled and smashed its way to the bottom and now lay as a crumpled disaster.

"I don't have the equipment to get you up from down there," the tow truck driver said. I knew he meant the car, but I was feeling pretty low myself.

Back home, I filed a police report and called the insurance company. The insurance company concluded that I'd destroyed the Duster myself in an attempt to commit insurance fraud. They closed my file, and that was the end of me owning cars until after I was married and had worked at the bank for nearly half a decade.

By that point, I had been physically assaulted both at work and in my personal life, I'd had my pay stolen by an employer, and I'd been robbed in a variety of contexts. So, while the insurance company's decision upset me, it fit a pattern. If I didn't have money or the right relationships, the world was not going to treat me well. That's not a good lesson for a heart to learn at nineteen, but it wasn't an experience unique to poverty or the 1980s either. Solomon noticed the same problem three thousand years earlier on a completely different continent. Here's how he put it:

¹⁶ I saw something else under the sun: in the place of justice, there was wickedness; and in the place of what was right, there was wickedness again! ¹⁷ I thought to myself, God will judge both righteous and wicked people, because there's a time for every matter and every deed.

ECCLESIASTES 3:16–17

Some commentators use this passage as proof that Solomon wasn't the author of Ecclesiastes. The argument goes like this: as king, he could have fixed everything, but instead, he expressed surprise at what was happening. According to these commentators, the author is criticizing a corrupt society from the outside, not the throne.

My response is that I suspect most of these critics are academics who have never led a modest government department, never mind an entire government ministry or country.

I've never managed a government bureaucracy either, but I have worked in and held leadership roles in one of North America's largest international banks for over three decades. I've also been vice-chair of a regional education committee in my area of Ontario and sat on a charity board and several related committees. Through those experiences of managing teams, processes, projects, and policies over time, I've been continually amazed at how the well-meaning efforts of myself and others wind up distorted, misinterpreted, misapplied, or outright abused—intentionally or not—downstream from the original decision-maker's chair. Downstream can mean down the hierarchy (a head office policy misapplied at the junior-employee level), across geography (a Toronto directive misinterpreted in a province several thousand kilometers away), or even time. I once came across a policy I'd participated in creating in the early 2000s a decade and a half later and was appalled at the way my plan had been corrupted from our original intention. Those changes hurt people. I learned from these specific experiences, but I also gained some sympathy for Solomon's complaint. He was a king who sorted things out—remember the Queen of Sheba's glowing praise for his administration in 1 Kings. But, with age and perspective, Solomon also saw his failures. Try as he might, there were places in his kingdom meant to enact justice that instead bred wickedness.

Verse sixteen speaks to a place of justice and a "place of what was right." That modern English phrasing sounds somewhat awkward, but the ancient

Hebrew idea was that wickedness lurked in both the courts (the place of justice) and the place of religious authority (i.e., the temple).

The world is broken. Solomon was the king, and he could fix what he found, but like a game of whack-a-mole, it was an unending fight. You can find corruption in church and state, school and courts, the local golf clubhouse, art studio, pickleball court, farmer's market, and library. He is not saying we should surrender to this reality. He is simply observing reality and calling it out in plain language.

So, in Solomon's existential quest to find meaning in life, we might expect him to get militant about how we need to picket, campaign, vote, or act against these crimes. He does do this in other places. Proverbs supplies some good lines on when to stand up and when to sit down. Other writers—the Prophets—speak to disconnects in their societies and address how to oppose them. Here, though, in Ecclesiastes, Solomon is remarkably self-focused. He's not trying to build a better society. In Ecclesiastes, Solomon is trying to heal a ruined mind. As an old man, how can he calm himself amid society's contradictions and find meaning (lasting benefit) when he hungers for more than this life can offer but must exist here in this unjust world anyway?

His answer is to start identifying broken things that hurt him and then put them in perspective so they don't overwhelm him. The perspective he offers, in this case, is "God will judge both righteous and wicked people, because there's a time for every matter and every deed" (3:17).

There is that time reference again. Do you see how this is all connected? His original themes are still in view here. There is a time for pleasure and a time for work. There is also a time for judgment. He can act calmly now because he isn't tasked, even as king, with being the ultimate fixer, right now, of every wrong, everywhere, immediately. He should work at doing what he can to fix what he can during his reign—particularly since he is the king—but he can also calm himself, knowing that God is the ultimate judge.

From broken human bureaucracies, Solomon moves on to questioning the value of simple human existence.

¹⁸ I also thought, Where human beings are concerned, God tests them to show them that they are but animals

ECCLESIASTES 3:18

Why is Solomon comparing people to animals?

¹⁹ because human beings and animals share the same fate. One dies just like the other—both have the same life-breath. Humans are no better off than animals because everything is pointless.

²⁰ All go to the same place:
   all are from the dust;

all return to the dust. ²¹ Who knows if a human being's life-breath rises upward while an animal's life-breath descends into the earth?

ECCLESIASTES 3:19–21

Ah. Solomon compares humans and animals due to our mutual mortality. Everything is breath (3:19). Everything is essential but also ephemeral and temporary. Both humans and animals face the same gasping vulnerability that inevitably ends in death, and in Solomon's day, eternity was not a clear and certain prospect for humans. As far as his human wisdom could forecast, both humans and animals returned to dust at the end of their lives. He had no concrete understanding of heaven to lean on.

So what does this grimly candid perspective cause Solomon to conclude?

²² So I perceived that there was nothing better for human beings but to enjoy what they do because that's what they're allotted in life. Who, really, is able to see what will happen in the future?

ECCLESIASTES 3:22

There's that mortal conclusion again: enjoy life; this is people's allotment, and there is nothing better. Not every moment, of course, is enjoyable. A tooth extraction is something to get through as best you can. There's a time for everything in life, and some things are more pleasant than others, but the call is to enjoy what we can in the moment.

The RSV's interpretation draws out an extra nuance in the Hebrew more clearly: "there is nothing better than that a man should enjoy his work."

I've had some terrible jobs in my life. But even after starting at the bank, it wasn't long before I found things to complain about. It took me a while to finally grasp that I was the common denominator across my various unhappy jobs. I was the one who needed to change.

I did have the ability to enjoy my work at one point in time. Working for Ed—tearing down a house and building a new one in its place—was a blast. But I seemed to lose that gift along the way. Maybe I should have learned from how much I loved working for Ed and gone on to study architecture in school. My wife and I together would have made a fantastic design duo. However, without some of Solomon's maturity, I suspect I would have found things to complain about as an architect as well.

This business of life is a tough assignment. Just slowing down and learning to enjoy lunch takes focus. Learning to find enjoyment in our work takes additional effort. Enjoying lunch and our job while existing in a world prone to injustice is a next-level life skill. Perspective helps. Sometimes the long view is the right perspective—recognizing that God will deal with injustice in his time. Sometimes the right perspective is a narrower focus—on lunch or the one friend who really cares about you.

There are always better jobs and more just situations. But better jobs, healthier environments, and more just societies are, on a certain level, a lot like fancier lunches. They will never fully satisfy. We will always want something more. If you do manage to upgrade—your lunch or job or social environment—the skill of enjoyment will be just as valuable in your new circumstances. We are always our own common denominator over the course of our lives, and the art of enjoyment is something worth prioritizing now. It's a talent that pays rich dividends at any age, whatever your circumstances.

23

DON'T CHASE THE WIND

WHEN MY SON Jackson was in elementary school, he had a lot more on his mind than most seven- or eight-year-olds. Sometimes he left the house with an ambulance in the driveway and emergency crews in the throes of reviving his sister. "Would she live to the next year?" was an open question that his parents could not answer.

That reality bred a sense of seriousness and care into him from a young age. It also sometimes contributed to challenges making friends. He didn't host as many things at our house because we never knew when medical drama might strike. A medical crisis is a downer during a hangout. The friendship challenge made those friends that he did make all the more special.

Along with his early sense of seriousness, Jackson developed an abiding passion for justice and protection. He cared about his sister and could do nothing to help her, so he redirected that sense of care to the world at large. I don't regret at all that his childhood gave him these characteristics, even though they came with a heavy burden for a young boy to bear.

During this period, Jackson had a friend at school that we'll call Paul. This Paul had a younger brother we'll call Billy. One day at school, some boys a few years older than Jackson were picking on Billy. The violence was low-key, but the pushing and words were the sort that leave marks later in life, and Jackson was having none of it. He left his fun with Paul and stepped between Billy and the older boys, and a mild fight ensued. This, too, was at the elementary school level of mostly mild words and pushing, but it was high drama for young lads. It helped that Jackson was big for his age, but he still stood against multiple older boys in defence of little Billy.

All the boys wound up in the principal's office that day with their parents called and warnings doled out. Eventually, both Jackson and Billy were exonerated, and things went back to normal, except for one detail.

At home, Billy shared the day's details and his parents noted that their older son, Paul, had done nothing to help his younger brother. Words were spoken. The parents came to meet Jackson and thanked him for intervening on Billy's behalf. It should have ended there, but Paul and Jackson were never friends again. Paul would have nothing to do with his brother's rescuer. Shame can be a heavy burden for kids in elementary school as well.

Elementary school should never be a place for bullying. Households should never be a place for shame—although it's often the first tool in a thoughtless parent's tool kit. And a boy struggling with the at-home pressures of a seriously ill older sister and already short of friends shouldn't lose one of those friends because he tried to help someone else in distress. Life isn't fair.

As Solomon continues to explore how to live in this broken world, he further develops his argument about wickedness existing in places where it should not. He does so by approaching this material from a surprising angle: he shows that perpetrators of corruption are no better off than their victims. He tells the story of Billy's bullies and the more serious oppressors that have characterized humanity in the millennia prior. It is a surprisingly modern take on a persistent social reality.

> *¹ When I next observed all the oppressions that take place under the sun, I saw the tears of the oppressed—and they have no one to comfort them. Their oppressors wield power—but they have no one to comfort them. ² So I declare that the dead, who have already died, are more fortunate than the living, who are still alive.*
>
> ECCLESIASTES 4:1–2

Both the oppressed and the oppressors go uncomforted. Solomon teaches here that we cannot find the solution to life's burden at the top of society's power hierarchy any better than at the bottom. Life plays very fair with the existential tension between the *hevelness* of life and the eternity that lurks in every man's and woman's heart. This isn't just an elementary school problem or a unique feature of your workplace, homeowner's association, or other wannabe power player environment.

If you doubt Solomon even a little, look closely at today's news reports. The latest politician, dictator, Hollywood star, or sports celebrity story will inevitably show a pattern of drugs, alcohol, infidelity, divorce, estranged children, peer recriminations, depression, or disaffection within their chosen sphere of influence on par with the general population. Here's a simplistic illustration: whether a soul drowns their sorrows with cheap beer or fine cognac, they are peers at heart, even if they come from a different economic class or have different tastes.

Said even more simply: rich or poor, oppressed or oppressor, under the skin, we are all the same. In this passage, Solomon is trying to help us see that reality clearly without being fooled into chasing an uncatchable prize. It's not just Jackson or Paul or Billy who lost that day. Billy's bullies lost too.

Understanding this reality, Solomon reaches what may seem like a gloomy conclusion. He states that the dead are better off than those in both high and low social classes. He assumes that humanity's existential angst is relieved only in the grave. At least there, our hunger is finally over.

Remember, Solomon is not trying to teach schoolyard ethics, nor is he expounding on a theology about heaven, hell, or anything of that sort either. Instead, he's trying to make sense out of life, here and now, in a broken world, despite its brokenness.

To make his point even more dramatic, Solomon takes his case beyond the considerations of social class or mortality and dabbles in speculation about complete non-existence.

> [3] *But happier than both are those who have never existed, who haven't witnessed the terrible things that happen under the sun.*
> ECCLESIASTES 4:3

At the beginning of his existential crisis, Job says something similar. In Job 3, he describes how it would have been better to have never been born than to suffer as he had.

Pursuing this theme further would probably lead Ecclesiastes to a gloomy conclusion, but Solomon is interested in figuring out how to live well despite this dark viewpoint. So he lets go of his pessimism about mortality (though he will remind us of its inescapable reality again later) and focuses instead on the next hard thing life throws at us.

> *⁴ I also observed that people work hard and become good at what they do only out of mutual envy. This too is pointless, just wind chasing.*
>
> ECCLESIASTES 4:4

Competition is not just ubiquitous; it is also just breath. There is always an individual or family who is ahead of you. There is always a bully that is on his way to the top of a hierarchy. There always exists a company with a better product, strategy, or sales force. There is always a better sports team. Teams and individual athletes don't wildly celebrate their successes because they were foregone conclusions. Every victory is a peak. Tomorrow, the insecurity starts again. Somebody else is training better, has more talent, has better funding, or has a better plan. The whole competition game—in commerce, athletics, social media impressions, or any other sphere—is ultimately pure *hevel*. Breath. Every good breath needs another to follow it or death results. Final satisfaction is always, ultimately, out of reach. Bullies never win—they just become more exposed and insecure. Even a Super Bowl victory, Oscars win, or CEO title is ultimately just wind chasing. Ultimately, there is nothing there to catch. The *hevelness* inside is a hunger that will never be satisfied.

So should we give up on working hard then? Should we focus on pure pleasure and not even try to succeed at anything? No, that's not the answer either, as Solomon tells us next.

> *⁵ Fools fold their hands and eat their own flesh.*
>
> ECCLESIASTES 4:5

Okay, Solomon is not advocating slothfulness as the solution to life's existential burden. So what is he advocating for?

> *⁶ But better is resting with one handful*
> *than working hard for two fistfuls and chasing after wind.*
>
> ECCLESIASTES 4:6

Balance. Solomon is talking about balance. Learning to enjoy life requires work, and as we learned in 3:22, work itself is something we need to learn to enjoy. This is humanity's lot in life. Satisfying our heart's existential need is not possible here, but learning to enjoy our life, including our work, is good. There's nothing better. And the right approach to that work is not obsession and workaholism but balance.

One handful of succeeding with an appropriate amount of accompanying rest is better than two handfuls of obsessively pursuing something that will ultimately reveal itself to be nothing. It is essential to ensure we don't chase the wind.

English has a euphemism for flatulence: "passing wind." While that wasn't the specific image Solomon was going for, it may help some of us reflect on the value of our obsessive passions. Pursuing two handfuls is like chasing a fart.

Some might argue, "But that's what it takes to win!" Solomon would respond with the question: "Win what?"

This is why I love Ecclesiastes. Solomon ignores heaven (other than acknowledging that our existential hunger for eternity cannot be satisfied in this life) and focuses instead on how to live here and now. As a super-rich guy with everything—possessions, money, fame, women—he's telling it to his readers straight. What was true about the human heart in Solomon's life three thousand years ago is still true today. Don't chase the wind. It's better to rest with one handful than to work hard for two fistfuls and spend your life chasing after the wind. If you catch what you're chasing, what have you caught? Nothing. Just wind.

Our technologies have changed, but the human condition has not.

PART SIX:

THE SEARCH DIVES INTO PRACTICAL MATTERS

24

REAL FRIENDSHIPS REQUIRE EFFORT

As MY FIRST year of university ended, I started on a spiritual search free of all romantic entanglements. This search initially led me nowhere. I wrote my last exam and then, with no immediate direction to guide me, decided that a trip home was in order.

Home was no longer California. My family had moved to Rock Springs, Wyoming, a place I had never visited. As a broke university student, I no longer had a car. So how would I get to Wyoming?

An Amtrak train ran from Seattle, Washington, through Washington State, Idaho, Utah, and finally Wyoming. The train left eastbound from Seattle early each morning. To make this trip work, I had taken a Grayhound bus from Vancouver to Seattle the night before, wearing an old pair of jeans, a T-shirt, running shoes, and a worn-out backpack, carrying whatever Stephen King novel I was reading at the time. I didn't have money for a hotel, so I bought dinner and endless coffees at an all-night diner near the train station. On the nights I was there, the place was mainly frequented by prostitutes and drug addicts. Years later, I visited Seattle as a tourist and discovered that the city is a very different place during the day, but that first experience was a night visit. Reading Stephen King for hours while the night traffic conducted its business around me was a strange experience for a country boy still not used to big city life. When I finally left the diner at two or three in the morning, I was wearing a blue-jean jacket with a sheepskin lining and collar to keep me warm against the cool Seattle air. I wandered in darkness to the train station near the old coliseum where the Seahawks used to play.

At that time of night, the area lay nearly deserted. I slept for a few shivering hours on an empty street bench and then woke in time to get on the train, where I slept through most of Washington State before waking up in Idaho. The trip was two days of being rocked to the train's rhythm while I dozed, read King, or stared out the window.

Looking back on those lonely hours walking Seattle's streets at night, declining invitations to sample the underbelly of the big city's nightlife, falling asleep on a cold bench in a dangerous section of the city with a horror novel as my pillow—well, that was an invitation to get mugged or killed. Neither occurred.

There is an old French proverb (or it might be a German quotation or have a Portuguese provenance; the literary backtrail is a bit fuzzy) that roughly states, "God loves fools, lovers, and drunkards." Variations of this quote swap out "lovers" in favor of "artists," some add in "children," and in some variants, God doesn't love these people but instead helps them. The general sense, however, is clear: there's a class of apparently incapable humans that God looks after despite their bad choices. There is no other apparent explanation for their survival.

Decades later, I concluded that I navigated Seattle's nightlife by the same principle, since this wasn't my last train trip to Wyoming, and each time I went, I followed the same pattern. I wore the same country boy, sheepskin-lined jean jacket among the city's dark-leather-clad night crowd, ate at the same diner until I'd outstayed my welcome, and slept on the same cold dark bench. Shadowy shapes seemed to coalesce out of the darkness and make offers and then fade back into the shadows as I cluelessly carried on, not even clutching my backpack more tightly.

It would be easy now to interpret my posture on those streets as that of a young man too naive to be afraid. The reality is that I'd been in fist fights as a teenager—had my nose broken in one—been sexually assaulted, and had endured the resulting courtroom proceedings. I'd been robbed at gunpoint and knifepoint several times over the years.

I don't think naïveté was the problem. In fact, I read a lot of Clive Barker, Anne Rice, Peter Straub, and Dean Koontz at that time in my life, writers who ought to have fuelled a fearful imagination. I had also once sat in on a murder trial as a companion for a witness. My posture was not a product of blissful ignorance but hunger. I craved a connection and yearned for something more meaningful in my life so strongly that I had no room for fear. For whatever reason, even at that young age, the night's temptations offered nothing that drew me. I didn't know what I wanted exactly, but I wanted whatever it was a lot. I wanted something more than Seattle's nightlife had to offer. I was intensely aware but not afraid and most certainly protected.

Looking back, I can see now that the friction of staying up through the surreal darkness and sleeping on a deserted bench were just new versions of my move to Canada and the later England idea. They were just another empty beach to search for what called to me. Looking and not finding was the only thing that claimed my attention. Sleeping on a bench in a rough part of town was just more input for a hungry seeker still searching. In retrospect, I was foolish, but I was also, inarguably, focused. Shady deals, an extended fishnet thigh, and sly offers found nothing in me to hang on to. However, the sound of dump trucks in a dew-soaked dawn and the flickering that drew bleary eyes to the muddy yellow lights inside the Amtrak station spoke to me like a piece of Tom Waits's urban poetry. It was all another signpost advertising, *This is something. This is not it. But it is something. Keep looking. There is this, and then there is something more.*

In the following verses, Solomon addresses a very different type of person: one with money. This is not someone sleeping on a bench but someone, nevertheless, equally alone.

> [7] *Next, I saw under the sun something else that was pointless:* [8] *There are people who are utterly alone, with no companions, not even a child or a sibling. Yet they work hard without end, never satisfied with their wealth. So for whom am I working so hard and depriving myself of enjoyment? This too is pointless and a terrible obsession.*
>
> ECCLESIASTES 4:7–8

By the end of my first year at university, loneliness had started to grow strong within me. I'd cut ties with the girls I knew. My older roommates had graduated and moved on to new lives, and I never heard from them again. My Jewish friend seemed to disappear from campus. The mature dental hygienist likewise quit school or moved away. This was in the days before cell phones and social media. Once someone stepped out of your social circle, they were gone unless you'd thought to get a permanent address or landline phone number.

After the Seattle streets and the long train ride east, I met someone in Wyoming I've remembered ever since. My parents introduced me to her. I think she was in her thirties, but perhaps she was older. She'd been a professional ice skater in previous years, the sort that dances on ice. I have no idea how my parents knew her or how she'd wound up in Rock Springs, Wyoming.

Going to an ice rink at the beginning of summer when you don't skate and no one in the family plans on skating either seems like an odd outing, but off we went. My folks weren't trying to arrange a date. For all I know, she was married. I remember her as about a decade or more older than me, and I was just a broke first-year university student living in another country.

Regardless, we went to the rink. If this was a public skate session, no one else hit the ice that day. The place was deserted. It seemed like a private event, except my parents didn't have money for that kind of thing. They were not the type to organize such a thing, even if they did, and as I said, this wasn't a setup for a relationship. I don't even know today who staged the event or why.

However it came to be, I put skates on, and this woman took me out onto the ice. Even though I'd never been able to ice skate before and have never successfully ice skated since, somehow, in her arms, I skated. It was magical. We danced on ice. Despite intense ballet training, I can't even dance properly on solid ground to popular music. I like the idea of it, but to my wife's chagrin, I'm no Fred Astaire. I've seen Instagram videos of four-year-olds with moves I'd pay good money to get into my limbs. But that afternoon, I not only danced but danced on ice.

I'm a novelist even more than a nonfiction writer, so these past few paragraphs sound even to me like a setup for a romantic drama, but it wasn't that. I was smitten, sure, but I never tried to contact her again and have no memory of her name or what she looked like. I don't even remember her hair color. Beyond suddenly—and very temporarily—being able to ice dance, what most stood out to me was that my second girlfriend at UBC, the one I'd most recently broken up with, had also been an ice dancer. She had been a beauty pageant winner, and ice dancing had been her thing before starting university. Her parents had even sent her off to Toronto for a season where she had competed in competitions, danced with some company, taken higher-level classes, or done something along those lines. And that was the point that struck me dancing with this woman on cold Wyoming ice: I didn't know. I'd never asked. My spiritual angst had consumed me, and I had never asked the human beings in front of me good questions. I was a selfish guy in his early twenties who had never explored a girlfriend's world and had never even once suggested putting skates on together.

Perhaps we might have danced. It doesn't sound probable, but it worked on Wyoming ice. UBC had a skating rink with presumably equally fine ice. But no, I'd had an ice-dancing girlfriend and never once entered UBC's rink.

This isn't an old guy pining after lost loves because there wasn't much in the way of love there. Selfishness was present. Self-focus of many kinds was evident. Love was absent from the equation. I told her I loved her once, since it seemed like the right thing to say at the time, and her response was "Oh, don't say that." Candor, I suppose, is a virtue. Maybe we had a "situationship" before the next generation invented the term, and I didn't even know it.

Returning to the Wyoming visit, my ice dancing experience was a one-and-done affair—a bit of strange magic as unexpected as it was unlikely. The days and nights on the train back to Seattle were spent reading, sleeping, and eating in the same upright seat along with many hours spent just staring out the window at the passing scenery. Thinking about that magical ice experience, I decided that I was deficient as a human being. I couldn't see the things that were right in front of me. I never re-encountered the Wyoming ice dancer, but I learned something from her that I've never forgotten.

> [8] *There are people who are utterly alone, with no companions, not even a child or a sibling. Yet they work hard without end, never satisfied with their wealth. So for whom am I working so hard and depriving myself of enjoyment? This too is pointless and a terrible obsession.*
>
> ECCLESIASTES 4:8

That was me. I didn't have any apparent wealth yet, but I had squandered the good things I enjoyed and shared them with no one. I was a quarter of the way through my university degree, and I didn't know why I was studying so hard.

Remember, Solomon is not saying that this business is pointless. He's saying that it is *hevel*. Breath. It is essential but transient, temporary, and hard to pin down. We have to work to live, but why do we live if we're simply alone?

I returned to Vancouver, determined to live better. I needed to stop being alone; by that, I didn't mean I needed to find a new girlfriend. Just the opposite seemed true. I needed to build genuine relationships not aided or altered by romantic considerations. I needed real friends.

25

REAL FRIENDSHIPS ARE IMPORTANT BUT NOT ENOUGH

NOT LONG AGO, I had the pleasure of sitting in on a leadership talk given by Dr. Kimberley Amirault-Ryan at the bank. Among other accomplishments, she has been a performance consultant for the NHL's New York Rangers and Edmonton Oilers, the NBA's New York Knicks, and Canada's Olympians. She is a gifted speaker and a joy to listen to. Her talk that day featured a powerful section on givers and takers in the context of team dynamics, using the selection process for Canada's men's Olympic hockey team from a previous year to illustrate her lesson.

Her talk focused on top NHL players jockeying for a position on Canada's team and how there were men who took and men who gave. The takers were dominant, self-absorbed, and hyper conscious of status. The givers offered help and encouragement, did not let their high- or low-status assignments affect their mood, and strove for the benefit of the team as a whole. Givers made the cut. Takers did not. The givers won gold that year.

Afterward, I reflected on how her assessment of hockey players also applied to friendships and Solomon's own commentary on this topic. This is the passage in particular that came to mind:

⁹ Two are better than one because they have a good return for their hard work. ¹⁰ If either should fall, one can pick up the other. But how miserable are those who fall and don't have a companion to help them up! ¹¹ Also, if two lie down together, they can stay warm. But how can anyone stay warm alone? ¹² Also, one can be overpowered, but two together can put up resistance. A three-ply cord doesn't easily snap.

ECCLESIASTES 4:9–12

The cynic could view these four verses as a defence of selfishness. The world is full of takers. Solomon could describe my romance-centered first-year university experiences as being self-focused and utilitarian, existing for my personal benefit alone. The world has enough humans only looking to get what they can from others. Do we really need verses like this providing justification for more self-interested manipulation of others?

In the case of my early romances, such criticism would have been fair. Hunger is innately self-focused. Those early relationships were too full of me looking for what I could get from my current girlfriend and not much else. But love and friendship are practical things, not just feelings. They do good. They provide a benefit. These personally beneficial aspects of relationships should not be discounted simply because they are often abused.

People need a hand up; they need warmth. They need protection. Even NHL pros being considered for the national Olympic team need help, encouragement, and friendship to succeed.

My experience with the Wyoming ice dancer was magical but not love or friendship. It was, at a stretch, infatuation, but we didn't know each other, we didn't exchange contact information, and I've long since forgotten her name. She was a drop of grace and joy in a life that needed it and a mirror that exposed deficiencies inside me that required correction.

A true friend, however, is not just magical and perhaps corrective. A true friend is there for the long haul, or as Solomon puts it, will help you up and keep you warm, and together, you can protect each other. True friendship is multi-functional and mutual. A friend who won't help and runs away when a need arises isn't a true friend. There is a legitimate level of self-interest in a quality friendship.

In *Even the Monsters*, I described the people who stepped into our lives after our daughter Mackenzie was born and trouble swamped my wife and me. We discovered who our friends were and who no longer had time for us. There is no judgment in that observation. It is simply an observation. You don't know the depth of a relationship until trouble tests it. Intentions don't count. Weddings are fun, and honeymoons by design should be splendid—but if you want to assess the quality of a marriage, take a look at it ten or twenty years after the honeymoon.

A few years after Mackenzie's birth, we moved from Canada's West Coast to Ontario, over four thousand kilometers away. That move taught me that it takes ten years to build a ten-year friendship. In fact, the older you get, it may take more than ten years to build the kind of bonds that can be formed earlier in life in the same amount of time. Some of that is probably just how basic neurological wiring works in our teens and twenties. Some of it, however, is an issue of available time. Child-free singlehood provides a lot more hours in any given week for friendship building than is available when marriage and parenting take over the calendar.

Solomon, however, is not writing a guide for friendship. What follows are not the top five things you can do today to make good friends, be a great friend, evaluate the quality of your relationships, or even assess whether you are a giver or a taker. Instead, Solomon deals with *hevel*, his insatiable hunger for something more, and the grim reality that he cannot have what he wants. Stuck in this state of desire and denial, he is picking life apart, analyzing its bits, and coming to conclusions on the best way to live within the boundaries of human limitations.

With that as his focus, Solomon moves on from loneliness and shows that solving loneliness, while necessary, is not humanity's ultimate life quest either. To do this, he tells us a short story.

¹³ A poor but wise youth is better than an old and foolish king, who no longer listens to advice. ¹⁴ He emerged from prison to become king, even though during his rule a poor child is born. ¹⁵ I saw all who live and walk under the sun following the next youth who would rise to take his place. ¹⁶ There was no counting the number of people he ruled, but those who came later aren't happy with him. This too is pointless and a chasing after wind.

ECCLESIASTES 4:13–16

To understand this story, it helps if you realize that there are three characters in this scene. First, there is Youth #1 (poor but wise), then there is the King (old and foolish), and lastly, there is Youth #2 (the next youth who it appears was very popular (4:15)). It's this last youth who ties this story back to Solomon's previous dialogue about loneliness.

Chronologically, in the background of this story, the King came first. Old age is typically associated with wisdom in ancient Hebrew stories, so this tale inverts standard expectations twice: the old king gets mentioned second and is foolish. So far, so good.

Next comes Youth #1, who further upends expectations by being young and poor but also wise. Eventually, Youth #1 emerges from prison to become king, a story not identical to Joseph's but certainly reflecting similar themes of a person finding wisdom in an unlikely place and then rising to power.

But notice the weird bit in verse fourteen. After Youth #1 becomes king, "a poor child is born." That next youth grows up and becomes Youth #2, who takes Youth #1's place.

Then the story ends with Youth #2 losing popularity as well.

In other words, old age didn't work to secure a nation's favor, youth and wisdom in tandem didn't work, and early-stage popularity had no long-term value either. It didn't matter what flavor of king sat on the throne because, in the long run, they all failed to win the hearts of their nation, and that, in Solomon's estimation (remember, he's a king as he writes this), is very frustrating. It's *hevel*. It's like chasing the wind. Anyone with a political career can probably relate.

So, Ecclesiastes 4 covers three topics: oppression, friendship, and royal succession. These subjects are not disconnected but part of Solomon's ongoing theme regarding mortality and his frustration with reality.

As wealthy, wise, and powerful as Solomon was, he could not force life to fit into a mold of his liking. Oppressors and the oppressed both suffer. In the end, Dr. Amirault-Ryan's givers and takers both suffer. Existentially speaking, people work without knowing why or for whom. Kings (and NHL stars and celebrities and artists and masters of industry) all fall out of favor. Generations go and generations come, and today's heroes become tomorrow's memories until even the memories are forgotten. Who was on that gold-medal-winning hockey team? I have no idea. My grandchildren one day probably won't even look it up. The planet moves on. This frustrating world won't let itself be yoked to Solomon's agenda of wanting to find satisfaction that lasts. Reality will not cooperate with even the king's command.

So how can a person live well in this life of hunger and *hevel*?

26

WARNINGS ABOUT EXCESSIVE WORDS

CHRIS IS A tall church leader in Canada's north whom I originally met as a young single guy in Vancouver. A friend of mine had invited Chris to the church that I'd begun attending, thus establishing our connection. At the time, he was studying to be a deep-sea diver and underwater welder.

After a service or two, Chris took a greater interest in what he saw around him and wanted to study the Bible as well. In response, some of the guys in that little church put together a study plan, and I joined the studies as an excuse to hang out.

After one study—which covered prayer, among other topics—I suggested to Chris that we go for a prayer walk together. Prayer walks were a fashionable thing in that small fellowship. Nowadays, if we see someone walking alone and talking out loud, we assume they've got earbuds in and are on a phone call. Back in the pre-cell phone era, such behavior made you appear, at best, mentally unwell. Two or more people, however, could go for a walk outdoors, praying out loud as they walked, and passersby thought nothing of it. Only the two people walking and praying knew that there was a third participant: the Creator of the Universe.

Except, before Chris, that's not how prayer worked for me. I'd grown up with a flavor of Christianity whose KJB-centered religious language extended even to its prayer life. As a result, I hadn't understood a lot of what had been said in prayer around our family dinner table. What I did understand struck a tonal balance between courtroom formality and funeral solemnity. There is not a lot of emotional range between those two poles. Later in life, when I spent some time studying the Psalms, I was struck by how the Psalms—when read as prayers—did not fit at all with the Christianity I'd learned as a child. The Psalms are dynamic and emotional and sometimes even alarming in their swings from one pole to another.

So Chris and I hit a local park for our prayer walk. I was theoretically his older spiritual brother who, through this walk, was going to help make our recent Bible study on prayer more practical. Instead, Chris taught me a lesson on prayer that still shapes how I pray three decades later.

This is how Chris started that first prayer.

"Hi God. It's me, Chris."

I have no memory at all of what he prayed after that. All I know is that my brain locked up in the face of his casual intimacy and sincerity. I was shocked. My shock was not one of offence but recognition. This was how someone prayed to God when they thought of God in terms of a loving relationship. Everything in my childhood experience of Christianity had been form and procedure, rules and requirements, King James language and stiff formality. Relationship had never entered the picture. My adult relationship with God had started to mend that damage, but Chris's prayer shone a light on one unaddressed religious habit: a rigid and sometimes ostentatious approach to prayer that was the opposite of what the Bible taught and who I wanted to be.

"Hi God. It's me, Daryl."

I've prayed that way ever since.

In his old age, Solomon did not face a formality issue but instead a verbosity problem. Here's how he raises this new topic:

> [1] *Watch your steps when you go to God's house. It's more acceptable to listen than to offer the fools' sacrifice—they have no idea that they're acting wrongly.* [2] *Don't be quick with your mouth or say anything hastily before God, because God is in heaven, but you are on earth. Therefore, let your words be few.*
>
> [3] *Remember:*
>> *Dreams come with many cares,*
>> *and the voice of fools with many words.*
>
> ECCLESIASTES 5:1–3

In my own experience, I valued learning from Chris's informal intimacy, but there is something for our generation to absorb from Solomon's instruction here as well. Imagine, for a minute, praying in such a way that you spend more time listening to what God might be telling you than speaking. In other words, imagine a private prayer that starts with Chris's intimate familiarity but adds pauses to think about what you want to say next and allows for response windows. This idea might inspire a protest along the lines of, "Well, that doesn't sound like prayer; that sounds like mysticism or meditation," to which I (and I think Solomon) would answer, "Precisely."

This isn't the place to unpack the history of Christian mysticism or to detour into the finer points of how meditation works. Disentangling Buddhist and Eastern styles of meditation from what the Bible describes is also not our mission. For our purposes here, let's just call it praying and listening. Do a lot of listening when you pray and not so much talking. That is Solomon's point, along with the sage warning to not be hasty with your mouth when you do speak.

Solomon has another bit to share with us on this topic of speech in the context of religion. This one isn't about general prayers but rather religious vows

> [4] *When you make a promise to God, fulfill it without delay because God has no pleasure in fools. Fulfill what you promise.* [5] *Better not to make a promise than to make a promise without fulfilling it.* [6] *Don't let your mouth make a sinner of you, and don't say to the messenger: "It was a mistake!" Otherwise, God may become angry at such talk and destroy what you have accomplished.*
>
> [7] *Remember:*
> *When dreams multiply,*
> *so do pointless thoughts and excessive speech.*
> *Therefore, fear God.*
>
> ECCLESIASTES 5:4–7

Chris subsequently moved to Calgary, then France, while I departed for Ontario. But I learned a lot from him when we shared Vancouver together and treasure those memories. He didn't just pray informally. He also prayed to God as a man would talk to a true friend, never making grandiose promises he would never fulfill, but speaking thoughtfully and without excessive words. I'm still learning about prayer from Chris. Some friends leave you with lessons that last a lifetime.

27

INJUSTICE EXISTS WHERE IT SHOULD NOT

OUR DAUGHTER ENTERED kindergarten in a wheelchair with very limited speech abilities. We were close enough to the school that bus services were not normally provided, but due to her physical disabilities, she qualified for transportation services. Jackson was a toddler at the time, so we were grateful for the help.

I came home from work one day to a distraught wife.

"Mackenzie went missing today," she said.

"What do you mean, 'she went missing'?"

"The bus picked her up at the normal time," Carolyn replied. "But the school reported that she was forty minutes late getting to school."

At the time, we lived two minutes from the school—five minutes on a really bad day.

"Where did she go?" I asked.

"No one knows. The driver said that he drove straight to the school. But there's no way it took forty minutes to get there. There were no other kids on the bus today. And Mackenzie can't communicate well enough to tell us anything."

"Well, we need to get a hold of the bus company," I said.

"I did that already," Carolyn said. "I'm already getting the runaround."

"The runaround" was our phrase for bureaucracies disinterested in responding to the concerns either of us raised. With Jackson, we never got the runaround. With Mackenzie, though, we either met amazingly interested and compassionate professionals who treated their jobs as a calling or people skilled at the runaround. We worked very hard not be "problem parents." We've always made an extra effort to develop strong relationships with all of Mackenzie's teachers, caregivers, and health care providers, but occasionally, we encountered the runaround. For runaround specialists, Mackenzie's needs were a bother and questions from her parents a great annoyance.

In the Case of Missing Mackenzie, the runaround quickly turned into a brick wall. The bus company opened and closed our file within twenty-four hours, having interviewed no one and explained nothing. It appeared that the easiest way to handle the case of a misplaced child was to ignore the problem and tell the parents to go away.

Our concerns were dismissed.

Solomon observed a similar problem in his own society, highlighting not the problems of special-needs children and their parents but the oppression of the poor in general.

> [8] *If you witness the poor being oppressed or the violation of what is just and right in some territory, don't be surprised because a high official watches over another, and yet others stand over them.* [9] *But the land's yield should be for everyone if the field is cultivated.* [10] *The money lover isn't satisfied with money; neither is the lover of wealth satisfied with income. This too is pointless.*
>
> ECCLESIASTES 5:8–10

It's not pointless. It is *hevel*. Breath. Temporary, fleeting, important but also insubstantial and elusive. Frustrating. The plight of the poor in society is *hevel*.

I take Solomon's point here to be one advising against naïveté. "Don't be surprised," the wise man says. "The world is corrupt, and that corruption comes in layers."

In the Case of Missing Mackenzie, we tried escalating our concerns by going up the layers in the busing organization. The company's supervisor informed my wife, with no evidence to back up the claim, that our daughter had not gone missing, and we should stop bothering them about it. For a second time, the case was closed.

This response made no sense. A non-verbal young girl had gone missing, and that could mean many things.

Solomon goes on to relate that corruption in the world often does not make practical sense. So often, the poor in Solomon's day were the lowest manual farm laborers, yet everyone benefited from their labor since everyone needed to eat. Inevitably, however, somebody made money off the backs of the poor, and this is as true today as it was then. Despite the universality of this observation, Solomon goes on to note the lack of satisfaction for all participants since there was never enough money for those who loved their bank accounts. Crushing one person for gain doesn't bring joy to anyone in the long run because greed is never satisfied.

Solomon has just described a circle: corruption in a domain, the bureaucratic layers of that corruption, the illogic of the corruption, and the dissatisfaction felt by everyone involved. Nobody wins. This whole scene is a bunch of *hevel*.

Likewise, with our busing complaint, there was nothing to be gained by the company refusing to investigate my wife's concerns. The best-case scenario was that the driver had stopped for a coffee or to chat with a friend along the way. Leaving our child alone on the bus would have been against policy and a risk, given her fragile medical condition, but the risk of it becoming an ongoing issue could have been easily remedied by giving the driver a warning. We had no evidence to suggest something more criminal had occurred in that forty minutes, but she couldn't tell us otherwise, and we fought hard not to let parental paranoia stir anxious imaginations. Regardless of the reason for the missing time, it was also in the busing company's interests to understand what had occurred and make sure it didn't happen again.

As in Solomon's day, injustice doesn't benefit anyone in the long run.

We saw that the last time Solomon raised the topic of societal failures, he didn't demand a cure for these problems. That is not Solomon's mission here. Other books in the Bible address that kind of material, including some of Solomon's own writings. But here, in Ecclesiastes, Solomon is trying to help individuals live in the society we have rather than the one we want. In this passage, Solomon tells us to "wake up; this is how the world works." Don't be naively surprised at how broken society is, and don't think that even the folks at the top are ultimately happy with their situation. Injustice and oppression exist in many places where they shouldn't be found, and those injustices don't ultimately create a lasting benefit for anyone anywhere.

When we're not surprised by injustice in the world, it makes it much easier to think through how to deal with injustice when we do encounter it. Racism and sexism are the injustices my community has talked most about. Beyond these sorts of headline issues, however, even garden-variety injustices, such as people stealing your ideas or blaming you for their errors, are examples where injustice will never see a courtroom but can still leave an emotional mark. Sometimes emotional responses are appropriate. Sometimes thoughtful reasoning is the most effective approach. A balanced mixture has usually served me best, emotion and reason both playing a role to address a situation. When your society supports it, there are occasionally legal, regulatory, reputational, or other accepted methods that you can use to help remedy bad situations. What is common to all these approaches, however, is the advantage that a non-naive, non-surprised, but also non-cynical attitude can have when trying to fix a problem.

In the Case of Missing Mackenzie, my wife started driving our daughter to school, since we no longer trusted the bus driver. She also arranged for a meeting with the bus company's supervisor to talk through our concerns in person. After much debate, the supervisor reluctantly agreed to the meeting and arranged a time at their head office location in a nearby city.

The supervisor was expecting a sleep-deprived young mother with a healthy toddler in tow while Mackenzie spent the morning at school. Instead, I showed up with Mackenzie. Carolyn could have handled the appointment, but she stayed home to recover from the night shift with Mackenzie and to look after Jackson. I'd taken time off work to attend this meeting.

When the president of the bus company met me at the front door, he was startled to find a father before him along with a special-needs girl in a wheelchair. The world is still too often a sexist place. From the look on his face and his awkward wording, it was clear that he had been expecting Carolyn and would have preferred to loom over her rather than face a six-foot-tall man in a business suit. His expression shifted from dominant to off guard and then quickly to embarrassment. The meeting had been booked to take place in a boardroom on the company's elevator-free second floor. As a result, I carried Mackenzie in her wheelchair up the flight of stairs while he looked on in dismay.

The boardroom was well staffed that day. In addition to the supervisor and president, there were over half a dozen other people around the vast boardroom table, including the head of HR, head of operations, and several other people who I paid little attention to. I'd seen this kind of thing in the business world before: put one troublesome soul in the hot seat in an intimidating room in front of a large panel of interrogators sporting senior titles, and watch that individual melt. It was stupid social manipulation designed to shut down or emotionally rattle a lone parent. Except I wasn't alone. I had Mackenzie with me. She might be special needs and non-verbal, but she's also cute. As much as the world is sometimes still too sexist, it's also vulnerable to cuteness.

The useless participants around the table—the window-dressing executive crowd—developed very uncomfortable demeanors. I think they wanted to be gone. When I ignored the crowd and focused only on the president—since he was the boss and the only one in the room now that mattered—the other members of the board moved from co-interrogators to witnesses. The president, too, seemed to suddenly regret their presence.

I started by asking him what he knew of the facts and made it very clear that I was only interested in what he did or didn't know so that he and I could have a clear conversation and come to a good resolution before I left. As he struggled to explain what he knew, one of the window-dressing witnesses literally changed sides of the table. Mackenzie had a small Winnie-the-Pooh with her, so that board member and Mackenzie played with Winnie while the president explained himself. He had the basic facts straight. Then, in a strange bit of autopilot programming, he repeated the supervisor's previous lines about how parents cannot dictate busing schedules or staffing, and there was nothing more they could do. As he said these words, it was clear he was repeating coached lines and no longer believed what he heard himself saying. But he said it, and did so in front of a room full of witnesses.

I then turned to the supervisor who had shut down my wife's queries twice. I reminded the room that the school itself had recorded and reported the forty-minute gap and then asked the supervisor, "Did you consult the teacher who made that time recording when you conducted your investigation?"

"No," she answered.

"Did you ever consult any of the other teachers or educational assistants regarding the missing forty minutes, asking to see the logbook or anything of that sort?"

"No," came the answer.

"Did you talk to the school principal or anyone else associated with the school board to validate their method of tracking and logging children's arrival times?"

"No." Her answer was almost a whisper now.

"Did you ask the bus driver to explain the missing forty minutes? Perhaps he went for a coffee or had some other errand to run."

"No," she said.

"Do you log the bus return times so that you can validate the time when a school bus returns to the yard and therefore spot anomalies that way?"

"No."

"Do you have cameras on the buses with time-stamps so you can go back and make your own assessments without involving witnesses?"

"No."

I then turned my attention back to the president, making sure I had his full attention before proceeding.

"So, on your company's watch, a young girl went missing for forty minutes, and your staff talked to absolutely no one who had any facts regarding this incident. Additionally, your company has no procedural or technical controls in place to catch problems early or investigate them after the fact. Twice your staff closed this file with not even one phone call's worth of investigation. And in your own words, there is nothing you can do."

I let that sit there for a minute, correctly reading that he wouldn't respond. The room was dead silent except for Mackenzie playing hand games with the one staff member.

"I think it's safe to say that there's not a parent in this room who wouldn't be alarmed and even infuriated by what has occurred here, and by the unanswered questions that remain." I didn't take my eyes off the president, but if a person can feel people nodding around him, I felt them. Looking at the president, I could see the supervisor at his side. She looked like she was going to throw up. Now, however, was not the time for kindness. Calm, yes, but not kindness. As Solomon has already told us, there's a time for everything, and this, in its very small way, was a time for war.

"I want to make sure I treat you fairly in this matter and don't misrepresent you at all," I said, eyes still locked on the president. "Is there a union rule that prevents you from addressing this problem?"

"No," the president said.

"Is there an educational system or transportation system regulation that ties your hands?"

"No."

"Is there a provincial or federal employment standard or regulation you risk violating—or a contract with the driver, the school board, or any other party—that makes it impossible for you to properly investigate and resolve this matter?"

"No," he answered, and now he, too, was nearly whispering.

"Thank you for your candor," I said. "It was important for me to ensure I fully understood the facts before I engage a lawyer. Prior to Mackenzie's birth, my wife used to work for a couple of major law firms—one in Mississauga and one in Toronto—so we'll tap that network and find a good fit for this case. With a lawyer's guidance, we'll then engage the media and potentially the legal system regarding a non-verbal child who went missing and a well-known local bus company that refuses to investigate the matter."

The president finally found his voice again. "That shouldn't be necessary," he said. "You'll have a new driver tomorrow morning, and we'll immediately launch a proper investigation." He turned and looked at his supervisor, HR manager, and operations manager. They all nodded in agreement. Someone said, "Definitely," though I didn't catch who.

When Mackenzie and I left, the president helped me carry her in her wheelchair down the flight of stairs. The staff all shook my hand and said kind words to Mackenzie. I sensed that the one who had played with her wanted to give my daughter a hug goodbye but held back.

Two new drivers in two separate buses showed up the next morning to take Mackenzie to school. When the investigation concluded, things with the driver were dealt with as they needed to be. This isn't the space to get into those side tales. Suffice it to say that if I met any of those boardroom people on the street today, we could talk kindly to one another. Not only was the problem resolved, but its resolution did not create new adversaries. I wouldn't hire anyone on that team into my own workplace, but I could visit with them in a grocery store aisle and not work hard to do so.

It makes it easier to deal with injustice in society when you're not surprised by it but also not cynical or hateful. Sometimes anger is useful. Sometimes, perhaps, it's even necessary. At other times, calm is what is required. That day, calm won the day.

Whether calm or carefully angry, it helps not to be naive. "Don't be surprised," Solomon said. He's right. It makes it easier to think.

28

WE CRAVE SOMETHING MORE THAN WEALTH

I'VE WORKED IN Canadian banking for over thirty years now. I started as a part-time casual teller in Vancouver with guaranteed Saturday and Monday shifts and occasional hours at other locations when opportunities arose. Over the decades since, I've worked in what seems like every area of the bank—from bank branches to brokerage offices, from customer service to investments and lending, and on to head office jobs in product management, IT, HR, operations, and strategy roles. However, over and over again, in all my diverse roles, I've repeatedly made the same disturbing observation: the rich are not any happier than anyone else. Banking privacy laws and common sense prevent me from sharing specific stories, but the tales money could tell are tales filled with sorrow and dissatisfaction, not joy and gratitude.

I've read numerous psychology articles over the years trying to make sense of the obvious pattern that I had the privileged access to observe. The data in those articles suggested that money could buy some happiness—food, shelter, and clothing did a lot for one's mood—but beyond the level of basic needs, there was very little correlation between money and happiness[74]. Once

---

74   For readers interested in exploring this literature further, the work of Daniel Kahneman, a Nobel prize-winning economist and psychologist is a good place to start. An internet search under his name will bring up a treasure trove of newspaper articles and YouTube lectures starting in 2010 that summarize the otherwise less accessible academic writings.

a person is fed, clothed, warm, and dry, money didn't go very far to improve their long-term enjoyment of life.

I saw that this nuance found in research papers matched my observations as well. So I rephrased my view: if money couldn't buy happiness, at least it could buy some misery reduction. But that was it.

Solomon—remember, he was a seriously rich man—made a similar observation.

> *[11] When good things flow, so do those who consume them. But what do owners benefit from such goods, except to feast their eyes on them?*
>
> ECCLESIASTES 5:11

The problem Solomon identified was the human incapacity to make any practical use of more and more success. We can only eat so much food before it becomes a health problem. We can only wear so many clothes before we get too hot. We can only drive one fancy car at a time. There may be no limit to greed, as Solomon talked about in the previous verse, but there is a limit to our ability to enjoy consuming the products we attain.

By contrast,

> *[12] Sweet is the worker's sleep, whether there's a lot or little to eat; but the excess of the wealthy won't let them sleep.*
>
> ECCLESIASTES 5:12

As a wealthy man who dived off pleasure's pier far more than was wise or reasonable, Solomon knows a thing or two about this problem. Not only is there a limit to how much one person can enjoy, but the accumulation of stuff can even produce displeasure. One can lose something as simple as the sweet satisfaction of a good night's sleep to concerns about protecting, maintaining, and growing that wealth. Sleep deprivation will steal the joy from every good thing in life and will do so fast. A day or two without sleep, and any human is in trouble at a fundamental level.

The Queen of Sheba's gift, which was tons of gold, illustrates Solomon's wealth quite nicely. He knows what he's talking about on the topic of money and its negative qualities. He goes on to give us some further practical insight on the topic of the super-rich.

> [13] *I have seen a sickening tragedy under the sun: people hoard their wealth to their own detriment.* [14] *Then that wealth is lost in a bad business venture so that when they have children, they are left with nothing.* [15] *Just as they came from their mother's womb naked, naked they'll return, ending up just like they started. All their hard work produces nothing—nothing they can take with them.* [16] *This too is a sickening tragedy: they must pass on just as they arrived. What then do they gain from working so hard for wind?* [17] *What's more, they constantly eat in darkness, with much aggravation, grief, and anger.*
>
> ECCLESIASTES 5:13–17

This isn't exactly the mai-tais-on-a-beach or black-tie-soiree image we usually associate with the super wealthy. Solomon instead gives us a scatter-shot collage of unexpectedly negative outcomes. A bad business deal erases wealth (5:14). Then, even if the wealth is kept or lost, the wealthy still depart life as naked and penniless as they entered it (5:15). Even if they hold on to their wealth in life, they don't gain any lasting benefit from it (5:15–16). A life of striving just leads to a life of darkness and aggravation. Solomon emphasizes his point by calling it a life of "much aggravation, grief, and anger" (5:17). Notice here that these wealthy people don't just experience "darkness, with much aggravation, grief, and anger" once or twice, but they eat in this state. Eating is something most people do every day, multiple times a day. Like sleep in verse twelve, eating is one of those pleasures that Solomon commends so highly and yet, for these burdened wealthy, even eating loses its capacity for joy and becomes a haunt of negativity.

Do you think Solomon is mistaken here? Are you captivated by the apparent success of the super wealthy as outlined in glamorous magazines and shows? Are you inclined to dismiss Solomon's social critique? If so, it doesn't take much of a scan of the world's headlines to find countless poor social, psychological, and health realities of the super-rich to prove that Solomon knows what he's talking about. People don't need drug rehab spas and divorce lawyers because things are working out. Sinéad O'Connor, the

Irish singer-songwriter, once covered the song "Success Has Made a Failure of Our Home" by Johnny Mullins and Loretta Lynn. Whether these artists intended the song to be autobiographical or not, their message certainly aligns with Solomon's point. The facade of worldly success perpetuated by entertainment shows, magazines, and social media is just that: a facade.

Once, I listened to a sports star lament about not having brought a high school romantic relationship with him into his professional career years. His net worth was now the subject of fan sites' estimations, and his sports and endorsement contracts were on the public record. As a result, he was beset with dating opportunities but trusted no one. He doubted now that he could ever get married.

I shared this story with my son when he was in second-year university and mentioned how blessed he was to be forming quality relationships at his age and life stage, free from money's influence.

"Money can't buy what you have," I said.

His response was, "Actually, Dad, money would be a barrier to building what I have."

He didn't mean that he didn't want to make money one day. He simply understood the sports star's problem. Money was that man's relational curse.

To Solomon—a member of this apparently successful but personally failing social class—O'Connor and that date-options-rich but relationship-poor sports star both had it right: success created failure. As a result, Solomon judged this whole business to be a "sickening tragedy."

Okay, Hollywood society or the top-of-the-food-chain elite in New York, London, Paris, Dubai, Hong Kong, or whatever other pinnacle city is currently in vogue are easy targets to critique. What is harder to imagine is an alternative aspiration—one that everyone can work toward regardless of their racial, gender, economic, or any other social class. Wouldn't it be nice if our philosophers had something practical to offer besides criticism?

Even better, wouldn't it be cool if God himself inspired someone well-suited to explore these topics—someone with the time, money, social standing, health, and even wisdom—to go deep, perform experiments, and thoroughly mine every option to find ultimate meaning in life and then report back to us in language we can all understand?

Ah, there is such a messenger: Solomon is our guy. He made a royal mess of his own life, but by doing so—and being gifted by God with wisdom along the way—he is our perfect guide to life's failures and the path we should take instead. The path he describes is the one he should have taken. Instead of admiring the rich—or if we are rich, being seduced into ruining our lives by the mesmerizing qualities of wealth—Solomon advises us about what we should focus on instead.

> *¹⁸ This is the one good thing I've seen:*
>
> ECCLESIASTES 5:18A

Okay, hold on. We know where this is going, right? Worship God, serve the poor, obey the rules—all the usual religious tropes on how to live well.

No, that's not where Solomon is going with this. Remember, he's focused on how to live "under the sun" (1:3). This isn't a book on salvation or heaven or even righteousness. This is a book on how to live the best possible life now, despite the broken state of the world and struggles of human society and the reality of mortality.

> *¹⁸ This is the one good thing I've seen: it's appropriate for people to eat, drink, and find enjoyment in all their hard work under the sun during the brief lifetime that God gives them because that's their lot in life. ¹⁹ Also, whenever God gives people wealth and riches and enables them to enjoy it, to accept their place in the world and to find pleasure in their hard work—all this is God's gift. ²⁰ Indeed, people shouldn't brood too much over the days of their lives because God gives an answer in their hearts' joy.*
>
> ECCLESIASTES 5:18–20

There it is again. In 3:22, Solomon put this same call to enjoyment in the "nothing better" category. Here it is positioned as "the one good thing" Solomon saw: enjoy your life. He doesn't tell us to enjoy our sweeping conquests or massively obsessive life goals but to enjoy lunch or a drink of cold water on a hot day. And while you're working on your amazing projects or huge goals or small tasks, enjoy the work. He says it twice, in verses eighteen and nineteen—enjoy your work, take pleasure in your work. Said almost too simply, focus on enjoying the journey, not the reward at the end. Let me say that again. Take pleasure in the journey, not the prize at the end. When you sit at the piano, don't worry about the upcoming performance; instead, love the sound now. Like my first-year calculus professor, find beauty in the numbers that are your career, the smell of wood shavings if you're a woodworker, the flex of muscle, the creative output, the agency and gift of work, and not the accolades that might come later.

The gift of work? Yes, gift. These things are gifts that "God gives [people] because that's their lot in life" (5:18) and "this is God's gift" (5:19). Enjoying life, including our work, is our lot and gift in life. That's the plan. The curse in the Garden of Eden was not the creation of work. Work existed before that tragedy. The curse in Genesis was for creation to fight back against the worker (with thorns and so on), but work itself was part of paradise before the fall. Healthy hearts and brains need work. Laziness with wealth is better respected and fed than laziness with poverty, but at a psychological and heart-health level, they are equals. The idle—rich or poor, able or disabled—suffer without meaningful work.

So enjoy your life—not the future life you're striving for, but this one right now. Sure, we should all be working toward something better, be that heaven or a life goal here and now. The Bible does discuss the value of planning and working toward future goals. The book of Proverbs provides plenty of practical advice in this regard. But our primary lot in this gift of life that God has designed for us is not to achieve something but to enjoy the process along the way—to enjoy the present. Our lot is learning to appreciate the present and then also enjoy that new situation when the future happens. That's the plan. God is not the great grumbly rule-maker in the sky saying "No" to everything fun. God is described elsewhere as love, and that moniker applies here in Ecclesiastes as well. Our loving God wants us to enjoy the world now, despite its broken state.

Learning to enjoy a meal and not just wolf it down takes some practice. It takes slowing down a little.[75] It takes focus. Learning not to let worry or anxious plotting consume our days requires mental effort. Learning to enjoy our work likewise takes some effort. For some of us, it may require switching jobs to something more suited to our nature or skills, but beware of the

---

75 I found Carl Honoré's volume *In Praise of Slow: How a Worldwide Movement Is Challenging the Cult of Speed* (Vintage Canada, 2004) an enjoyable extended read on this topic.

recent siren call of ever searching for that dream job. Go after a meaningful and rewarding career change if that's appropriate to your situation, but whatever you put your hand or mind to, it will still be hard. Work is hard. The mental friction of labor—be it physical, emotional, or mental labor—takes effort, so any job is likely to require times of dutiful diligence without an ideal emotional state or creative flow. But in Solomon's words, learning to enjoy our work is part of the "one good thing" that humanity can focus on. There's nothing better.

Let's be honest: that's a bit disappointing. After all, God put eternity into our hearts—we always want something more. But, even if we get that dream job, it won't be enough. And that's Solomon's point: nothing in this world will be enough. It's all *hevel*—it is breath that is elusive, essential, fleeting, repetitive, insatiable in its demands, and life-giving but intangible. However, recognizing the *hevelness* of life is precisely why we need to learn to enjoy what we have now. This is not just sound advice; this is an art. It's an essential life skill. It's God's plan.

Enjoy dinner. Enjoy a glass of something refreshing. Wear clothes you enjoy. Enjoy your work. These things are your lot in life, and they are gifts from God.

29

YOU CAN'T BUY HEAVEN OR *YITHRON*

"Stairway to Heaven," the legendary rock anthem by Led Zeppelin, was released in 1971 and went on to become one of the top rock songs ever recorded. Roughly ten years later, our family moved to California, and my father took on his first role as lead pastor. When he was asked the following year to handle his first funeral in that new role, our whole family attended even though none of us had met the deceased young woman. The woman's family arranged the sound system for the outdoor service and decided that "Stairway to Heaven" would feature prominently in the service.

My father knew nothing about rock music and approved the selection based on its title alone. The resulting drama at that sun-drenched California funeral was imprinted on my early teenage brain, and the memory is as vivid today as it was then.

First, it was hot. Our Canadian family was not yet used to California summers. While my father, the casket, and the deceased woman's immediate family sweltered under a tall shade, the rest of us, including my mother, sister, and I, stood baking in the sun. My father's KJB-flavored language poured out over the assembly of people. As that seventeenth-century religious phraseology wrapped up, Jimmy Page's quiet guitar work replaced my father's voice, and then Robert Plant's voice began describing a materialistic woman who was sure she'd be able to buy her way into heaven.

What that young woman's family at the funeral were doing—using a song that, upon reflection, seemed to be a takedown of her spirituality and character—I had no idea. I was thirteen or fourteen at the time. What I did know was that my super conservative preacher father was suddenly realizing that this wasn't a hymn from any approved psalter.

As the song progressed, the quiet guitar accompaniment developed electrified layers. Then the drums came in at about the four-minute mark. At about the six-minute mark, Robert Plant's increasingly abstract and metaphorical lyrics paused, and the building tension of the song climaxed. At that moment, my mother passed out. Later it was called heat stroke. At the time, I was pretty sure that Jimmy Page and Robert Plant had struck her dead by the power of their voice and electric guitar. We didn't listen to rock music at home, and I'd never seen someone faint before, so it wasn't a completely unreasonable conclusion.

Led Zeppelin continued to wash over that black-dressed crowd amid a garden of pink, white, and red flowers. A full minute of instrumental work oversaw the crowd's reaction to my mother's back-of-the-funeral drama, and then Robert Plant's voice floated back in, returning us to the story of the woman trying to buy her way into heaven.

"The song is about an LSD trip," my father informed me later. "I didn't know. This was totally the work of Satan."

That sounded a bit much to me, but that was in the days before the internet, so I couldn't download or stream the song at home or search the lyrics to critique the accuracy of my father's statement.

That same year, the Trinity Broadcasting Network, as part of their general campaign against rock music, announced that the song "Stairway to Heaven" had been backmasked with satanic messages. To discover the song's secret satanic message, you had to play the record backward. I remember as a young teenager wondering how you played a record backward. My record player only went one way. I figured that if I had the record, I could manually drag the turntable the opposite way, but needles were expensive, and I didn't know if dragging the record the wrong way would wreck the needle. This was also the era before rap music had popularized that kind of vinyl manipulation, so it was not at all obvious at the time that the experiment would be anything more than a plan to set money on fire. I was interested in understanding this controversy better, but buying the record while living in my house was out of the question, so getting to the stage of wrecking a needle on it wasn't going to happen.

The next time I encountered "Stairway to Heaven" was about a decade later in the movie *Wayne's World*. In that movie, the main character, Wayne, tries out the song's opening riffs in a guitar store beneath a sign that says, No Stairway to Heaven. The movie came out twenty-one years after the album, and that *Wayne's World* joke apparently had a basis in real life. There's an unwritten rule in guitar stores that you don't use "Stairway to Heaven" to try out a new axe. The world has apparently become a bit weary of the song, yet it still ranks high in surveys of the greatest rock songs of all time. Maybe the world just doesn't like amateur renditions of the classic.

And there's the rub. If it weren't for Led Zeppelin's bad-boy reputation and its distinction as a forerunner of hard rock and heavy metal; and if it weren't for conservative Christianity's resistance at that time to any music composed after the 1800s; and if that same vein of Christianity had done more work to understand art (starting with maybe reading lyrics before vilifying them), "Stairway to Heaven" might actually have become a Christian anthem. Okay, it probably would not have been played on Sunday morning in church, but in the same way that the Apostle Paul quoted pagan poets, the song could have served a powerful role in helping the Christian world articulate some very basic spiritual truths. Those truths include that: you can't buy your way into heaven; the Pied Piper (never named in the song but repeatedly alluded to) will deceive you; however far you've gone down a false road, you can still come back; and finally, the writing is on the wall if you think you can buy your way into heaven. There is more than one biblical allusion in the song.

I suspect that the family at that funeral had no better idea of what the song was about than my indignant preacher father and fainting mother. When the internet was invented and I could google song lyrics, I happily studied them and found a message I could relate to.

Solomon was not focused on heaven in Ecclesiastes, but he was in tune with the general point of Led Zeppelin's song. Change the word "heaven" to "*yithron*" (lasting benefit), and the song could have been written by the ancient and wise king himself. You can't buy *yithron* with money.

> *¹ I saw a tragedy under the sun, and it weighs heavily upon humanity. ² God may give some people plenty of wealth, riches, and glory so that they lack nothing they desire. But God doesn't enable them to enjoy it; instead, a stranger enjoys it. This is pointless and a sickening tragedy.*
>
> ECCLESIASTES 6:1–2

Beyond simply being unable to take things with us when we die, Solomon considers another tragedy that "weighs heavily on humanity": the inability to enjoy our blessings while we're still alive.

If you cannot take your life's work with you when you die, and you cannot enjoy it while you're alive, then pursuing wealth in Solomon's view was not just *hevel* but *hevel* plus a sickening tragedy. He went on to expound more on this idea.

> *³ Some people may have one hundred children and live a long life. But no matter how long they live, if they aren't content with life's good things, I say that even a stillborn child with no grave is better off than they are. ⁴ Because that child arrives pointlessly, then passes away in darkness. Darkness covers its name. ⁵ It hasn't seen the sun or experienced anything. But it has more peace than those ⁶ who live a thousand years twice over but don't enjoy life's good things. Isn't everyone heading to the same destination? ⁷ All the hard work of humans is for the mouth, but the appetite is never full. ⁸ What advantage do the wise have over the foolish? Or what do the poor gain by knowing how to conduct themselves before the living? ⁹ It's better to enjoy what's at hand than to have an insatiable appetite. This too is pointless, just wind chasing.*
>
> ECCLESIASTES 6:3–9

For those who have lost a child, Solomon's illustration here might prove hurtful and distract the reader from his main point. Solomon aims not to reopen old wounds but to contrast short life with long life: a stillborn child whose life never got started versus someone who lives "a thousand years twice over."

Typically, in biblical literature, a long life is considered a divine blessing, but Solomon states here that it is only a blessing if an individual can enjoy it.

Previously, Solomon had recommended that the remedy for the *hevelness* of life was food. There is, however, a problem with this advice: "the appetite is never full" (6:7). The drive to find satisfaction in money, sex, career achievements, and so on cannot simply be transferred to a quest for the perfect lunch. After all, it's "better to enjoy what's at hand than to have an insatiable appetite" (6:9). Gluttony is not the new goal. Appreciation, though, is.

Perhaps a personal example will help illustrate this point more clearly.

I like bonsai. Yes, I'm referring to the little trees grown in specialized, often Asian, pots. I have a fine collection of trees and enjoy working on them. My wife and I also have a four-season conservatory at the rear of our house, complete with a green wall, tropical plants, and of course, small trees. The room hosts a total of nearly two hundred plants and trees of all sizes. The room is a source of great pleasure for us. My favorite time of day is first thing in the morning when we enjoy a coffee together among the trees, vines, and beautiful tropical leaves, chatting about the previous day or the one to come. Due to our daughter's slowly degenerating condition, those chats often concern medical challenges and nursing schedules. Still, this is a special quiet time for us at the beginning of our day. In the winter, surrounded by this greenery, with snow falling outside and the fireplace beside us to keep us warm, even if the topic is necessarily practical and dark, the experience contains an element of magic.

However, long before we created this special oasis, my wife and I learned to enjoy each other's company. Our first apartment was 490 square feet in size. The entire apartment was barely bigger than our conservatory is today. One morning when we were getting ready for work, we tried to pass each other at the foot of the bed, one of us heading for the closet, the other for the bathroom. Our apartment was so small that we had to shuffle sideways to make it work. As Carolyn was trying to pass between me and the bed, I turned too early, and my shoulder accidentally caught her chin and sent her backward onto the bed. It would have been funny if it hadn't nearly knocked her out. She wound up missing a day of work as a result, fighting nausea and dizziness, and I spent the week mortified—feeling like a wife-abuser and getting hassled about it by our friends.

Four homes later and five years into our marriage, with one child already born, we found ourselves with a kitchen so small there was no room for a fridge—we kept the fridge in the unfinished basement. To live together in such small spaces, we didn't just need to learn how to better execute the foot-of-the-bed sideways shuffle. It was also about cooperation, kindness, and courtesy. We learned to run up and down the stairs to help whoever was cooking, to stay quiet when the other was ill or asleep, and to enjoy each other's interests and conversation since there was no other end of the house we could retreat to if we weren't getting along. The butterflies-in-your-stomach infatuation stage of love is great, but you need a lot more than that to navigate close quarters year after year.

We enjoy a much grander living situation now, but our indoor forest, though fun, would be useless if she and I didn't get along. The broad view of winter's snow in the season's low light would simply be depressing, the fire another expense to maintain, the space just one more room to sweep and dust, our mornings together yet another opportunity for friction and contempt.

Likewise, if I didn't like tending the plants and trees, the work of watering, fertilizing, repotting, pruning, and occasionally battling insects or other infestations would be a significant burden. Life would be terrible with this useless labor-creating room that nobody enjoyed. Hanging pictures would be more time and cost effective, and then I could ignore the watering schedule and spend more time away from the family and the house. Not building the addition at all would have been an even better choice. We would have saved a lot of money.

I've known too many people over the decades who have bought a new house or upgraded the old one to no avail. The problem wasn't the home's design. The problem was the inhabitants' relationships and their internal wellbeing. Their interpersonal conflicts and soul-level wounds would follow them wherever they went until they faced their problems and healed.

My wife and I learned to love each other and communicate with each other long before we had extra square footage to move around in. And I do enjoy looking after the plants. I put on a set of high-quality headphones and dial in a playlist or audiobook that suits my mood and go to work, pruning shears and other tools in hand, to tend to what my wife calls my "old man's hobby." During those minutes or hours, my wife focuses on her own interests while I tend miniature trees.

The enjoyment of bonsai, however, had its drawbacks. One of the things I discovered early on was an insatiable desire to collect more and more trees. A meme recently went around the Ontario bonsai community stating, "You practiced self-control and didn't buy a plant today. Congratulations. You should reward yourself with a new plant." It made me laugh because it rang true.

I eventually started losing trees due to inadequate watering, poor planting choices, or pest invasions caught too late. I wasn't enjoying what I had. I wasn't observing the existing collection closely. I was just gathering more and more stuff and always shopping for a new species or more advanced specimen. I had to slow down. I had to take a lesson from Solomon and learn to "enjoy what's at hand" (6:9) and stop chasing what I didn't have. I will not satisfy the yearning for eternity that God intentionally lodged in my heart with small trees any more than the next person can fulfill their hunger for eternity with sports, achievements, or any other hobby or distraction.

Robert Plant sang about a woman trying to buy a stairway to heaven. Ignoring heaven, Solomon wrote about the inadequacy of money to buy lasting benefit in this life. More trees, even though I liked them, didn't make me happier.

That doesn't mean I should abandon bonsai. Remember, God wants us to enjoy ourselves. As we learned in the previous chapter,

> *19 Also, whenever God gives people wealth and riches and enables them to enjoy it, to accept their place in the world and to find pleasure in their hard work—all this is God's gift. 20 Indeed, people shouldn't brood too much over the days of their lives because God gives an answer in their hearts' joy.*
>
> ECCLESIASTES 5:19–20

Wait a minute. What's that bit about God giving "an answer in their hearts' joy" all about? That is a slightly opaque phrase, and we didn't cover that when we looked at chapter five.

The question answered in our hearts' joy is the "What does it all mean?" question. In this often enigmatic and frustrating life, the *hevelness* of it all can eat away at a soul's endurance. Always chasing what is around the corner or over the horizon and never learning to enjoy this life now is a "sickening tragedy" (5:13) and invites the question of how to live better. In answer to this question, Solomon insists again that finding joy in the days of our lives, in the moments now, over lunch, even, is a gift from God. This is the salve we require for our otherwise unendurable existential pain. We will never satisfy the eternity lodged within us in this life, but we can learn to enjoy the moment.

That's cool. But did you fully understand it? Think about it for a minute.

My lot in life is to enjoy the things God has made available to me and not get unrelentingly wrapped up in what's next. But while I'm enjoying what I can enjoy, I must ensure those things do not take over my entire existence. "It's better to enjoy what's at hand than to have an insatiable appetite" (6:9a) because an insatiable appetite is also *hevel* and "wind chasing" (6:9b). Like breath, you'll never have enough. Like wind, you'll never catch it.

In my case, while I enjoy bonsai, I need to remember that they're just little trees. By following Solomon's advice here and dialling back my insatiable appetite, I discovered more enjoyment in the trees that I did own, and they grew better with more focused, meditative attention.

Let's make this even more practical. The medical student needs to enjoy medical school as much as the objective of becoming a doctor. The parent has to practice enjoying parenting while the kids are young because it won't magically happen in the teenage years or later. If a parent is always looking ahead to graduation, career success, grandchildren, and so on, the relationships will die before the children reach those milestones. Like the medical student, it's fine to work toward a goal, but enjoy what's at hand in the moment. If you don't, when you win the prize, you may discover you can't enjoy the reward in the end. That is the sickening tragedy Solomon is trying to help us avoid.

For many of us, developing this conscientious enjoyment requires a season of prayer and listening. Practically applying Solomon's teachings to our individual lives and circumstances will take effort. But, as Solomon reminds us repeatedly, there's nothing better. You can't buy heaven. Led Zeppelin knew that. You can't buy *yithron* either. Solomon told us that. All you can do is enjoy what you have now.

This is your lot in life, God's gift to you. Don't miss the gift.

PART SEVEN

EXPLORING PSYCHOLOGY AND TRANSFORMATIVE EXPERIENCES

30

GOD KNOWS US BETTER THAN WE KNOW OURSELVES

As a guy in the second half of my life, I look back on my early days in Canada with a knowing smile. At the time, I considered myself to be unique: a Californian living in British Columbia, a guy with long hair when long hair wasn't common, a preacher's kid turned atheist, an artistic mind studying chemistry and physics, an aspiring intellectual with several years of Alexandrian Greek studies and ballet training under my belt, who had also worked as a framer and driven tractors for a living. But I wasn't as different from my peers as I thought. I was twenty-one years old and still finding my footing socially and philosophically, as were most of those around me. And like them, I was hormone-addled, relationship inept, and still deciding what I wanted to be when I grew up.

As Solomon put it,

> *¹⁰ Whatever happens has already been designated, and human beings are fully known. They can't contend with the one who is stronger than they are.*
>
> ECCLESIASTES 6:10

Human beings are fully known. In my own mind, I was a one-off and veiled work of art, a mystery, a wonder, and an unknown potentiality waiting to blossom into just about anything. To God, though, I was already known—

to be precise, I was fully known. My life's future options were shaped by factors such as when I was born, where I was born, who I was born to, and what opportunities came my way.

I was hungry that first year at UBC—even as a novice atheist—hungry for something more than what I had found so far in life. The eternity in my heart was singing a song I heard clearly without recognizing the tune. I didn't know what it was at the time, but I heard it nonetheless. I read books on philosophy, Buddhism, Islam, and Christianity. I visited a Catholic Mass and a Pentecostal healing service. I went to clubs where women wrapped in neon lights danced in cages suspended over the DJ, and the dance floors were filled with pulsing light and swirling shadows. I went skiing and mountain climbing in British Columbia's beautiful wilderness. I even jumped out of an airplane.

For my one and only skydiving experience, I made sure to be the first out of the plane and into the air because I feared that if I watched someone go through that door before I did, my nerves would override my sense of adventure. No one in that plane knew my name. No one would egg me on. I'd ride up in the passenger seat and land back on the ground in the same seat, alone. I couldn't let that happen, so I jumped first.

I was at about the two-thousand-foot level when the thought entered my mind that this wasn't it. I was looking for something, but this wasn't it. As soon as that realization came to me, I wanted the experience to be over. I wanted to get back on the ground. But there is no aborting a jump halfway through. I had to ride it out.

I had friends whose sense of worldly adventure took them more into the one-night-stand category of experiences, and they reported something similar: after successfully seducing someone, they lost interest partway through the experience. It's not that the chase was the real joy. It's that the pursuit promised something that it could not deliver in the end. Like my experience with skydiving, these friends' disillusionment came early and clearly, though some chose to ignore what they learned and kept pursuing the same path repeatedly, looking for a different result each time and not finding it. It was as if I'd kept jumping out of planes thinking I'd find something better in a different cubic kilometer of air. God help the soul that won't listen to its own desperate signals and continues to search in the wrong places.

I dived back into books and started showing up more at the residence pub nights, looking and looking for what could satisfy my need. If yoga had been a popular and available activity in that decade, I would have probably taken up yoga. Hunger is like that, always looking for an object or activity it can respond to.

But God did not make pub nights, library marathons, skydiving, or any other activity under heaven able to satisfy the hunger we all feel. We can try to replace our need for God with something else, perhaps even get violent or aggressively defensive about our chosen life posture, but we "can't contend with the one who is stronger" (6:10). God knows us better than we know ourselves, and any attempt to outwit God and the way he has set life up is doomed to fail. Why? Solomon explains it this way.

> *¹¹ Because the more words increase, the more everything is pointless.*
>
> ECCLESIASTES 6:11A

Keep the translation issue here at the top of your mind. The more words increase, the more everything is *hevel*. Breath. Elusive, repetitive, enigmatic, essential, but never enough. The answer was not that yoga needed to become more widespread and that it would have satisfied me had I found it. All of life is breath. Nothing in life will fulfill the eternal hunger implanted within us. We can cauterize that need but not fulfill it. The point of that hunger is to drive us to seek God (3:14), as unpalatable as that conclusion is to your average atheist seeker. The more we try to outwit God, the less successful we will be at finding the *yithron* (lasting benefit) that our souls seek.

Solomon continues his theme this way:

> *¹¹ Because the more words increase, the more everything is pointless. What do people gain by it? ¹² Because who knows what's good for human beings during life, during their brief pointless life, which will pass away like a shadow? Who can say what the future holds for people under the sun?*
>
> ECCLESIASTES 6:11–12

Solomon acknowledges elsewhere that God is the ultimate answer to humanity's hunger (3:14), but that is not his focus here. Here, he focuses on how to live now, under the sun, amid the *hevelness* of life and the ultimately elusive quality (in this life) of humanity's existential hunger. It is important not to over-spiritualize Solomon's message. He genuinely wants to know who in the world knows how to live and who can predict the future.

Obviously, God knows these things, but I believe Solomon intended the answer to his rhetorical questions to be: nobody.

Nobody knows for sure what is good for us to do. We might have good intentions and create a great tragedy by accident. We might pick what looks like a good path and discover that we've made a wrong turn. We might make a colossal mistake that somehow turns out positively in the long run. We cannot know what the future holds for people in this life. Good and bad luck complicate reality so much that surprises are the norm.

As a direct consequence of this uncertainty, the book of Ecclesiastes suddenly shifts here. In our modern English translations, this passage is positioned as the midpoint of the book as it was in the ancient Jewish versions as well.[76] This midpoint also marks a turning point.

Solomon will continue to probe the *hevelness* of life and occasionally return to broad philosophical themes, but for most of the rest of Ecclesiastes, he will get downright prescriptive. Self-help material will start to outweigh philosophical musings. He will try to answer his question, "What is good for human beings?" As a result, what follows will read like the short verses in Proverbs interspersed with parables and poetic discursions. All these varied literary digressions are meant to help us understand how to live well in this broken *hevel*-filled world.

I had a copy of Ecclesiastes when I first moved to Canada. I wish I had understood it in those younger years. The wise old king had lessons I needed back then, lessons I need now, and lessons that apply to you as well. All of life is *hevel*. What Solomon does next is begin to answer some of his own questions on how to live well in a clearly broken world, despite the *hevelness* of life.

---

76 Per Tremper Longman III, *The Book of Ecclesiastes*, The New International Commentary on the New Testament (Grand Rapids: William B. Eerdmans Publishing Company, 1998), p. 176

31

THE PATH TO JOY IS COUNTERINTUITIVE

Long before COVID-19 swept the globe and made the word *pandemic* a common term, AIDS was the scourge of the land. The fear and paranoia that initially greeted this deadly virus were widespread, sometimes aggressive, and often overlaid with layers of victim shaming and social isolation.

I met Don while I was still a single guy in Vancouver, and he was already infected with AIDS. Don hadn't expected to make new friends, and he enthusiastically hosted several of us in his home. It meant a lot to him that he was not untouchable, that he was a friend and even a brother. We were careful. You don't fool around with deadly viruses that we don't understand yet. Even so, AIDS in those days was more than just a disease: according to some churches, it was a God-given curse. The shame and social isolation I observed personally and through the media at the time were driven as much by some Christian communities as by secular sources. For those fuzzy on the distinction between Christianity and the Bible, note the stark contrast between the shaming condemnation of AIDS victims and the way Jesus engaged with the untouchables of his generation, such as lepers.

Don was not isolated within our circle of friends. Our community cared for him and about him. With us, his name was good, regardless of what virus had taken up residence within his system. Within the context of his illness, having a good name meant nearly as much to Don as his physical health. Perhaps more. Solomon seems to understand how important care and recognition are as he starts this next chapter.

¹ A good name is better than fine oil,
  and the day of death better than the birthday.

² It is better to go to a house in mourning
  than to a house party,
  because that is everyone's destiny;
  and the living should take it to heart.

³ Aggravation is better than merriment
  because a sad face may lead to a glad heart.

⁴ The wise heart is in the house that mourns,
  but the foolish heart is in the house that rejoices.

⁵ It is better to obey the reprimand of the wise
  than to listen to the song of fools,

⁶ because the fool's merriment
  is like nettles crackling under a kettle.
  That too is pointless.

ECCLESIASTES 7:1–6

In this second half of Ecclesiastes, Solomon's first good thing to draw our attention to is a good name, meaning a good reputation. That, however, is not his point, as the following five-and-a-half verses make clear. He merely ushers onto the stage the excellence of a positive reputation to serve as a comparison. Fine oil is good, and a good name is better. In the same way, a birthday is good, but the day someone dies is even better.

What?

To understand what is going on here, we have to slow down. Our problem with verse one starts with the first bit about names and oil.

Proverbs that say "this is better than that" usually compare things that are related to one another, perhaps things that sit at the opposite ends of a continuum. For example, hard work is better than laziness. Wisdom is better than foolishness. Those are the kinds of this-is-better-than-that comparisons that sound natural.

When we hear that a good name is better than fine oil, it should startle us and make us pay closer attention. Why did Solomon compare personal names to commercial grades of oil? What kind of continuum could they both fit within? Does fine oil signify wealth? If so, is he saying that your reputation is worth more than money? Is he using a poetic image to imply that a bad name is like cheap smelly oil? Or is he just comparing two completely unrelated things as a literary way of grabbing our attention and making us read carefully?

Whatever Solomon's intention might have been, if we are reading carefully now, then he's got our attention just in time to tell us that the day of someone's death is better than that of their birth. I highly recommend never quoting this verse at a baby shower or someone's funeral. The opportunities to create social calamity here are nearly endless.

The verse that follows, however, starts to clarify Solomon's intention. The house of mourning is a better place because that is where we all wind up in the end.

Hmm. I also recommend that you do not quote verse two with verse one, not at a baby shower or a funeral. Is Solomon depressed here? Is he on a mission of social destruction? If all we had were verses one and two, we might conclude so, but verse three comes next.

> *3 Aggravation is better than merriment*
> *because a sad face may lead to a glad heart.*
> ECCLESIASTES 6:3

Okay, so a glad heart is a good end goal. He was not counselling in favor of gloom. However, Solomon's prescription on how to get to a glad heart is counterintuitive. If you want happiness, you go to a party, right? Surely not a funeral.

"No," Solomon says, "go to the funeral."

How is that a good idea?

Throughout my friendship with Don, we must have celebrated birthdays and other occasions together, but decades later, I don't remember any of them. However, I do remember sitting at his hospital bedside near the end when he asked me what would happen to him after he died. In response to that question, we read the relevant passages in Corinthians together. I will remember that time with him forever. I'll rejoice with him in heaven one day because of those very conversations. It brings me a teary, quiet joy, decades later, to remember those hours alone with Don in the hospital.

By contrast, I also remember that, in the final weeks of Don's life, he tried to stage a solo hospital breakout to attend church. He was a rather conspicuous escapee, still wearing his hospital gown and towing an IV pole. He didn't get far. The hospital staff quickly returned him to his bed. Don just wanted to spend time with God and his friends. In retrospect, without Solomon telling me so, I now realize that I should have been at the hospital that morning, not at church. Our "church" should have been at Don's hospital bedside.

What was I thinking?

I was thinking of my immediate joy and not his. I chose to spend time with healthy people in an atmosphere guaranteed to be merry and fun. By contrast, I should have been talking with Don beside his bed, listening while he spoke, taking him more safely about the hospital garden in a wheelchair, or perhaps reading Psalms to him this time instead of Corinthians.

I don't remember anything about the church service I prioritized over time with Don. However, I would have remembered that morning with him in the hospital garden to this day—had it occurred. It would have changed my life for the better, forever. I would have more joy today in my memory of Don now. I would feel good knowing I'd made good decisions, prioritizing meaningful time with my friend rather than tainting the joy of that friendship with one poor choice on a Sunday morning long ago to prioritize the party of the church crowd's small talk over my friend's need.

That's the secret to what Solomon is saying here. He's not advising his readers to go exclusively to funerals. Instead, he says that if you want lasting joy, go be with those who mourn. Joy is not a by-product of parties but of meaning and selfless engagement. We build lasting good memories on substance, not froth.

On a similar note, Solomon then points to another seemingly negative experience: a reprimand from a wise person. We should prefer the experience of a wise person's correction over a karaoke party. Why? Because, like that Sunday morning I should have spent with Don, the wise person's reprimand will mean something for a lifetime. The karaoke party, less so.

Solomon beautifully illustrates this principle by referencing "nettles crackling under a kettle." This phrase may not resonate for non-campers, but the key thing to know about nettles in a fire is they make a lot of noise, burn out fast, and leave a lot of ash behind, but they don't produce much heat. Good luck getting enough hot water for your tea from a nettle fire. Parties are like that. Songfests are like that. To use an old cook's phrase, there's a lot of sizzle there but not much steak. Or, for a nutritional illustration, it's a sugar water diet.

Funerals and rebukes from a wise person do not recommend themselves as attractive experiences, but they can give us the opportunity to meaningfully engage with life. This, too, however, is *hevel*. How much sorrow is enough to temper a soul? How do we learn to savor a morning in the hospital with a dying friend instead of a morning having fun with healthy friends? How do we learn to like reprimands from the wise over the input of those who only say positive things? You can get too sour if you focus only on what's wrong and needs changing.

We also need times when our hearts are glad (remember verse three). We also need encouragement. It's a tough assignment to learn how best to balance and navigate these varied life experiences, especially since life is primarily composed of unpredictable surprises. Trying to concoct the perfect life recipe that combines sober and joyful experiences is a *hevel* job. It's a heavy burden. It's like chasing the wind. This kind of living takes conscious effort.

32

OPPRESSION, BRIBERY, AND IMPATIENCE ARE INTERCONNECTED

I GOT MY driver's licence at fifteen years old (par for the course in Northern California in the 1980s) and was driving long before getting my licence (also par for the course for a country boy). A decade later, I had a commuting companion who micromanaged my speed, city navigation choices, braking timing, signalling, and so on, to the point that I became frustrated and my driving skills deteriorated. It wasn't just the distraction of relentless input. I later realized that, for the sake of peace, a part of my brain had started outsourcing decision-making. I should have ignored my fellow commuter or told them to knock it off. Instead, when the verbal direction to "turn right at the next light" always came a split second before I hit the turn signal, I started waiting for the verbal prompt before taking any action. As a result, my companion essentially started driving even though I was behind the wheel. In my head, a missed turn started becoming my companion's fault instead of mine. As you can imagine, trouble followed. A therapist could probably make a lot of hay about what this meant for my intellectual maturity or sense of self at the time, but regardless, that was my reality back then.

Solomon wasn't a therapist, but he did touch on this odd dynamic.

> [7] *Oppression turns the wise into fools;*
>   *a bribe corrupts the heart.*

ECCLESIASTES 7:7

Of course, driving micromanagement is only one type—and admittedly a mild type—of oppression. Many of us deal with more severe flavors, such as racism, sexism, and economic oppression. For many people, even more extreme versions are their experience. These may include the challenges of political or military tyranny, false imprisonments, or worse. For now, though, let's stick with a milder form of oppression and discuss micromanagement.

As a group manager in the head office of a large international bank, I take all kinds of lessons from Solomon's warning here. If I want to create a team of fools, all I need to do is oppress them. Were I to embark upon such a foolish mission, many already wise team members would resign and find new places to work. Similarly, quality staff from elsewhere in the organization would discover my reputation and avoid my job postings. Those on my team who lacked the résumé, requisite skills, or network support to leave would be stuck under my leadership and risk becoming, in Solomon's language, fools. This foolishness might be an actual, a reputational, or simply a practical consequence of my restrictive control. In the same way that my driving deteriorated under the influence of my relentless companion, my staff would likewise suffer were I to oppress them in this manner.

I don't want fools working for me. I want the mature to stay on my teams and those with a learning runway still in front of them to blossom under my leadership. To ensure I don't act oppressively, I need to do more than act ethically—I need to listen, take input, and adjust to that input. Doing so encourages wisdom, provides growth opportunities, and encourages the full energy and brainpower of those I collaborate with. In this way, I avoid forming teams of fools.

Wait—how did we get from Solomon to modern management theory?

> [7] *Oppression turns the wise into fools;*
> *a bribe corrupts the heart.*
>
> ECCLESIASTES 7:7

Human history provides an endless flow of more serious examples that reinforce Solomon's point. Totalitarian leaderships—in government, churches, workplaces, or families—eventually run themselves into a metaphorical brick wall or off a cliff. No matter how successful or captivating that approach may seem in the short term, it always fails in the end.

Likewise, the second half of this verse should strike a chord for anyone with basic business sense: "A bribe corrupts the heart."

It is not a small thing to give or take a bribe. It corrupts the heart of both the giver and the taker.

Solomon doesn't speak here about the legal or reputational risks associated with bribery, nor does he speak to the impact of corruption across generations, organizations, and societies. He is narrowly focused here on individual hearts. Chopping garlic makes your fingers smell. A bath makes you wet. A poke in the eye hurts. A bribe corrupts your heart. Like gravity, these are just basic and inarguable facts about reality. There is no getting around these truths. In the case of accepting bribes, any additional factors—such as your likelihood of getting caught, the culture's social acceptance or rejection of bribery, and your personal spin on the situation—are entirely irrelevant to the corruption that a bribe creates. A stubborn soul could say, "Well, this particular poke in the eye won't hurt," but it will. That's how pokes in the eye work. Likewise, bribery is bad for your heart, whether you intellectually accept that as truth or not. Again, getting caught is irrelevant to that corruption.

I've applied these bits of wisdom to a corporate work context, but they also apply to other social relationships, including those within churches, communities, families, and marriages. Oppression and bribery are bad.

And that's about all Solomon chooses to say here on this topic. Like a sharpshooter hitting the mark and then moving on to the next target, Solomon states his facts, then hits us with his next observation.

> [8] *The end of something is better than its beginning.*
> *Patience is better than arrogance.*
>
> [9] *Don't be too quick to get angry*
> *because anger lives in the fool's heart.*
>
> ECCLESIASTES 7:8–9

I think it's significant that Solomon moved from talking about oppression and bribery to patience. Let's take this slowly to understand what he's doing in these verses.

First, it's not a given that the start of any new endeavor will go well.

Making progress on just about anything takes effort. A good start, however, is irrelevant in the long run. You don't have to live for very many decades to learn that a big flawless wedding says nothing about how the marriage will turn out. Likewise, a business's grand opening offers zero guarantees that the venture will lead to a multi-generational success story or any kind of success at all. As a novelist, I've read countless first chapters from fellow writers that were great starts, but the writer never finished the book. Starting is easy. Finishing is hard. And in Solomon's judgment, finishing is better.

Solomon celebrates the end of things not because he's gloomy but because he knows you can't judge the ultimate worth of a thing by its initial potential. You know the value of a thing by looking back on it over time. You know if a movie was any good at the end, not by its impressive opening sequence.

With that in mind, Solomon counsels in favor of patience and against anger. Patience gives the worth of a thing time to materialize.

By contrast, impatience is arrogance materialized. Anger can short-circuit discovery. I believe there is a righteous indignation or a call-for-justice kind of anger that, properly channelled, is a positive, not a negative, emotion. God gets angry sometimes, and Solomon is not calling God a fool. Instead, he speaks of anger in the context of impatience, and in that context, it is something that "lives in the fool's heart" (7:9). Anger has its time and place but should not live within us as a resident. Ephesians 4:26 says, "In your anger, do not sin" (NIV). It doesn't say, "Don't ever be angry at all."

This is where verses eight and nine on patience and endings relate to verse seven's warning about oppression and bribery. Building well takes time. Careful planning takes effort. By contrast, oppression and bribery are a way to force reality to go faster or move in a preferred direction while skipping necessary social obligations toward the needs of others. Part of why my relentless commuter co-pilot couldn't be quiet was because he wanted to be at work now, not five minutes from now. His need for me to signal a turn preceded my move to signal by half a second, so a drama unfolded between us that was unproductive and damaged our relationship. Getting to our destination was the good thing. Getting there half a second earlier and feeling tense were not valuable.

When politicians or business leaders or even friends veer into oppressive or corrupt behaviors, it helps to recognize that what we're seeing is not always coming from greed but sometimes just from basic impatience. The end is what matters: keeping our relationships healthy and whole, constructing safe and uncompromised buildings, getting to work on time, and so on. When we understand that, we're in a better position to filter out the negative forces that try to influence our choices. To quote an old proverb, the ends don't justify the means. Character and reputation matter, even if they don't seem to in the moment. The patient way that doesn't deploy oppression, bribery, or any other corrupt tool is always the right way in the long run.

I long for Solomon to slow down here and dive deep into these points with illustrations from his own family life, business ventures, or political experiences. Impatience is perhaps my most native sin, and I could benefit from an entire book focused on that topic, but that kind of detailed analysis is not Solomon's method in Ecclesiastes. If you want to learn how these things are true and manifest themselves in various spheres of life, you will have to meditate on his points yourself or find other places in scripture that get into the details. Some books in the Bible that speak to the nature of corruption and oppression—either directly or indirectly—are Proverbs, Job, Ephesians, and James. You can also gain insight on this topic through a contemplative study of God's works in the historical accounts of Samuel, Kings, and Chronicles. Here in Ecclesiastes, Solomon is not interested in a granular study of these topics but is instead interested in answering his *yithron*—lasting benefit—question. Avoiding impatience and not letting beginnings distract us are tools to help us on our *yithron* quest.

33

MEMORIES CAN BE ROAD SIGNS FOR THE FUTURE

I'VE BEEN CARRYING a sealed box around with me for over thirty years. Over the course of twenty-seven years of marriage, my wife and I have moved eight times. After the first few moves, my wife started asking what was in the box. I would mumble something about it being childhood mementoes or journals or something like that.

A few moves on, my wife started asking me why I never opened it.

"Oh, I don't know. It doesn't seem important," I would reply.

"Then why do we keep moving it?" she'd ask. "Just throw it out."

"Yeah, I should probably get rid of it," I'd reply. "But not yet."

This past August, I finally opened the box. The originally clear packing tape had aged to an amber color and didn't require a knife to cut. The brittle material fell apart into flakes and crumbs with the slightest pressure. That box ended up containing the journals I described earlier in chapter eleven, the ones that documented my young life with the precision of an archivist. I got a lot of value from reading through those aging pages.

Solomon says something next, though, that seems to contradict my personal experience.

[10] *Don't ask, "How is it that the former days were better than these?"*

because it isn't wise to ask this.

ECCLESIASTES 7:10

This verse used to bother me a great deal. Why is inquiring about the past a problem? If the past was better, shouldn't we learn from it? I learned a lot about myself looking back on my childhood journals. Some parts were better than today. Others were not.

Over time, I began to interpret this verse not as a statement against research but as a judgment on the rose-colored glasses humans sometimes wear when invoking the past. There were stories I'd "remembered" for decades that my own accounts proved to be false. My memory was no good. My handwritten record told the truth as I had lived it, and that record contradicted my late-middle-age memory.

The original Jewish escapees from Egypt had a similar experience, without the benefit of journals or therapists to help them self-correct. They complained to Moses about how life as slaves in Egypt had been so much better than their current trials in the wilderness on the way to the Promised Land. Similar stories repeat throughout human history. We often quote the past selectively to support a particular narrative or argument. We remember what serves us or helps us survive. We bury the rest.

Solomon didn't need childhood journals to understand that memories are sometimes unreliable, and people are at risk of burnishing the past. So he cautioned us regarding how we use memory.

With more time and study, however, I've come to see this verse in yet a different light. Solomon's quest, you'll recall, is to address the *hevelness* of life under the sun. He's not interested in whether a particular social structure, economic system, political posture, engineering approach, or other technical stance would have worked better in the past. Insofar as he has tackled these topics, he did so to address the eternity placed within the human heart and the existential hunger felt by everyone on earth, rich or poor, man or woman, wherever they might live.

With this goal in view, another way to interpret this verse becomes clearer. I think Solomon is saying that it's not wise to inquire about why former days were better than today because, in the context of addressing the *hevelness* of life, neither the past nor the present has changed anything positively or negatively. Humanity operates with the same unsatisfiable hunger, whatever the circumstances or era. Imagining that we had satisfied that hunger in an unrecoverable past merely distracts us from what we truly desire now. It is not wise to distract a searching heart with uncatchable phantoms. The past was just as hungry as the present, whatever economic, social, political, or other lessons it might have to offer.

If you're an engineer and your bridge falls down, by all means, do some research to figure out what went wrong. Learn from successful bridge builders of the past. Likewise, chefs, parents, lovers, farmers, and all manner of occupations and human interactions can benefit from counsel that includes lessons from the past. If you've got a childhood journal, read it and learn from it. But when you search for the meaning of life, the past has nothing on the present. They are equals. Your heart is a unique work of art, existing today and hungry today for what cannot be satisfied by something that was and is no more.

Going back to C.S. Lewis's analogy of road signs pointing us onward, if we get thirty minutes past the sign to Algonquin and start longing for that sign again and moaning about how the feelings and experiences of being at that sign were better than this current stretch of road—well, that's not helpful. The goal is Algonquin, not the sign that points us there. Once we're past the sign, keep going.

That is good advice. So is Solomon's next bit.

> [11] *Wisdom is as good as an inheritance—*
> *an advantage for those who see the sun.*
>
> [12] *Wisdom's protection is like the protection of money;*
> *the advantage of knowledge is that wisdom preserves the*
> *lives of its possessors.*
>
> ECCLESIASTES 7:11–12

In other words, as a follow-up to the previous verse about memory, don't let the past become your focus but do use wisdom to think carefully about how you live now. Its protection is not absolute, but it is very helpful. Wisdom won't solve the *hevelness* of life, but it can help keep you from driving off the road into the ditch. Think of wisdom as akin to painted lines along the edges of a country road. We've got an old and battered Ontario Snowmobile Association road sign in our house that tells us to "Stay on Trail." That's good advice.

34

GOD SOMETIMES MAKES THINGS CROOKED ON PURPOSE

ON ONE BEAUTIFUL Saturday afternoon, sunlight flooded the open floor plan of our local garden center. Carolyn and I had a nurse to look after our daughter. Our son was off visiting friends. During these periods of respite, we usually either slept or got basic household chores done. This day we had enough energy to go shopping for plants. Even if we didn't buy anything, this kind of outing was a salve for our relentless stress.

As we talked and walked hand in hand through the indoor part of the nursery, a small display of what looked like miniature trees with woven trunks caught my eye. They were only twelve inches tall, planted in disposable plastic pots, each pot sporting four trunks that had been woven together. I pulled up my plant app to identify the unique specimens. They were Suriname Cherry Trees—a subtropical version of the cherry trees that grew in Canada with the drawback that they could not withstand a northern winter. This was likely why I'd never seen them before or since in our local garden centers.

To a bonsai fan with a substantial four-season plant room, this drawback was actually a benefit. Canadian cherry trees have to drop their leaves and freeze each winter as part of their annual rest cycle. The Suriname Cherry, however, would be happy to spread its branches and grow in our plant room and keep its leaves year-round.

By the way, a pro tip for newbie bonsai enthusiasts: the most popular and readily available starter bonsai options tend to be some form of northern evergreen. Junipers are what I see most commonly in local stores. They must freeze each winter, or they'll keel over and die. Trying to grow one on a windowsill or even a nice plant room indoors year-round is like trying to keep a mammal awake for weeks on end. You'll kill your pet. Likewise, it's torture for northern-acclimated evergreens to never have a frozen winter sleep, and it's hard to tell that they're sick until after they're long dead. So don't buy northern junipers unless you're planning to care for them outdoors in a climate that gets cold for at least a few months of the year.

Back to my Suriname Cherry Tree. It quickly came out of the cheap plastic pot and into a nice Japanese bonsai tray. I pruned the roots and removed a few select branches to encourage it to grow the wide canopy I had in mind for its future. One thing I didn't do was untangle the woven trunks and try to straighten out the individual trees. The woven design was part of the tree's charm. The four trees would eventually fuse, and the crooked result would have exactly the character that its early shape foretold.

Solomon talks about something similar in the next verse.

> [13] *Consider God's work! Who can straighten what God has made crooked?*
>
> ECCLESIASTES 7:13

God is not just omnipotent; he is sometimes frighteningly so. He deliberately makes some things bent that we would prefer to have straight. It's one thing to have a twisted tree, but when a person has an unexpected difference, we tend to be less enthusiastic.

With good reason, the Bible tells us in many places to fear God—but, of course, balances that fear by also exposing God's love for us, his wisdom, and his long-term thinking. Because of the combination of God's implacable power and deep love, we can approach him with fear but also with confidence and trust. He is admittedly incomprehensible at times but also perfectly capable and deeply compassionate with a beautiful end result as his aim. That is an essential mix.

There is, however, a practical outcome of God's sovereignty that sometimes leaves mere humans in a quandary. How do we deal with the *hevelness* of life and its attendant lack of existential comfort when our souls hunger for so much more? How can we interpret what is happening around us or in us when God doesn't explain himself as often or as clearly as we would like him to?

My wife sometimes stresses out when I take clippers or a wire to one of my bonsai trees. "Trust the process," I say. "I'm clipping or wiring it for what it will look like in five or ten years, not today." She has to tell me something similar when she takes a perfectly good handbag she got at a thrift store and starts chopping it up into pieces to get at its vintage hardware for one of her own bespoke creations.

When it comes to the crooked or broken things in our lives, Solomon doesn't do much to explore God's power or intentions in Ecclesiastes—the book of Job covers that—but instead, as it befits his mission here, Solomon focuses on how people should respond to this reality.

> *¹⁴ When times are good, enjoy the good; when times are bad, consider: God has made the former as well as the latter so that people can't discover anything that will come to be after them.*
> ECCLESIASTES 7:14

In other words, if you think you know what's going on or think you're in control, think again.

I got a lot of positive feedback after publishing *Even the Monsters*. Still, as with anything available for public consumption, there was naturally some negative feedback. The negative feedback came down to a group of people unable to deal with the lack of real knowledge and control that the book of Job reveals as the actual human condition. God clips us and wires us as he sees fit and doesn't ask our permission along the way and rarely lets us know where the design is going. Job's friends argued with him precisely because they could not relinquish their insistence that human agency is supreme—the idea that if we try harder and do better, things will always work out in a way that keeps us in control.

According to Job's three friends, God needed to be programmable or at least manipulatable. Without this sense of control, the human experience would have been unbearable because it required a level of trust that terrified them. That trust was precisely what Job (and Elihu) insisted was the true state of human affairs. This view of reality did not offer the benefit of a divine explanation when things appeared to go wrong. God did not offer humanity a seat at the heavenly counsel that was featured at the beginning of Job and that shaped later events in the story.

Some who read *Even the Monsters* reacted to that message with the same anger that Job's three friends demonstrated. In one case, the angry words written against me were almost identical to those of Eliphaz himself. As I considered the feedback, the irony was obvious and heartbreaking.

Solomon was not like Job's three friends or the critic of *Even the Monsters* who could not accept the reality it discussed. Instead, Solomon understood and accepted the principle that God does what God does, and people are powerless to thwart him. As he put it, God makes good and bad things "so that people can't discover anything that will come to be after them" (7:14). In the language of software developers, this aspect of reality is a feature, not a flaw.

Job learned this through intense suffering. By contrast, Solomon learned it through success after success until he'd burned himself out with success and still had not satisfied the eternal hunger that burned inside him. And so, in a characteristically practical manner, Solomon's advice is: don't fight God's choices for our lives but make the most of them. When times are good, enjoy them. When times are bad, trust God. As stated in the book of Job, God sometimes shuts the doors to understanding to disabuse us of any real sense of control. The point is not to destabilize our psyche but to avoid letting us anchor it on the wrong thing. He keeps us hungry to keep us moving onward. The signs are not the goal. A deep investigation of the sign misses the point. God works to keep us on target—moving on to Algonquin and not turning around to go back and repeatedly visit the same mileage marker.

Solomon goes on to say,

> [15] *I have seen everything in my pointless lifetime: the righteous person may die in spite of their righteousness; then again, the wicked may live long in spite of their wickedness.*
> ECCLESIASTES 7:15

Solomon calls it as he sees it. Once again, the book of Job explores these ideas in greater detail, so we'll let this verse rest without further commentary other than to remind the reader that it's not a pointless lifetime that Solomon is referencing here. Instead, it is a *hevel* lifetime. A breath-like, vaporous lifetime. A fragile, temporary, very important, but also ephemeral lifetime. In this lifetime, things don't always go the way we want them to.

My Suriname Cherry might prefer to be an eight-meter (twenty-six-foot) tree on a South American slope with a view of the Atlantic Ocean. Instead, it is woven together with three other identical trees, will never get taller than my knee, and sits alongside a Brazilian Rain Tree and an Indian Laurel in similar Japanese pots. Instead of a tropical ocean view, the snow of wintry months whips across broad windows mere feet away while flames flicker in the nearby fireplace. If trees had feelings, it could bemoan its fate. Or rejoice that it will never fight wood-boring insects, be cut down for firewood, or be starved for nutrients. If trees suffered from our native human angst, it could find ways to be unhappy with either fate. Solomon here counsels for the opposite. Sometimes life doesn't work out the way we would prefer, and sometimes God makes things in our lives crooked that we'd rather have straight. Some of us are planted on slopes and some in pots. Solomon's message teaches us to keep working toward our goals, but don't obsess about them at the expense of the life right in front of you.

35

AN ANTI=EXTREMISM WARNING

I MADE A new batch of friends between first- and second-year university, one of the longest lasting being a science student that I'll call Valerie. She was part of a close circle that formed that year, and we stayed friends long after we both got married to other people and had children. Later in life, I used my memories of those early UBC friendships as a yardstick to measure my son's social progress. Jackson and I had meaningful talks throughout his high school and early university years about the importance and value of the relationships formed in our late teens and twenties. Proper investment pays dividends that can last a lifetime. Valerie was one of those friends who helped shape who I am today.

Valerie also has a gift for blunt, though not unkind, candor. Sometimes the things she says called to mind the following verse in Proverbs.

> *Trustworthy are the bruises of a friend;*
> *excessive are the kisses of an enemy.*
> PROVERBS 27:6

One afternoon, I was in the back seat of a red Acura. My family doctor, who was also a friend, was driving. Valerie was in the front passenger seat. As I recall, there were no other witnesses to our discussion.

The three of us had been conducting a rather intense dialogue about personal growth and areas of character development that applied to the three of us. On its own, this kind of conversation wasn't unusual. We were all young and keen to figure out how to be better humans and part of a church that, at the time, was laser-focused on subjects of personal responsibility. Later, that focus became authoritarian and unhelpful, but on that afternoon, the dialogue wasn't corporate but organic. We genuinely wanted to become better people.

In a moment of inspiration, Valerie turned around so she could look me in the eye and said, "You know, Daryl, the main problem with you is that you walk around and live your life like you have a stick up your butt." Oof.

I don't get carsick, but in that Acura's back seat, I think I would have welcomed the distraction.

Valerie's words would have been merely offensive if she hadn't been such a good friend. Like that proverb says, "Trustworthy are the bruises of a friend."

In my deepest self, the message resonated. I was too stiff. I found it hard to relax in groups. I was rule bound and often stubborn in my thinking. When it came to matters of religion, I tilted fundamentalist. For those who don't understand that term, it means many things in a Christian context, but in my case, it manifested as a kind of unloving rigidity. I didn't like that part of me, but it was there all the same. In the next few chapters, I'll share some of the keys that helped me discover the sources of those unsavory parts of me and unwind the resulting behaviors. However, I first needed to understand that such a posture in life wasn't good, that it existed within me, and that other people could clearly see it. I needed a friend like Valerie to call me out on it.

Solomon calls us all out on the same thing in his next verse.

> [16] *Don't be too righteous or too wise, or you may be dumbfounded.*
> ECCLESIASTES 7:16

Dumbfounded is not a common word in modern English. The Complete Jewish Bible's translation is easier to grasp.

> *So don't be overly righteous or overly wise;*
> *why should you disappoint yourself?*

The Christian Standard Bible (CSB) offers another translation that is closer to the original Hebrew.

> *Don't be excessively righteous, and don't be overly wise. Why should you destroy yourself?*

The KJV, NIV, RSV, and my translator's handbook all agree with the wording of the CSB. Solomon's question is, "Why destroy yourself?"

If something this startling had appeared in the book of Job, I would have immediately suspected that one of Job's misguided friends said it—men who God rebuked at the end of that book. If someone had told me, as a young Christian, that the words were from the New Testament, I might have wondered if they were from Satan tempting Christ or from a Pharisee challenging Christ or even from Romans trying to dissuade the early Christians from professing their faith.

> *Don't be excessively righteous, and don't be overly wise. Why destroy yourself?*

However, these words don't come from these questionable sources. Solomon is offering these words, purporting to teach practical wisdom within the context of faith. Admittedly, Solomon did a poor job of living that faith during much of his lifetime, but Ecclesiastes is his corrective text. He is teaching practical righteous living with God-given wisdom and from a platform of personal experience.

His surprising message, however, is not what we might expect. We might expect conservative and orthodox instruction along the lines of, "Act more righteously than I did in life and stick to the narrow path at all costs." Instead, his message is that we need to avoid overdoing it in the areas of righteousness and wisdom. He then underscores that teaching by claiming that the stakes are personal destruction. That is an odd message from a spiritual teacher trying to set us on a good life path.

C.S. Lewis offers insight that is helpful here.

> *Human intellect is incurably abstract. . . . Yet the only realities we experience are concrete—this pain, this pleasure, this dog, this man. While we are loving the man, bearing the pain, enjoying the pleasure, we are not intellectually apprehending*

Pleasure, Pain or Personality. . . . This is our dilemma—either to taste and not to know or to know and not to taste—or, more strictly, to lack one kind of knowledge because we are in an experience or to lack another kind because we are outside it. As thinkers we are cut off from what we think about; as tasting, touching, willing, loving, hating, we do not clearly understand. The more lucidly we think, the more we are cut off: the more deeply we enter into reality, the less we can think. You cannot study pleasure in the moment of the nuptial embrace, nor repentance while repenting, nor analyze the nature of humor while roaring with laughter. But when else can you really know these things? "If only my toothache would stop, I could write another chapter about pain." But once it stops, what do I know about pain?[77]

Lewis is getting at the reality of different types of knowledge: experiential versus abstract. There is an uncrossable divide between these two modes of thinking. It is the problem we encounter when learning a new skill, such as how to play the guitar. You don't get to experience the joy of making music when first learning that art. Instead, your fingers hurt, your brain is confused, and nothing goes well. But when you learn to play well, perhaps after years of training, and are playing a piece you know and love, you have little conscious awareness of how your fingers perform the complicated magic that creates beauty and emotion from strings and a wooden box. In fact, conscious awareness would short-circuit the flow and ruin the piece. You can play, or you can think about the mechanics of play. You can't do a good job of both at the same time.

Lewis's example of lovemaking (nuptial embrace) is a bold example for his era (mid-twentieth century), culture (British), and profession (Oxford professor), and I wonder if a prudish editor might have protested his choice at the time. Protest or not, his text was published as we have it. Had Lewis been overly righteous, he would have used an illustration less likely to offend the prudish. Had he been overly wise, he might have come up with an equally accurate way of making his point, perhaps drawing on our modern

---

[77] To access Lewis's full article, see "From 'God in the Dock'—Clive Staples Lewis," Myth Became Fact, accessed August 7, 2023, *http://mythbecamefact.com/*.

understanding of the brain's limbic system and pre-frontal cortex and thereby losing most of his audience. But sometimes, not being overly righteous or wise is righteousness and wisdom in perfection. Jesus often deliberately used parables or particular words that alarmed and even offended his audience, but those shocking methods got his points across in ways that more palatable or predictable approaches would have failed to.

Jesus's words, however, were never spoken at the head of a mob to condemn. Some readers might remember "angry Jesus"—the one who made a whip out of cords, flipped over tables in the temple, and drove out the money changers (John 2:13–16). If the story is unfamiliar to you, give it a read. Google will give you the verses for free if you don't have a Bible handy. What is important to understand in this verse is that Jesus performed these actions alone, not as part of a mob. Additionally, he did so at least in part as a public defence of the poor who the temple authorities were scamming, trapping the public between their religious obligations and their leadership's greed. Sometimes, the oppressed need someone to stand against oppression on their behalf. That stand, however, in a mob, can quickly become its own problem. Jesus wisely acted alone here.

Many stories in the Gospels explore a similar vein: the father celebrates the Prodigal Son's return; the Good Shepherd goes in search of the lost sheep; the widow celebrates the recovery of her one coin. Jesus pulled Zacchaeus and Matthew into fellowship instead of condemning them as outsiders. He sent the woman caught in adultery away with gentle words. The truly wise and the genuinely righteous in scripture stand more often against authority rather than at its head, and they do so not by stubbornly defending the status quo with a mob behind them but by standing alone and in support of the weak or marginalized. Even the Old Testament prophets, often remembered for their anger, spoke alone against authority and not for it or at the head of a crowd.

Solomon builds on this message in the next two verses.

^{17} Don't be too wicked and don't be a fool, or you may die before your time. ^{18} It's good that you take hold of one of these without letting go of the other because the one who fears God will go forth with both.

ECCLESIASTES 7:17–18

A comically large number of commentaries I consulted pounced on verse seventeen as the antidote to the out-of-control immorality that verse sixteen risks. The counsel to avoid wickedness or foolishness is undoubtedly wise. However, the word "too" in this verse still makes many uncomfortable. It implies that a little wickedness and a little foolishness are fine. Just don't sin it up too much.

Is that what Solomon is communicating? In verse eighteen, he counsels that we should "take hold of one of these without letting go of the other because the one who fears God will go forth with both."

How can that be right? The godly person will deliberately act both righteously and wickedly, wisely and foolishly?

I'll quote William P. Brown here.

> *[Solomon] suggests an alternative to these two extremes. . . . Godly fear forges a middle ground, but not as some muddled mean, as if righteousness should be tempered with a modicum of wickedness, or folly mitigated with a healthy dose of wisdom. Reverence is neither a matter of fanatical fear that raises the bar of moral conduct to unobtainable or excessive levels, nor a matter of indifference or moral complacency. Rather, the fear of God is based on an accurate awareness of human finitude and a realistic assessment of life's vicissitudes.*[78]

Finitude is not a common word in regular speech. It describes a state with limits or bounds. We could just use the word *limits* and get close enough for our purposes here.

Likewise, *vicissitudes* is not a word we use in everyday life. That word basically has two potential meanings: something that is changeable or something that is challenging. It's actually unclear in this quote whether Brown

---

78 William P. Brown, *Ecclesiastes: Interpretation; A Commentary for Teaching and Preaching* (Louisville: Westminster John Knox Press, 2011), p. 82.

is using the more neutral or negative meaning here. To keep things simple, let's replace it with the everyday word *troubles*.[79]

So Brown's point here is that a proper fear of God "is based on an accurate awareness of human [limits] and a realistic assessment of life's [troubles]."

Jesus had a similar point when confronting the Jews of his day: unless your righteousness exceeded that of the Pharisees you wouldn't make it to heaven.[80] Too many of his hearers took the point to be that they needed to try harder. Jesus, however, was making the opposite point. Trying harder wouldn't work. You can't do it. You can't earn your way to heaven. It is a hopeless task.

Later, Jesus told the parable about how it's easier for a camel to get through the eye of a needle than for a rich person to get into heaven.[81] As a kid, I learned about a gate in Jerusalem's tall stone walls that was called the Eye of the Needle. In this ancient context, gates were less like garden gates and more like castle doors. As it was explained to me, this gate apparently had a stone header so low that camels needed to get down onto their knees to get through the opening. This low gate supposedly prevented raiders from charging through and invading the city, thus showing that a rich man could enter heaven, but the process was difficult and presumably humbling as well. Also, they would have to do it as individuals and not in groups.

The problem with this interpretation and its baggage of applications is that there was no such gate in Jerusalem, and camels don't walk on their knees. Camels only have two knees—on their front legs. They would have had to drag their rear legs behind them. Camels don't move this way. Ever. It anatomically does not work. The interpretation I grew up with was a stunning display of preacherly laziness and is utterly laughable to anyone who grew up in the Middle East or knows anything about camels.

Jesus's immediate point was that the situation for rich people was hopeless. You're not going to make it. Jesus was literally talking about an actual eye in a needle that camels will obviously never fit through—the hole so

---

79   This is what drives me crazy about standard commentaries on the Bible. They're full of rich insight but written so that even above average readers will struggle to digest the language. Insight is useless if it is indigestible.

80   Matthew 5:20.

81   Matthew 19:24.

small that it's hard to get thread through it, let alone one of the region's largest land mammals.

Jesus's ultimate point was not to block rich people from heaven but to demonstrate that people need him to get there. Without him, we can't make it to the Father. Jesus is the gate (John 10). He is the way (John 14). He is the solution (John 14). Unpacking this teaching is a lesson for another book, but Jesus's points align nicely with Solomon's and thus Brown's interpretation. Becoming extra, extra, ultra-righteous is not the solution. That route leads to self-destruction and not heaven. A swing to the opposite extreme is likewise a fatal mistake. Instead, the path forward for Christians is Christ.

But Solomon didn't have Christ, and he's not trying to get himself or anyone else to heaven either, so his advice doesn't lead to baptism or similar salvation-oriented teachings. Those were not discussion points in his day and age.

Let's go back to why Solomon wrote this book again. He wants to understand the *hevelness* of life and how to deal with humanity's existential hunger throughout that life as we search for *yithron*—lasting benefit. His advice for humanity, in that context, is to move forward on a path of righteousness and wisdom but not to become obsessive about it. You'll make mistakes. Okay, mistakes made; straighten out and press on. A Christian will say that grace and mercy cover those errors. Solomon references practical reality. You can't be perfect, so get on with life and don't sweat missteps. Don't be a religious fanatic or the person in the room that must always be right. Likewise, don't deliberately engage in evil or stupidity. Just live your life the best you can, and course correct as you go, always aiming for better. By contrast, the religiously proud are way off course.

Going back to Jesus, the few times he did get angry in the Gospels, it was always directed at the religiously strict. Adulteresses, thieves, and even Roman oppressors he treated kindly. Pharisees and Sadducees, however, he called "whitewashed tombs" and worse.[82]

Jesus and Solomon were in sync. Fanaticism and extremism of any type—religious, political, or cultural—are not just unattractive; they are also wrong and lead to destruction.

My life did not immediately take a new course after Valerie's observation.

---

82 Matthew 23:27–28.

What she said wounded me, but it was one of those Proverbs-style bruises that could be trusted. It exposed something that ran deep within me and needed to be dug out. Discovering the roots of that stiffness and unwinding its damage took years. I'll talk about some of that a few chapters from now.

In the meantime, I remain grateful to Valerie for saying what she and others saw, and for Solomon's counsel that this is no way to live. I had been on a path that would have destroyed me in the end. It took years of reshaping and pruning to address the flaws, and the work continues, but it started with Valerie.

36

WISDOM LEADS TO GROWTH, BUT GROWTH IS SOMETIMES SLOW

THE EVENT I described in the previous chapter was a gut punch for me. It hit me when Valerie spoke to me in my mid-twenties, and over the years, her lesson was repeated in the contexts of performance and personal development appraisals at work, in disagreements in my marriage, and even in discussions with friends.

I worked hard to curb the negative behaviors that others pointed out personally and professionally, but no matter how hard I tried, it seemed that the metaphorical stick within me—and the sharpness of my tongue—were as native to my nature as my need for air. I invited corrections because I really did want to do better, but at times, I despaired and felt even suicidal as this flaw within me resisted all attempts to fix it. It felt like the world needed me to do fine calligraphy with my left hand when I'm a clumsy right-handed writer. I was bad at it. I couldn't get good at it no matter how hard I tried. I could not be as relaxed and warm as I and the world around me wanted me to be. In fact, the harder I tried, the worse I became.

Then, after a very long period of preparation—using the metaphor of bonsai, after a lot of personal pruning and wiring—God dropped an emotional bomb in my life that changed everything. My psychological surgery was happening at such a high speed that I could hardly endure it, but I welcomed it all the same. I'm going to devote two upcoming chapters to that bomb: chapters thirty-eight and thirty-nine, called "The Extraordinary

Nature of Internal Transformation," parts one and two. For now, though, how was I to live when I had extremist flaws within that resisted correction and extraordinary personal transformation had not yet occurred? That is what Solomon tackles next.

> *19 Wisdom makes a wise person stronger than ten rulers who are in a city.*
>
> ECCLESIASTES 7:19

Later in Ecclesiastes, Solomon will tell a story that expands on this point, so I won't unpack this verse too much except to say that part of what prepared me for the internal transformation to come was spending many years investigating wisdom. When the emotional bomb dropped into my life, I was ready. I recognized what was occurring, even though the events surprised me. I could not have predicted the bomb that went off in my life, but I'd studied how to grow enough to recognize growth when it occurred.

The human heart is sometimes like my bonsai trees. Sometimes it needs to be pruned. Like a pruned tree branch, the work creates wounds that are open and raw at first. But when you see the wound heal over—and even better, when you see the bud swell, signalling new growth—it gives hope.

Wisdom makes you strong, in part, because you learn to recognize the signs for what they are: this swelling is an infection; that one is a new bud. It helps to understand what is going on.

One way those with a growth mindset prepare themselves to grow is by seeking out wisdom. Change may come from unexpected sources, but wisdom helps you recognize what is happening when it does occur.

On the path to seeking wisdom, however, we will all make mistakes. We'll read the wrong thing, listen to the wrong lecture, commit to the wrong teacher, draw the wrong conclusion, and in so doing, prune off the bud that was important for our future or just fail to execute the practice steps properly. Solomon knows this, and so he cautions us against being too hard on ourselves as we grow.

> *20 Remember: there's no one on earth so righteous as to do good only and never make a mistake.*
>
> ECCLESIASTES 7:20

Verse twenty stands on its own just fine, but still remember its context in the text. The previous verses describe the need to avoid excessive wisdom, foolishness, righteousness, and wickedness. In this context, verse twenty is also working to correct judgmentalism. If our posture in the world is that of a full-time critic (of ourselves or others), verse twenty reminds us to cool it. Growth and healing are processes, not one-time miracles.

If we're in danger of worshipping those who appear to live exemplary lives, verse twenty can help us correct that posture as well. Regardless of appearances, our heroes and heroines are flawed. As a follow-up to verse nineteen, it also reminds us that the one wise person and the ten rulers are all flawed as well.

Okay, so we've had our self-criticalness and idol worship tempered. What, however, are we to do when those voices, internal or external, still clamor for our attention? For these situations, in this *hevel* life, Solomon offers up this advice:

> *21 Don't worry about all the things people say, so you don't hear your servant cursing you. 22 After all, you know that you've often cursed others yourself!*
>
> ECCLESIASTES 7:21–22

Solomon, though not elected, was essentially a politician and thus faced his share of critics. He didn't have social media to contend with, but that made the news and gossip less transparent and quantifiable.

It is noteworthy, however, that Solomon doesn't say to ignore everything people say about you. Instead, he says we shouldn't worry about *everything* said. By inference, considering some things people say is okay, perhaps even advisable. Valerie was worth listening to. Some of my bosses had good counsel. My wife has true points to share. Others are sometimes just hurtful. Solomon teaches us here to filter our input sources.

Finally, Solomon sums up these teachings about extremism, growth, and gossip.

> *23 I tested all of this by wisdom. I thought, I will be wise, but it eluded me.*

*²⁴ All that happens is elusive and utterly unfathomable. Who
can grasp it?*

ECCLESIASTES 7:23–24

Solomon's use of the word "eluded" in verse twenty-three is essentially repeated in twenty-four when he describes these lessons as both "elusive and utterly unfathomable." In other words, it's all *hevel.* Then he asks explicitly, "Who can grasp it?"

This is one of the qualities of Ecclesiastes that I love the most. Right in the middle of his text, the philosopher-king acknowledges that the business of life is hard and trying to understand it is harder yet. The wisest of men found that wisdom eluded him. He's doing his best, but the whole package of human reality that God has made is a lot of *hevel,* and any sense of certainty is tough to pin down.

So far, Solomon's arguments, understood within the context of his quest for *yithron*—lasting benefit—in the face of all the *hevelness* of life, have stitched together beautifully. He has laid out both spiritual and practical philosophy, hedged with uncertainties and the understanding that God has deliberately hidden some of what humanity most deeply desires to force us into the embrace of our maker. Solomon's material is as relevant to modern-day sensibilities and concerns as they were three millennia ago.

But what comes next clashes with everything we know today to be true. What comes next is one of the most jarring and controversial passages in scripture—or at least that's how they read to most modern readers.

Let's tackle Solomon's startlingly sexist material next.

37

WISDOM OPPOSES MISOGYNY AND SEXISM

I WAS IN my fifties before I realized that some of my best friends were women, in large part because of my experience with sexual assault at twelve years old. It wasn't just the assault itself that set me back but the behaviors of the males around me that compounded the problem. The middle-aged California men who populated the sheriff's office and courtroom were largely Vietnam veterans who likely had their own unaddressed traumas they carried with them through life. They had no training or personal ability to comfort or heal a humiliated and confused preteen. They were businesslike and generally avoided making eye contact with me, except for my assailant's defence attorney, who subjected me to a withering stare and mortifying questions on the witness stand.

In addition to being a local pastor, my father was the chaplain of the sheriff's department. As a result, he inexplicably provided Christian counselling for the pedophile who assaulted me but never talked with me about my pain other than to report that I'd got a detail at the trial wrong. My assailant criticized my testimony personally to my father in these private sessions, and my father reported that criticism to me without ever telling me what I got wrong. Did I get the color of his pants wrong? Did he claim that I'd identified the wrong suspect in the police lineup? I never knew. I just knew that I'd accurately identified the guy, and he went to state prison for his crime. Later in life, I learned how rare it is for these kinds of cases to ever be reported and for the few that are reported to ever go to trial, let alone achieve a conviction that leads to a state prison sentence.

For the legal result, I'm grateful—those otherwise clueless men got their legal job done—but the personal result was that a preteen boy washed out of that process more damaged than he'd been going in. Boys that I'd previously known fled my social circle. That was an era when homosexuality, even the unwanted victim type, left a stain that protests could not erase. Six months later, I was ushered out of the house to that seven-nights-a-week nursing job. I felt like I'd been banished and left to raise myself from then on.

My later construction job was just me and Ed and the occasional contract laborer. No friendships came from that job. My follow-up jobs in a nursing home, a hospital, and restaurants surrounded me with women. I felt safe with women. I could talk deeply with them. I understood their fears and vulnerabilities better than some of my male peers who found locker-room talk so easy. There's a reason it was Valerie who could puncture my stiffness when my male doctor friend had been unable to.

In 1992, Harper Collins published a book by John Gray called *Men Are from Mars, Women Are from Venus*. The book went on to sell fifteen million copies. It intended to use the idea that men and women are from different planets as a humorous metaphor to describe differences between the sexes. The book hasn't aged terribly well as psychologists and sociologists have taken issue with its misrepresentations of much of the data on human personalities and behaviors. Gray was inadvertently sexist in a book that likely wasn't trying to be. Nevertheless, the fact that the book has sold more than fifteen million copies suggests that Gray's book and its underlying metaphor resonated with the public.

Solomon's next bit is likewise often understood in a sexist way. In this case, the problem is not with Solomon's language or choice of metaphors but rather with how time and religious conservatism (and at least one suspect translation choice) have subverted his message. Let's investigate these controversial verses.

> *25 I turned my mind to know, to investigate, and to seek wisdom, along with an account of things, to know that wickedness is foolishness and folly is madness.*
>
> ECCLESIASTES 7:25

So far, so good. What's the problem? No problem. Not yet. The next bit is the problem.

> *26 I found one woman more bitter than death: she who is a trap, her heart a snare, her hands shackles. Anyone who pleases God escapes her, but a sinner is trapped by her. 27 See, this is what I found, says the Teacher, examining one matter after another to account for things. 28 But there's something that I constantly searched for but couldn't find: I found one man among a thousand, but I couldn't find a woman among any of these.*
>
> *29 See, this alone I found: God made human beings straightforward, but they search for many complications.*
>
> ECCLESIASTES 7:26–29

The CEB translation we're using here does a really good job of handling these verses. Where readers get into trouble is when translations (like the NIV) throw in an extra detail: it's "one *upright* man" (emphasis mine) that Solomon found in a thousand while he did not find a single righteous woman. The word "upright" is the bonus word some translators insert that is not found in the original Hebrew.

When I was a young single guy in Vancouver, a female art-student friend of mine brought the NIV version of this passage to my attention. She challenged me to explain how it was that there were no righteous women in the world but you could find the occasional good guy. Why was the Bible so sexist? I was caught off guard at the time. The message didn't line up with my own experiences of how humanity worked, and so I fumbled my reply. As I recall, I basically argued that Solomon had surrounded himself with a lot of lousy women, so what could you expect? He wasn't a misogynist; he was just reporting on his bad experiences.

To my shame, lacking a better answer, I held that view for decades. Thankfully, during the writing of this book, Amelia, one of my editors, refuted my early argument and pointed out that sexist ideas derived from bad personal experiences were still sexist. The source didn't change anything. She then pointed me toward some reference material that augmented information from my translator's handbook and other sources. Together, they helped me finally understand this passage in a way that was clear, internally consistent, and meaningful.

Let's start to unpack this verse by looking at the big picture and outline Solomon's argument in five bullet points.

1. He's got a plan to really figure everything out. He's going to unpack everything: wickedness, foolishness, madness, and folly— the whole deal (7:25).
2. The first thing he finds on this quest is a really horrible woman (7:26).
3. Then he summarizes or emphasizes that this is what all his searching uncovered (7:27).

Right away, we have a problem. His mission's scope is massive, but the study stops at one woman who is apparently a real train wreck of a person. That's it? The sum total of his investigation is this one woman? But then, weirdly, after summarizing this conclusion, Solomon restarts his own argument.

4. He can only find one man in a thousand and not a single woman (7:28).

One man in a thousand of what? People? That doesn't make sense, since it would mean he randomly sampled a crowd of a thousand people and found one man and no women. This is where the NIV inserts the word "upright" here to try to make sense of the sentence. According to the NIV, there is only one good man in a thousand, and no good women at all.

By translating the verse this way, the NIV took a mysterious line and made it misogynistic. The problem here is that the original Hebrew doesn't say "upright," and there is just as much literary justification to insert the world "wicked" as there is "upright." With "wicked" inserted, the verse would state that only one man in a thousand is wicked and no women are wicked at all. That's demonstrably not an accurate depiction of reality either, so what is going on here? Solomon's not done yet, so let's continue with our outline.

5. God made humanity upright to begin with, but they keep making a mess of things (7:29).

If you're anything like me, your head might be spinning a little. What is that passage trying to say? Let's go over this again quickly.

1. Solomon has a plan to figure things out.
2. He figured out that one woman was particularly bad.
3. He confirmed that this was everything he discovered.
4. Then he states he only found one man in one thousand, but no women, without telling us what category "one thousand" is referring to.
5. He wraps up by saying this isn't God's fault—it's people who are messing things up.

Wow. That's a pretty chaotic argument, even for Solomon. What's going on? Something seems off about the way these verses are laid out. They don't hang together to create a coherent idea. Are women bad and men good, like the NIV has made up here? Or is everyone making a mess of things, as verse twenty-nine states? And who is this one woman who was particularly evil? Is she a class of women, one of Solomon's seven hundred wives, or someone else?

Let's start over here, one verse at a time.

> [25] *I turned my mind to know, to investigate, and to seek wisdom, along with an account of things, to know that wickedness is foolishness and folly is madness.*
>
> ECCLESIASTES 7:25

Okay. Deep breath. What's the scope of his search here? I like the very loose translation that my translator's handbook offers here.

I turned to giving myself fully to the quest for wisdom and a logical explanation for things.[83]

Right. That's clear. Next verse.

[26] *I found one woman more bitter than death: she who is a trap, her heart a snare, her hands shackles. Anyone who pleases God escapes her, but a sinner is trapped by her.*

ECCLESIASTES 7:26

Do we have misogyny here? Not necessarily. He's talking about one woman, and there are plenty of women in history Solomon could have been referring to. Jezebel came just over a century after Solomon, so he couldn't have been referring to her, but several of his seven hundred wives could likely have fit the bill.

Whoa. Is it fair to say that one of Solomon's wives was this kind of hellish individual? Do we know that?

Yes, in fact, we do.

The book of 1 Kings describes Solomon's home life in this way:

[4] *As Solomon grew old, his wives turned his heart after other gods. He wasn't committed to the Lord his God with all his heart as was his father David.* [5] *Solomon followed Astarte the goddess of the Sidonians, and Milcom the detestable god of the Ammonites.* [6] *Solomon did what was evil in the Lord's eyes and wasn't completely devoted to the Lord like his father David.* [7] *On the hill east of Jerusalem, Solomon built a shrine to Chemosh the detestable god of Moab, and to Molech the detestable god of the Ammonites.* [8] *He did the same for all his foreign wives, who burned incense and sacrificed to their gods.* [9] *The Lord grew angry with Solomon, because his heart had turned away from being with the Lord, the God of Israel, who had appeared to him twice.*

1 KINGS 11: 4–9

---

83 Graham S. Ogden and Lynell Zogbo, *A Handbook on Ecclesiastes* (New York: United Bible Societies, 1998), p. 266.

Notice verse four makes it clear that his wives were the ones who introduced Solomon to this idol worship, which makes sense, given that he married women from all over the ancient world. They brought their religions with them. That's why the Jewish king wasn't supposed to marry foreign women to begin with, but we've already covered that. But let's be fair. They were just following their home religions, so is it reasonable for him to refer to one or more of these women as "more bitter than death" and "a trap" just for worshipping idols? It's not like this behavior should have been a surprise to him when he married her.

To answer this question, let's just focus on verse five and the reference to Astarte worship.

It is difficult to know precisely what Astarte worship looked like in the tenth century BCE due to the scarcity of surviving records. We do, however, have reasonably good information from early in the first century BCE and later into the era of the Roman Empire. I have a significant Astarte chapter in my historical fiction novel *Blind Man's Labyrinth*, which covers the practices of a temple at Ashkelon where the local name for this goddess was Ashtaroth. Other regions gave her the name Ishtar.

The level of institutional abuse associated with this cult made even the Romans shudder. For example, infant sacrifices were part of its rituals. Likewise, to mark their entrance into womanhood, teenage girls had to prostitute themselves to the first male who claimed them at the temple. That's how they lost their virginity. Men were permitted to serve as priests in this religion, but only after they had been castrated (in an era before modern medicine and anesthetics). Abuse in this religion was horrific, came with equal opportunity, and operated on the power of fear enhanced by the selective use of hallucinogenic drugs. As a result, at times, the Romans banned this form of worship. Did you get that? Even the idol-worshipping authors of coliseum death matches, public crucifixions, and institutionalized torture found Astarte worship too much to stomach.

And Solomon married a woman devoted to this kind of madness. She would have wanted to sacrifice some of her own babies or those of her servants. Her idea of how to introduce her daughters to society would have been for them to take a turn as a one-night prostitute at the Astarte temple, accepting the first random guy that came along. Remember, these girls would have been Solomon's daughters as well. Good heavens. Some of Solomon's bad marriage matches must have been made during the heavy drinking phase of his life. Can you imagine the marital disagreements in that palace?

Anyone who pleases God escapes her, but a sinner is trapped by her.
ECCLESIASTES 7:26B

Solomon did not escape because, as we saw earlier, Solomon was not a man who pleased God. He seriously messed up both his nation and his home life during his pleasure quest decades.

Okay, so we've covered verses twenty-five and twenty-six with no misogyny so far, but Solomon definitely regrets inviting at least one really awful woman into his life.

Here's the next verse.

27 See, this is what I found, says the Teacher, examining one matter after another to account for things.
ECCLESIASTES 7:27

This verse is basically a rephrasing of verse twenty-five. Here's what I think has happened here: in verse twenty-five, he stated his mission, then immediately got sidetracked by one of the biggest mistakes of his life. Then in verse twenty-seven, he calmed himself down and repeated the overall mission.

27 See, this is what I found, says the Teacher, examining one matter after another to account for things.
ECCLESIASTES 7:27

Okay. The wisdom quest is back on track. What did you find, Solomon?

28 But there's something that I constantly searched for but couldn't find: I found one man among a thousand, but I couldn't find a woman among any of these.

29 See, this alone I found: God made human beings straightforward, but they search for many complications.
ECCLESIASTES 7:28–29

This is where most commentaries go the route of the NIV, give up on Solomon, and declare that he was a misogynist. That, however, doesn't make sense to me for three simple reasons.

First, God is the ultimate author behind this book. When people say obviously bad things in the Bible—like Job's three friends or Satan or a corrupt king—God makes sure that the record is corrected or that the false speaker is clearly understood to be a false speaker. That never occurs here. Jesus himself even references Solomon, so it doesn't make sense to me that Solomon wrote misogynistic material into scriptures and it was allowed to stand.

The only way that would make sense is if God was a misogynist. But God isn't a misogynist. That's my second point. God starts the Bible pointing out that he "created humanity in God's own image, in the divine image God created them, male and female God created them" (Genesis 1:27). God's image isn't inferior to something else. Likewise, throughout the rest of the Bible, we see women blessed by God as national leaders,[84] prophets,[85] deaconesses,[86] and so on.[87] The first person in history that Jesus revealed himself to as the Messiah was a woman.[88] I could go on.[89]

---

84   Judges 4–5, Micah 6:4.

85   Isaiah 8:3, 2 Kings 22:14–20, Nehemiah 6:14, Joel 2:28, Luke 2:36–38, Acts 21:9.

86   1 Timothy 3:11 and Romans 16:1. In both of these instances, modern translations often obscure the original language and say "servants" in place of deaconess. But elsewhere, when talking about men, our English translations swap out servant and use deacon instead. There may be misogyny in religion, but that's man's doing, not God's. See Ecclesiastes 7:29.

87   There are two passages by Paul in the New Testament that are often considered misogynistic as well. Any interpretation of these two passages, however, needs to account for the status of women revealed in all the rest of scripture. There are specific audiences for Paul's two controversial passages (the church in Corinth and Timothy, who was in Ephesus). Time does not permit a thorough digest here, but suffice to say, the cities in question and local goddess cults dominating those cities go a long way to explaining what he's targeting in those letters. Women were not Paul's issue, as is made plain by the personal remarks in many of his letters, addressing and praising many close women friends and fellow ministry workers by name.

88   John 4:25–26.

89   A book that does go on is *Two Views on Women in Ministry* by numerous authors, edited by Stanley N. Gundry and James R. Beck (Zondervan, 2005). My

Thirdly, verse twenty-eight is vague. It's not clear what was unique about the one man. Verse twenty-nine is the verse that gets specific, and it clearly states that "God made human beings straightforward, but they search for many complications." According to Solomon, both sexes were fouling up God's work. A misogynist doesn't usually go after both sexes.

The problem here is a translation complexity. These verses can legitimately be translated as they are—except then the flow of the argument doesn't make any sense.

However, there is another perfectly accurate way of translating these verses that results in a flow that is internally coherent. I owe a debt to my editor, Amelia, for pointing out a good reference that made this clearer and making a copy of that paper available to me.[90] The original article is full of Hebrew technicalities, and I had to read it multiple times to unpack its meaning. Here, however, is my simplified version of what its author is communicating.

When Solomon says, "there's one thing I constantly searched for and couldn't find," he's trying to find the truth behind a contemporary saying from his time period: "you can find one guy in a thousand, but no women." Whether that was a good guy, a bad guy, a smelly guy, a musical guy, or a happy or sad guy, he doesn't say.

Whatever the category of guy, there was only one of them in a thousand. It appears there must have been a phrase in Solomon's day along the lines of "I could find one X-kind-of guy in a thousand and not one woman" that locals used as a formulaic way of expressing some popular idea about differences between the sexes. I take it that it was a "men are from Mars and women are from Venus" kind of phrase that was used (and probably misused) regularly in popular culture circa 1,000 BCE.

If my reconstruction is accurate—that Solomon is dealing with his own culture's popular truism on gender—then John Gray wasn't the first guy to come up with pop psychology concepts to simplify something complicated.

---

thanks to an old friend, Kim Boehlke, who repeatedly recommended this title to me. When I never got around to obtaining it, she finally bought me a copy. I read it and was glad to have done so.

90   Roland E. Murphy, "On Translating Ecclesiastes," *The Catholic Biblical Quarterly* 53, no. 4 (1991): pp. 571–79, http://www.jstor.org/stable/43718346.

In his era, Solomon had a stock phrase instead of a book to respond to, but like Gray's critics, he took issue with the concept expressed.

Gray tried to divide the sexes: men are from Mars and women are from Venus. They are psychologically different species. The message Solomon was reacting to had the same mission: there's only one man in a thousand (pick your subject or quality) and no women—one good man, one bad man, it doesn't matter. The point was that when you're looking for something rare (good or bad), you'll occasionally find it in a man and never in a woman. In other words, men are rarely exemplary (super good, bad, talented, rich, whatever the subject) and women (along with the majority of men) are always average. Only men populate the extremes. You can see how such a false pop psychology expression might gain traction in a population. Remember, this isn't Solomon's view but an idea prevalent in his day that he wants to address.

Solomon's take on this is that, no, men and women are not different in that way.

> [29] *See, this alone I found: God made human beings straightforward, but they search for many complications.*
> ECCLESIASTES 7:29

Both men and women go astray from how God made them to be. Men and women are not that different.

With this understanding, let's outline the flow of these verses again.

1. Solomon is on a mission to figure things out (7:25).
2. He got distracted by one completely awful woman who he failed to escape (7:26).
3. He refocuses back on his stated mission (7:27).
4. He inspects a stock Mars-versus-Venus kind of phrase popular in his day that encourages him to expand his negative view of that one woman to all women (7:28).
5. He rejects the stock phrase as wrong (7:29).

Yes, he had one awful woman that really upset him. And yes, there was a stock phrase in his day that he could have leaned on to reject all women and most men in his life. But no, upon evaluation, Solomon rejected that idea. His view is that people in general make mistakes. Women and men are the same in that regard.

My translator's handbook had that explanation for this passage written in plain language right from the beginning of my studies.[91] I'd read it multiple times and failed to grasp what it was trying to tell me. That's the problem with academic works—even diligent students who spend years on the material can fail to understand when the language is so dense. It took Amelia's criticism and the fresh lens of her Catholic Quarterly article to help me see my way through these verses. Only later did I realize the solution had been in my library all along; I just hadn't seen it.

Good editors are gold.

Oh, and let's be realistic. Solomon was probably a misogynist when he was young. Seven hundred wives and three hundred mistresses are indefensible. But the old man had sorted himself out, and he's trying to write down the proper way to think about these things now. He directs us here to stop putting women in special categories of good or bad. The virgin-versus-whore dichotomy, the pedestals or dumping grounds of idealistic or toxic popular positioning are just wrong. People are people, whether they are men or women or prefer not to tell you how they identify and wear gender-neutral clothing. They are all still just flawed people.

I had the opposite lesson to learn on this topic than many of my peers. It took me years to develop close friendships with men. Solomon's words cut just as cleanly into my own prejudice as they do into our society's generally patriarchal nature. Not all men are bad. One went to prison for his crime against me, and the others around me failed to help me heal when I needed them, but that does not make all men inherently awful. I needed to learn to find and befriend good men and stop keeping them all at a distance as though they were an undifferentiated class. I had to find male versions of Valerie to incorporate into my life. And I did. But it took time. Instincts planted deep in early years can take decades to completely uproot. It's hard work, but good work, and work that, if you have your own children, passes good things on to the next generation. My son has good relationships with male and female peers, and it sometimes makes me teary eyed with joy to see that my flaws have not been passed on to him.

---

91   Ogden and Zogbo, *A Handbook on Ecclesiastes*, p. 272.

As far as Solomon was concerned, all of humanity is a mess, and I can't disagree with him. God made people in a straightforward way, filled with an internal hunger to serve as road signs that should drive us to him. Instead, we often go searching for detours that take us off course. In this regard, men and women are not from Mars or Venus. We're all from Earth and make the same mistakes.

38

THE EXTRAORDINARY NATURE OF INTERNAL TRANSFORMATION: PART 1

Now, we're starting a section that contains serious personal disclosure. This is the first of the two chapters where I talk about an emotional bomb that went off in my life that helped me accelerate changes that had already begun to occur after Valerie's candid assessment of my main character flaw.

Originally, I'd intended for these chapters to dive straight into a discussion of Ecclesiastes chapter eight, probably covering half a dozen or more verses in the first chapter. Instead, we're only going to look at one verse for two chapters. These two chapters are very personal, and the one verse we'll look at has been unexpectedly and shockingly meaningful to me. After all, bombs—both emotional and literal ones—tend to leave a significant impression. First, let me share the theme verse with you:

> *¹ Who is wise? And who knows the meaning of anything?*
> *A person's wisdom brightens the expression;*
> *it changes the hardness of someone's face.*
>
> ECCLESIASTES 8:1

Had I gone from working on chapter thirty-seven of this book straight to chapter thirty-eight, I wonder what I might have made of this verse. I'd like to believe that my thoughts would have been Spirit-led regardless of circumstances. After finishing the previous chapter, however, and before

I could start this one, an extraordinary series of personal events happened that accelerated the change that Valerie's observation started. Together, the changes made this verse read very differently to me. I understand the verse experientially now and not just academically. I believe that experience is the most intimate way to understand anything.

It just so happened that when I sat down to write this chapter, that emotional bomb went off. It literally happened as my Word document was loading on my laptop. And it changed everything.

Before I tell you about it, you'll need to know some personal background.

I grew up in a household that practiced a version of Christianity that is fundamentally disconnected from what I now understand Christianity to be. A few anecdotes can only scratch the surface of a much larger story, but they should be enough to paint the general picture.

I knew growing up that my paternal grandfather had not attended my parents' wedding. My parents explained to me many times throughout my childhood how much pain this caused both of them. So when the time came for my wedding and both of my parents refused to attend, I was shocked.

I made long-distance calls from Vancouver, British Columbia, to their home in the United States, trying to get them to change their minds or explain themselves. The first explanation was theological: my father did not wish to attend a wedding led by a minister from another denomination. He quickly abandoned that explanation in favor of the excuse that the trip was impractical. "You'll be busy with your friends. We'll meet her later." They sent plane tickets so we could visit the following summer. We did, and it was a remarkably uncomfortable experience. After over twenty-seven years of my marriage, they still have no relationship with or interest in their only son's wife or children. When it came to attending our wedding, money was not the issue. Indifference was.

We visited my parents for the second time a little over four years later. My wife, Carolyn, was pregnant with our first child. That pregnancy would lead to Mackenzie, my parents' first grandchild. One morning, in my mother's kitchen, my pregnant wife made herself a slice of toast without asking my mother for permission.

You might think, "Wait a minute, who needs to ask for permission to make a piece of toast?" Well, nobody does until suddenly they do. The rules were never clear in the household I grew up in, but infractions were dealt with fast and harshly. Welcome to my birth family.

My wife was simply a pregnant woman needing food, but suddenly there was a new rule about toast. My mother was livid at this violation of a previously unknown rule, and after rebuking Carolyn for an extended period, my mother sought a way to make her anger clearer. She pointed at my wife's belly and announced: "You are not my daughter, and therefore, that child will mean nothing to us."

Other than not asking before making toast, there had been no provocation for this outburst. This was simply my mother's typical manner of communicating with family members. That's just my mother. That was another Sunday afternoon or Monday evening or Friday morning in the Potter family. We didn't swear in our house because we were "good Christians" after all, but living there, my sister and I developed coping behaviors that are maladaptive in healthy contexts but common among people who went through childhood abuse. We have no physical scars and bore no bruises, but emotional abuse can be as damaging as physical abuse. It took years to undo the damage of growing up in such an environment.

With a bit more maturity and wisdom, my wife and I might have pushed to either find a resolution or commit to cutting off my parents, but we were young at the time, and shortly thereafter, our daughter was born. For the next two decades, more pressing medical concerns consumed our time. In the following years, we saw my parents only rarely. Years passed between visits, and when they did occur, we conducted them carefully. They were not vacations but anxious obligations.

Fifteen years after our daughter's birth, still trying to be a good daughter-in-law, my wife said to my mother, "Tell me stories about Daryl's childhood. I'd like to hear what he was like as a boy."

My mother's response was to look at Carolyn for a moment and then, with her characteristically cold stare, to say very slowly and clearly, "I know they're mine. But I do not have a single memory of their childhood." That was the end of the conversation.

My father's response to his wife's scorn and biting words throughout our childhood, and even in our adulthood, was to pretend not to have heard her or to leave the room and go for a walk. Not that size should matter, but he's a 6'3" man with a 5'0" wife, but he never said a word or even silently stood as a physical presence between his children and her words.

Growing up, I took this dynamic for granted. It wasn't until I moved out of the house and on to Canada that I learned this was not how healthy families operated. My second novel, *Blind Man's Labyrinth*, is dedicated to some of the families who helped me see differently.

No criminal acts were committed in my childhood home—at least none recognized by any civil authority—but growing up and living in that house was like trying to sleep nude on sandpaper. Casual cruelty, calculated coldness, and savage scorn were the operating model. You grew calluses in that house or you died. There never appeared to be a reason for this icy household temperature other than when my mother once announced that she didn't like children, her own included. Perhaps that was explanation enough.

When working on my fourth novel, my editor pointed out that "None of your protagonists have parents. They are either dead before the book starts or die within the first two chapters." I had only just noticed the pattern myself a few months earlier. It's strange, the things we carry when we don't even realize we're carrying them.

There's one final piece of background you'll need to know, but it's a general state of affairs rather than a particular episode. I grew up without aunts, uncles, or cousins. My father had a sister who was eight years younger than him. My mother was the second oldest of five; she had two brothers and two sisters. Neither side of the family was part of my childhood beyond roughly age eight. No one spoke of my cousins, their births, their names, their existence. No one gave me a clear explanation for why this was our reality, although my parents hinted many times about the evils these people embodied. This isolation, apparently, saved my sister and me from all kinds of trouble.

Given the casual acidity of our home, as a kid, I had shuddered to imagine what these other people must be like. Later, my parents' ghosting of blood relatives became the nature of their relationship with my wife and children and with their own daughter. I've learned over the years that the decision to isolate can become a habit and then a skill until it eventually takes the wheel and drives a path through the lives of many unwitting victims. When you grow up in that context, the skill of isolation seems essential to the human tool kit. You don't even notice it controlling you after a while—rejecting others becomes as natural as breathing.

If you had asked me about my parents over the years, I would have offered generalities on the state of their health. I believed that I had long since worked through the strangeness of my upbringing. My parents had never offered or asked for any real relationship with me, so I remained oblivious to anything beyond surface-level details. After moving to Canada and then meeting my future wife, she and I created our own replacement families[92] in the form of strong lifetime friendships, many of which were with either immigrants to Canada or people coming from similarly dysfunctional families. We became family to each other, and we all also became extended family to each other's children. I knew my past was broken, but I was happy enough trying to figure out how to live going forward without trying to fix what didn't want to be fixed. I was the only blood relative still in contact with my parents. I saw no need to become estranged from them since they had no meaningful part in my life, nor did I in theirs. They'd long since lost the power to upset me, and I had an international border between us that created a natural barrier to regular contact. The occasional holiday phone call to catch up on the surface-level news was all the relationship required. Essentially, we were vaguely related strangers who shared some DNA and exchanged appropriate greetings when the calendar suggested it.

I say this in case any readers are concerned that I intended the first part of this chapter to be a bitter takedown. That is not my intention. People choose their way of being in the world, and this was the way of the senior Potters. Honestly depicting these realities from my childhood is important—not just to contrast them with the life and family my wife and I sought to build but also to make sense of the story that now follows.

In August 2007, when I was thirty-eight years old, I received a message from a woman named Louise. She identified herself as my father's long-lost sister. She stated that she had been looking for me for decades. She was not on any form of social media at the time. I have no idea how she tracked me down. I was eight years old the last time I had seen or heard of her. She lived in Kemptville, Ontario, about four hours away.

We started a surface-level correspondence, and then shortly after that, my Aunt Louise came by train to Toronto for a conference, and we had tea

---

92   The term "found families" is often used to describe this sort of do-it-yourself family creation.

after work one day. "I wish she lived closer," I told my wife afterward. "It would be nice to have them over."

As a result of our meeting, I found one of her children on Facebook: her daughter Julie. So began a year of very infrequent notes between the three of us. Social media and email were not on phones yet. I only powered up my home desktop occasionally, so the gap between the message and response was around a month to six weeks. I looked back on those messages recently and saw that we had shared nothing of consequence. We'd exchanged basic biographical details but did not establish any meaningful connection.

My life then was full of work, financial stresses, and life-threatening medical issues impacting both Carolyn and our daughter. In addition, I had a healthy three-year-old son who needed my attention. Everything seemed to be a crisis during those years. My communications with these unexpected and physically distant relatives faded out within the year. Contact made was soon lost. I never discovered what evil had banned them from my childhood, and I had other concerns that claimed my attention at the time. I eventually forgot about my aunt and cousin.

Cue August 12th, 2022. While I was waiting for Word to load so I could start writing this very chapter of this book, I opened Facebook. I was sitting alone in a Boston Pizza and engaging in a bit of pre-writing procrastination.

At the top of the feed that night was a post from my Aunt Louise. I don't think I'd ever noticed a post from her before. She had put up a note about her daughter Julie. It was a birthday post, but I didn't notice that then. Instead, I noticed the pictures attached to the post, and one in particular caught my eye: a picture of a book with her daughter Julie on the cover.

My cousin had co-authored a book. Wow. Very cool. I had a fellow author in the family. I decided to drop her a congratulatory note. Upon opening Messenger to do so, I discovered a "checking in" message from Julie that had been waiting for ten years. I'd never got the alert and never opened the message.

In my note to congratulate a fellow author, I also confessed my deficiency as a cousin. Her response was nearly immediate: she was helping staff a workshop that weekend and would be on camera in thirty minutes, so she couldn't give me a good reply right away, but she'd send me a proper note the following week.

Something about her response left me stumped. Perhaps it was guilt at not answering her ten-year-old message. Maybe it was the realization that I had a writer cousin leading a weekend workshop, and I did not know her or anything about her. Perhaps I was finally ready.

I stared at my computer for a few moments longer, then decided that if I'd been a deficient cousin, I'd probably been a bad nephew as well. By this point, my sister had been estranged from our parents for over a decade, and I'd become old enough to see the pattern across all my parents' relationships. I was fifty-three years old. My youngest child was leaving the house to attend university in a few weeks. Something about my son preparing to move out, my aunt's post, and my cousin's brief reply made me want to know who my extended family were. I decided at that Boston Pizza table to reach out to my aunt.

I sent her a note thanking her for the Julie post (which I still hadn't noticed was a birthday post) and confessed to being a deficient nephew. She responded immediately. For the next several hours, instead of working on this book, I traded messages with my aunt. That series of communications quickly went from the kind of shallow topics we'd covered fifteen years previously to more serious matters, and it became apparent that shortly after losing her mother (from leukemia) and father (from a heart attack), my father, her only surviving immediate family member, had ghosted her. As a result, she'd spent almost half a century hurting and wondering what she'd done wrong.

"No, no, no!" I was able to counter. "You didn't do anything wrong. That's just how my parents relate to human beings. They weren't interested enough in their only son's wedding to attend it, don't know their grand-children, and haven't talked with their only daughter in over a decade. So shunning you is just normal for them."

Those first few hours of sharing notes contained deeply moving exchanges, during which I discovered a seventy-one-year-old woman who was far more like me than I could have ever imagined. She thought and communicated the way I thought and communicated. I understood what she said but also what she didn't say. I understood her as though we'd been close for decades. We were similar in startling ways.

For readers with a close family, that observation may mean nothing to you—of course blood relatives share commonalities. For me, it was a shock. There was someone in the world like me. In five decades, I'd never found someone like me before.

My Aunt Louise ended that first evening's exchange with this line: "Love you and always have." Anyone watching me in that Boston Pizza would have seen a fifty-three-year-old man go pale and wobbly. A four-by-four post could have hit me on the back of the head, and it would not have impacted me more than those five words.

My daughter's condition makes her non-verbal, and so, outside of my son, I had never had a blood relative say those words to me—not like that. The four letters of the *love* word had probably been pronounced in my presence, but a blood relative who was not my child had never spoken those words to me in a way that was meaningful or believable. But that night, reading her message, I believed my aunt. She had spent decades, without the aid of social media, trying to find me. She had searched two countries: Canada and the United States. No one had ever searched for me before. When that connection failed to spark, she didn't push but let it rest. But as soon as I reached out again fifteen years later, she said it plainly. "I've loved you since you were a baby." Her words hit me hard. She told me she loved me, and I believed her in a way I had never believed anyone with my blood before. I wept in that restaurant while shutting down my laptop, paying the bill, and trying not to make a spectacle of myself.

The following days involved marathon exchanges on Messenger, during which I accomplished zero writing on this book. This woman, my aunt, was beautiful in every way. How had she not been a part of my life? What would my life have been like with this kind of maternal affection and kindness as part of its milieu? How much of the acidity and coldness of my childhood could have been overcome with just this one woman's presence as a refuge and counterpoint, offering up a space for self-worth, a heart full of acceptance, and hugs that gave warmth? She showed me a picture of myself when I was three years old that she'd kept for over half a century. It was a picture of me, her, and her husband—my Uncle Bob. There we were, fishing along a shoreline. They'd been a part of my life once, then they were gone.

Deep inside me, a wall collapsed. I spent the next two months in tears as I experienced a part of my soul, starved for decades, returning to life. This was a hunger and a roaring pain that my wife, children, and friends had never been able to satisfy. This was pain and joy at the same time. This was a blood relative from a generation before mine who cared. I'd seen such things in movies. I'd experienced those films as having the same spirit as science fiction: people have amazing imaginations. None of those things, though, were real. At least, not for me.

Six days later, my cousin Julie reached out. At the time, she was four years out of a painful divorce and had three children and two grandchildren. She had earned a master's degree in counselling, worked as a clinical counsellor in New York for a period, and now lived in Texas with a day job as a school teacher, carrying on side projects as a writer, workshop creator, and personal transformation coach. She was super interesting.

Toward the end of that first evening's exchange of notes with Julie, she shared a line that she later admitted to having typed and deleted four times.

Vulnerability brings the risk of being hurt—Julie explicitly defined that for me nearly a month later in a paper she had written but not yet published. That night, on August 18th, 2022, she practiced her paper rather than teaching it. "I was going to ask you," she wrote. "I'm open to a full connection/relationship! lol We don't have a large family so this is nice!"

I learned later that the "lol" in this message was actually a reflection of Julie's nerves. I was the son of the man who had deeply injured his sister—Julie's mother—decades before. I was the missing side of the family that had not come to her wedding and had not celebrated the birth of her children, come to her daughter's wedding, or celebrated the birth of her grandchildren. I was that man's son.

I was a risk. There was no reason, decades later, for Julie to want to know me. But she was willing to take me in anyway. The family that raised me took no one in. No one. It specialized in rejection. This cousin, like her mom, invited me in. "I'm open to a full connection/relationship," she said. She deleted that dangerous offer four times. But she retyped it a fifth time and pressed Send.

These exchanges were not a repeat of our sporadic contact years before. Instead, this was a love story. This was a love story between a nephew and his aunt and uncle, a love story between cousins, and a love story that quickly extended to that cousin's children and grandchildren.

Aunt Louise's statement of love shook me in ways that still make me cry. Julie's expression of basically the same sentiment flattened me. Nothing would ever be the same again.

39

THE EXTRAORDINARY NATURE OF INTERNAL TRANSFORMATION: PART 2

BEFORE CONTINUING THIS story, I want to remind us what verse this personal story relates to.

> *¹ Who is wise? And who knows the meaning of anything?*
> *A person's wisdom brightens the expression;*
> *it changes the hardness of someone's face.*
>
> ECCLESIASTES 8:1

The weeks following my reunion with my aunt, uncle, and cousin were a blur of multi-hour Facetime chats, phone calls, and marathon texting (having finally moved off Messenger as our communication vehicle of choice). I was walking on a cloud. I had discovered people like me in so many ways it boggled my mind. Some things that had always stood out as slightly odd about me turned out to be normal in my gene pool. They, it turned out, were like me. We were blood. And my blood was not cold or natively scornful. Instead, this new family exuded something foreign to my upbringing but perfectly matched a hole inside me. These were my people, discovered at fifty-three when I had no idea such people existed.

One night a few weeks into this adventure, I went for a walk. I'd long given up trying to tell God what to do in my prayers. *Even the Monsters* covers some of the background to that. I had requests occasionally, but more and more, what I prayed for now was the ability to hear and see where God's spirit was directing me and for the clarity and wisdom to act on that direction. I wanted to be part of the plan. He had all the monsters—and good things too—within his control. I had learned to be happy with him in charge, and I didn't want to be a fool getting constantly run over by God's bus. I wanted to be onboard, maybe even, in minuscule ways, doing my bit to help or at least cheer its progress on. I'm a fan of God's work, but the ride is sometimes bumpy, and I occasionally get overwhelmed on the way. So I prayed for eyes to see, ears to hear, and a strong stomach to handle the curves and bumps in the road.

So that night, overwhelmed by the joy of new relationships and the pain that came with understanding the hurt my family had caused others and how that unique brand of hurt had played out in my adult life, I went for a walk and talked with God. I cried, as I'd already been doing for a couple of weeks, and while I cried, I prayed.

"God, this hurts more than anything I've ever experienced in my life. Something is changing inside of me that's good, so don't let it stop, but God, it hurts. I don't know how to endure it. Please help me get through this and feel this and show me what to do. Please help me get to the other side and show me how to live with this new, broken, torn-open, and remade heart."

We're not Pentecostal. I didn't hear an actual voice, as one of my Pentecostal friends describes, but I might as well have. Something close to an audible voice said, "Call your sister."

I wasn't going to call my only sibling. My sister was part of the problem I was glad to leave behind me. She wasn't the problem itself, but she was from that same household, had lived those same experiences, and was as damaged as I was. Recall that I started sleeping elsewhere at thirteen (that strange seven-days-a-week night shift job), officially moved out of that house at eighteen, and then moved to Canada at nineteen. My sister, who was five-and-a-half years younger than me, stayed in that house until she was twenty-seven and moved from there into her husband's home. She'd had no transition period for personal soul-searching along her version of Vancouver beaches. So that night, I ignored the voice and kept walking and praying.

Yet the voice—or thought or Spirit's call—came again. "Call your sister."

No. I wasn't going to call my sister. I had tried reaching out to her for over a decade after she got married, but she seemed incapable of reciprocation or sustained warmth. She later said the same about me. Neither of us had what it would have taken to develop a relationship with the other. We had survived our sandpaper childhoods and created new lives to the best of our abilities, but connecting with each other was impossible. We were still sandpaper to one another.

I wrapped up praying, put my headphones on to let a new playlist drown out my emotions, and kept walking. A song or two in, the Spirit poked me again. "Call your sister." Then again, "Call your sister."

I gave up. I called my sister. She answered on the second ring. She was available. She wanted to talk.

"It's funny you should call," she said. "I dreamed about you last night. I've only ever dreamed about you once before."

"What did you dream?" I asked.

"I dreamed that we were doing all sorts of things together. That we were having the most wonderful time. And then I woke up and was sad because it wasn't true."

We talked that night for over an hour. I walked her through my experiences of the previous two weeks, and at the end of it, she said, "I'm happy for you."

"No," I replied. "You're not supposed to be happy for me; you're supposed to join me!"

What followed was another near hour of rehashing the same material and adding to it all the times I had tried to be a brother to her and been rebuffed, all the damage done by the coldness of our upbringing, all the things I'd recently found and that she needed in her life as well, and how much I wanted her to be part of this new beginning. I wept. She finally did too.

I won't tell her tale, but suffice it to say that, with some fearful and tentative starts, she began to reach out and soon joined the story. What stood out to me most from that night's discussion was her response to the final question I asked her. "You said you'd only dreamed about me one other time before. When was that?"

"Two weeks ago," she said. "It was the same dream."

Two weeks ago was the night I first started corresponding with Aunt Louise. I was thrust into this new family adventure by surprise, drawn in by the idea that I had a cousin who was a fellow author, and then shocked into tears by a confession: "Love you and always have." My sister's journey involved not surprise Messenger notes but two warm-up dreams and then a phone call. God approaches us differently, according to our needs. I'd had a chance fifteen years before and done nothing with it. I'd needed an emotional four-by-four beam to the head. My sister needed a gentler approach. She got two dreams and then a phone call.

The weeks following this conversation were full of phone calls and messages that expanded to include not just my father's sister and family but also my mother's relatives. I can thank my Uncle Bob for cracking that door open and my Aunt Louise for hosting the first reunion for both sides of the family. Kemptville is a small town, and both sides of the family knew each other from high school days onwards. My uncles on my mom's side had even worked as young men for my paternal grandfather. My aunt still had old black-and-white photos of them all together on Grandpa Potter's farm.

A surprise work trip to Dallas came a month after our first contact, and I spent time with Julie, her children, and her grandchildren. It was a beautiful visit, and it hurt to leave. Around the same time, a respite hospital called and suddenly wanted our daughter to come for an unplanned visit. My wife suggested we take a trip to Kemptville. We went and planted seeds with both sides of my family that will continue to grow in the years to come. Less than two months later, my sister landed in Ontario, and the Kemptville crew from both my father's and mother's sides came to my place to see us both. When I put the missing puzzle pieces together, I discovered and recognized that my extended family is nothing like the household I grew up in. These gatherings continue to be overwhelming experiences. Each discovery generates a positive change that continues to affect my heart and soul.

I used to tell myself that our family was English, that English people had a history of travelling the globe founding empires, and that they were not known for close family relationships. I literally believed that for five decades. It was my way of explaining my childhood to myself. After talking with my actual relatives and finding them to be beautiful and funny and giving and warm, I started talking to all my English friends about their families and realized that my weird bit of English mythology was a complete fabrication. I had invented it when I was very young to make sense of senseless things.

Then I talked more with my new family and dug into ancestral records and discovered that I was only part English. I was mostly Scottish, Irish, and French. I had descended from kings and queens of Scotland, Denmark,

Norway, and Sweden, two lords of Milan, and German counts as well as English gentry. Irish farmers, a king of the Picts, and even Robert the Bruce featured in my family tree. My false English mythology, had it even been true, would have only applied to a minority of my bloodline.

So what does all this have to do with Ecclesiastes?

I finished chapter thirty-seven of this book just before my first contact with Aunt Louise. After that first contact, I lost all ability to write, fiction or nonfiction, for seven weeks. Family matters claimed my attention.

After my Dallas trip, I shared with one of Julie's adult children how I felt like a door had been opened inside me. Through that door came a pent-up roaring of pain that had been bottled there my entire life without my conscious awareness. The roaring now seemed endless. A month in, its volume had not been checked. Seven weeks on, the roaring continued but had lessened. In its place appeared a gentleness that I've always believed was a latent potentiality in my personality but was either well-hidden or completely overrun by a brusqueness I had wrongly attributed to genetics. It turns out I had not carried a stick around inside me but a dam. Its bursting was unexpected and dramatic.

Through those weeks of dialogue and discovery, almost as an after-thought, I discovered that anger was one of my abiding qualities. Few would have pegged me as habitually angry. Stiff, yes, but not angry. I was also confident. Authoritative. Reliable. Strong-willed. Fearless. But now I understood that underneath all these positive qualities lay not a base of good character but the steel of anger. I had been starved for affection, and my starved soul knew it even if my conscious mind did not. Anger was the by-product, and that anger, carefully camouflaged as more positive qualities, had become the backbone of nearly everything else.

Gradually, as I experienced a kind of love I had never known before, I softened. The roaring emptied itself. The anger packed up and moved out. The stick was gone.

On the downside, insecurity and anxiety replaced anger for a while—a reborn and refilling heart makes for a disoriented mind. Without anger to bull through every barrier, I felt ill-equipped to deal with life's challenges. Deep down, where no one could see, anger had been my secret weapon. Anger was my jet fuel. Without it, I felt defenceless.

Gentleness is a different creature altogether. I had to relearn business and leadership skills using a heart that was now gentle.

What does Ecclesiastes say?

> *¹ Who is wise? And who knows the meaning of anything?*
> *A person's wisdom brightens the expression;*
> *it changes the hardness of someone's face.*
>
> ECCLESIASTES 8:1

I don't know what I would have written about Ecclesiastes 8:1 on August 11th, 2022. I was incapable of writing anything on August 12th. Finally, by October 7th, I understood something about this verse that I would not have been able to notice, let alone write about, previously.

My expression had brightened. The hardness of my face was gone. Friends and close coworkers commented on it. Everything changed. I had not yet engaged with traditional therapy nor practiced behavior-modification exercises. I had not experienced yet another religious conversion. Instead, I'd discovered blood relatives and was immediately, unconditionally, unreservedly, and unreasonably loved by them. Love changed me. And that love led to a new understanding of who I am and who cares for me, and the experience changed my expression. My parents' household dynamic is not my family line. It is just them.

The change I'm describing felt like it happened immediately, but in reality, God had been tunnelling into that dam for years prior and making it ready for the impact of August 12th, 2022. *Even the Monsters* was part of that. Working through things in my marriage was part of that. Publishing my first three parentless novels was part of that. And when the time was right to blow the dam, God used my Aunt Louise to trigger the first charge. He didn't need my help to do it. He didn't ask for my permission. He just did it. Then, when I was still off balance, he had my cousin Julie lay and trigger the second. A cleansing flood followed.

My relatives' lives had likewise changed so that they, too, were ready for August 12th. This time, the exchanges were not casual and infrequent. My new family led with vulnerability, and we went to the level of tears at our first contact.

God plays 3D chess and then some. Proverbs puts it this way:

It is the glory of God to conceal a matter;
to search out a matter is the glory of kings.

PROVERBS 25:2 (NIV)

Searching for and discovering the small corners of what God might be up to makes me feel like a king. It brightens my expression. It removes the hardness from my previously angry, anxious, hurting face.

¹ Who is wise? And who knows the meaning of anything?
A person's wisdom brightens the expression;
it changes the hardness of someone's face.

ECCLESIASTES 8:1

Sometimes, all a soul needs to know is that they have an aunt who loves them and always has.

40

GENTLENESS IS BETTER THAN ANGER

About two months after making contact with my Aunt Louise, I experienced a mental health crisis that left me fearing for my career and personal well-being, in that order.

As I previously described, anger had been my backbone, the secret steel lodged at my core that gave me an edge in any and every situation. I had chaired project-steering committee meetings remotely from my daughter's hospital bedside while she lay inches away on life support in a medically induced coma. I'd worked in a sleep-deprived state for months straight due to rolling medical crises and walked into work meetings filled with senior executives who were one hundred percent opposed to my message and walked out again later with signatures, funding, or other forms of approval despite my exhausted brain.

Even in my spare time, a hidden-even-to-me anger fuelled me. For example, I knocked myself out one summer when building a deck on my own. When I woke up some time later, I had no idea how long I'd been out. I finished what I'd been doing, got some water and an Aspirin, then went back to work and finished the deck. Three months later, when the fog cleared, I realized that I'd been living with a concussion for those dark months. Unbeknown to me, anger—masked and subverted into something powerful—carried me through, regardless of the risks, the odds, or sometimes even medical sense. Of course, God was there at my side as well, but psychologically, it seemed that anger had been my crutch and my secret sauce. To use a car analogy, you can ruin a vehicle by using fuels that are too powerful for the stock engine. I was like a car running on buried anger, even though I had not been conscious of it before Aunt Louise came into my life.

After Aunt Louise, the anger melted. It happened very suddenly. I felt it. Then I showed up for work on a Monday morning without my secret sauce and felt naked. I was scheduled for a series of battles over the next few days and knew I couldn't do the job. I was a gunslinger with no guns. I had nothing now to help me but weak and trembling hands.

I sat at my desk that day in a state of terror. I couldn't face the week. I couldn't show up to the meetings that I was expected to either lead or win with no strength inside for the contest. Just the fact that I thought of meetings as something to win illustrates the mindset that had carried me through the three prior decades of my banking career. I deferred most of Monday's meetings using various excuses. Tuesday came, and the problem was worse. I cancelled more meetings, but I couldn't keep doing this forever. I was a decade away from retirement. I didn't know how I was going to make it through the week, never mind another ten years. I would eventually be fired. I'd be unemployable. We'd lose our home. I wouldn't be able to finish paying for my son's university education. Mackenzie would eventually be taken from us. We'd wind up living under a bridge. The panic attack that gripped me was both exhaustive and creative.

A mental health crisis is no laughing matter. Suicide seemed like a good idea again, which is insane given all the good that had come into my life through my aunt, cousin, and other relatives. But overwhelming good, when you've learned to live with unending complex trauma from childhood onward, is foreign and hard to bear. The grindstone of pressing on, bulling through the barriers with a determination fuelled by subverted anger, is what kept me moving forward and alive. I now understand that my stiffness, my concealed anger, Valerie's metaphorical stick inside me, my life of relentless productivity and progress were trauma responses and a socially approved way of managing both severe anxiety and depression.

But with the anger gone, I was now nonfunctional. I was a gunslinger with no guns, a carpenter with no tools, a voiceless singer. I needed to learn how to lead meetings again and how to brave executive panels opposed to my recommendations and do so from a place of inspiration or joy or some other emotional state. My tool kit of bullheaded determination had deserted me.

Solomon's next verses were the beginning of the instruction that I needed.

² Keep the king's command
      as you would keep a solemn pledge.

³ Don't be dismayed; leave his presence.
      Don't linger in a harmful situation
      because he can do whatever he wants!

⁴ Because the king's word has authority,
      no one can say to him, "What are you doing?"

ECCLESIASTES 8:2–4

That the king wrote this material about interacting with the king makes it a bit suspect. It seems, on its first reading, self-serving. In this passage, "Do what the king says" is equivalent to Solomon saying, "Do what I say."

The logic Solomon provides, though, is sound. He can do whatever he wants. Okay, fair enough. Likewise, in my workplace, the bank's senior executives could do whatever they wanted. I had no ability to force them to my will. What had seemed to work for me (bullheaded determination bolstered by a secret anger) perhaps had nothing to do with my previous successes. Perhaps the business cases I presented spoke for themselves, or God was my guide and somehow my proposals made it through the gauntlet despite me or the leaders above me. What am I supposed to do with these verses practically? How did this help me with my mental health crisis? How was a confirmation of the dominant authority's power helpful?

As a Christian, I expected Solomon to offer some kind of "remember Joseph before Pharaoh or David before Goliath" pep talk to calm my anxiety. At the very least, some kind of "trust God" message seemed to be in order. But that's not what Solomon does in this passage. In fact, the next verse starts in a way that makes the apparently pro-totalitarian slant here seem even more pronounced.

⁵ Whoever keeps a command will meet no harm,

ECCLESIASTES 8:5A

With a surface reading, the false notes in this verse ring loud. Isn't this how Nazi soldiers in the mid-twentieth century tried to justify their atrocities at Nuremberg? They claimed that they were just following orders. How was this going to help me survive until retirement with crippling and unrestrained anxiety as my new companion?

Well, there is a context to consider here. To bring that context into scope, let's finish verse five and keep reading beyond it.

> [5] *Whoever keeps a command will meet no harm, and the wise heart knows the right time and the right way* [6] *because there's a right time and right way for every matter. But human misfortunes are overwhelming* [7] *because no one knows what will happen, and no one can say when something might happen.* [8] *No one has control over the life-breath, to retain it, and there's no control over the day of death. There's no release from war, and wickedness won't deliver those who practice it.*
>
> ECCLESIASTES 8:5–8

What are these verses saying?

First, the obedience thing comes up again. Solomon says that obedience is a good idea. But then the rest of verse five states that the wise heart knows the right time and the right way. The right time and right way for what? The right time and way to be obedient? It doesn't say that. Presumably, the king's command included a time and way, so why do the wise also need that skill set? Aren't they just supposed to do as commanded? If I took the passivity that I initially read in this verse into my work life, my management role at the bank would be forfeited before long. I wasn't paid to be a drone that just took orders. I was paid to think and lead, in that order.

Verse six explains that, whatever the king's command may be, there is an ultimate right time and way for every matter. Not just the king's matter but every matter. The following verses go on to talk about the unpredictability of reality (8:6–7) before turning to the fragility of human existence, the implacable march of war, and the ultimate self-harm that comes from doing evil (8:8).

Did you catch that?

The charge to obey the king because keeping a command won't produce harm (8:5) is balanced by a warning about the fragility and unpredictability of life (8:6–8) and the ultimate punishment that evil will inflict on its practitioners.

Did you catch it that time?

Let's turn this around a bit and see if that helps make Solomon's message here clearer. The wise in heart will know what to do in every situation. They will know the right time and the right way, and often, the king's presence is not the right time or place to protest a lousy direction. As verse three puts it: "Don't be dismayed; leave his presence. Don't linger in a harmful situation because he can do whatever he wants!"

This puts verse one in a new light:

> *¹ Who is wise? And who knows the meaning of anything?*
> *A person's wisdom brightens the expression;*
> *it changes the hardness of someone's face.*
>
> ECCLESIASTES 8:1

The wise are not shocked or overrun with defensiveness, dismay, or any other emotion in the king's presence. They don't need anger to fuel them through obstacles. Anger is sometimes impatience materialized, as discussed earlier, but sometimes anger is also fear materialized, our internal trauma externalized. Anger is sometimes a useful emotion to galvanize action, but in my case, it was a corrosive emotion, born from hurt and resentment and long-buried periods of isolation and neglect that had become the hardness within me. It was my tool for getting things done and hiding the pain within me from myself and others. But the wise—those with softened faces and brightened expressions—they understand what is happening. They can think clearly. As a result, they are not overrun by negative emotions. Executives in a boardroom say, "No," and the expression on a wise person's face remains bright. No hardness clouds their appearance. They know the right time and way to deal with whatever the king is commanding, whatever the boardroom is rejecting, or whatever the boss is ignoring. There is no point in arguing with a dictator. As it says elsewhere in scripture,

> *Therefore the prudent keep quiet in such times,*
> *for the times are evil.*
>
> AMOS 5:13 (NIV)

Remember the purpose underlying all of Ecclesiastes. In this book,

Solomon is trying to understand how to live in a broken world. He's not writing a book about political revolution or even about trusting God. He's not writing a book about ethics either. He's trying to understand how to live amid broken systems, among broken people, haunted by a hunger that this life cannot satisfy, no matter how much effort we put into the mission.

With this as his context, Solomon's advice is to manage every situation not with alarm or with anger but with the calmness that comes from understanding.[93] The right thing to do and when to do that right thing are gifts the wise can give the world. War and wickedness are implacable, but wisdom is unshakable. In this conflict between a king and his subject, only one has a calm face and soft expression: the wise person.

Gentleness carries with it next-level authority. A kind expression is a résumé more solid than an ivy league education. I've run projects for the bank across three countries and two continents, and I can attest to the truth of this passage with example after example. The most intelligent and influential people I've ever worked with, whatever their country, did not refer to their alma mater. Who they were as human beings carried them forward, not their certifications or paper credentials. Those things work for a while, but not for a long while. Solomon knew what he was talking about. The wise know what to do and when to do it. Knowing calms the heart and softens the face. Knowing is effective.

Sometimes what the wise know isn't even about the job at hand or what the king (or the boss) requires. Sometimes what the wise know is outside the immediate crisis. Sometimes what a person knows is that they have an aunt who loves them. Alarms about a hundred business matters suddenly fade when a broken heart starts to carry that truth with it.

Books can record wisdom, but wisdom is only really known once experienced. So if these last three chapters did not resonate with you, I hope they do one day. It's a beautiful place to live.

For the record, my anxiety crisis lasted about a week. I took most of the rest of that week off work. By the time I got back to the office the following Monday, I was prepared to start learning Solomon's way. After three decades, it's hard to learn how to do your job all over again, but I accomplished more

---

93   For readers interested in exploring more deeply the idea of remaining calm in the face of trials, I highly recommend *The Anatomy of Peace* by the Arbinger Institute (Oakland: Berrett-Koehler, 2022).

in the following eighteen months than I had in any previous eighteen-month period of my career. Apparently, I didn't need that steel of anger after all. Along the way, I started conversations with a registered therapist who also holds a master's degree in theology to help me think through the implications of some of what I was experiencing and learning.

As G.K. Chesterton put it, "The Christian ideal has not been tried and found wanting. It has been found difficult; and left untried."[94] In my case, I wasn't given an option on what I wanted to try or when. Via Aunt Louise and my cousin Julie, without any warning, God ripped out my anger. As a result, all I could do was lean on him as I relearned how to live without it. Slow or abrupt, God's way works.

---

94   See *What's Wrong with the World* by G.K. Chesterton (London: Cassell and Company, 1910).

PART EIGHT:

BRINGING IT ALL TOGETHER

41

HOW TO LIVE WELL DESPITE UNFAIR CIRCUMSTANCES

THINKING ABOUT ANGER—BOTH the subconscious and explicit kinds—made me think back over my life and career. I was interested in understanding myself better, but the behavior of others also appeared in a different light. Impressive leaders lost some of their shine as I began to interpret their methods not as forceful but fearful. If leadership is fuelled by negative emotions (anger, anxiety, selfishness, buried traumas, and so on), then the role might have power, but the person does not. I'd seen that often enough over the decades—titans of industry or political leaders with great power were suddenly dismissed when the world no longer wanted or needed them. When facing these sorts of people, the wise can keep their hearts (and thus their faces) calm, even bright, because they know the right way to get good things done whatever the circumstances. People come and go, as Solomon talked about early in this book. There's no need to get into an existential panic about one mortal person or situation.

But what do you do when you're facing a tyrant—a boss, a teacher, a relative who has economic or other power over you—and you can't escape right now and you don't yet know the right time and place and way to handle your situation? How do you deal with that kind of trouble?

There isn't an easy answer, but that doesn't stop Solomon from helping us think through the situation with wisdom and clarity.

⁹ I observed all of this as I paid attention to all that happens under the sun. Sometimes people exercise power over each other to their detriment.

ECCLESIASTES 8:9

Wait. To whose detriment? I don't like verses that are unclear like this.

Is this verse just stating the obvious: oppressors harm their victims? Or is this a subtle psychological statement suggesting that oppressors wind up also hurting themselves? Who is harmed here? In other words, who is the "their" referring to?

Understanding this nuance changes the nature of the passage that follows. You would think this uncertainty would be quickly resolved by simply consulting other translations. However, a survey of the thirty-six English translations I had available to me revealed the following confusion.

Nine translations clearly state that oppression's damage is borne by the oppressed, which seems to be the obvious reading. Why bother even chasing this down any further? The Good News Translation, the God's Word Translation, and the New Revised Standard Version all fall into this camp. These versions, however, only account for twenty-five percent of our survey.

The New Living Translation and The Message translations both state that the harm is mutual: both the oppressor and the oppressed are injured by oppression. These two texts, however, are outliers.

Twelve translations are a bit vague about who bears the injury of oppression. Our ESV translation is an example of this ambiguity, and it's what sparked my question to begin with.

Fourteen of the thirty-six translations clearly state that it is the oppressor who suffers by their own hand. This is the largest choice and accounts for thirty-nine percent of the translations I surveyed. The KJV offers a clear example of this when it says, "there is a time wherein one man ruleth over another to his own hurt." His own hurt. The ruler hurts himself. Thirteen other translations use more modern English but make the same point.

So what is the answer? Should we decide how to interpret the Bible based on what translation is most common? Unfortunately, the original Hebrew text is just as vague as the English here. We don't know Solomon's intention, which implies that leaving the door open to all interpretations is the right choice.

Once again, I don't like these kinds of conclusions when I study something. I like the clarity of a precise answer, but Solomon did not provide precision here. His statement is now scripture, and the bottom line is that oppression is bad, but who suffers is variable. We can probably all come up with stories from general history or personal experiences that illustrate how variable harm can be. Oppression is a weapon whose aim is erratic.

Following this uncertain conclusion, Solomon rattles off a list of other things that seem dysfunctional to him.

> *10 Then I saw the wicked brought to their graves, with people processing from a holy place, while those who had lived honestly were neglected in the city. This too is pointless.*
>
> ECCLESIASTES 8:10

This, too, is not pointless, but *hevel*. Breath. Wind. Vapor. Ephemeral, fleeting, temporary, insubstantial, elusive. Things do not work the way they should. Wicked people are honored with grand funerals while simple, honest folk are forgotten. Do I need to draw on recent news stories or ancient histories to illustrate this? This observation rings as true today as it did three thousand years ago.

Next on Solomon's list of broken things is a problem with an obvious root cause.

> *11 The condemnation for wicked acts isn't carried out quickly; that's why people dare to do evil.*
>
> ECCLESIASTES 8:11

Next up, Solomon names a problem without stating a cause.

> *12 Wrongdoers may commit a hundred crimes but still live long lives.*
>
> ECCLESIASTES 8:12A

The next verse and a half paint a more conventional and optimistic picture of divine justice.

But I also know that it will go well for those who fear God, for those who are reverent before God. ¹³ *But it will not go well for the wicked; they won't live long at all because they aren't reverent before God.*

ECCLESIASTES 8:12B-13

Hold on. Wrongdoers live long lives in verse twelve, but then they don't in verse thirteen? Pick one, Solomon. Which is it? God punishes the wicked, and they live short lives as a result, or they "commit a hundred crimes but still live long lives"? Is it answer A or B? Solomon's answer is, "Yes. Sometimes A and sometimes B."

Sometimes oppression hurts the oppressed, sometimes it hurts the oppressor, and sometimes it hurts both. Sometimes the wicked die young, and sometimes they live a long life. The world does not operate on a formula, and things are not clearly predictable. Solomon would completely agree with some of Job's most passionate speeches on this topic.

Solomon goes on to explain himself further.

¹⁴ *Here's another thing that happens on earth that is pointless: the righteous get what the wicked deserve, and the wicked get what the righteous deserve. I say that this too is pointless.*

ECCLESIASTES 8:14

Notice that he begins and ends verse fourteen by saying this is *hevel*. In other words, this is super *hevel*. It is *hevel* at the beginning of the statement, and it is *hevel* at the end. There is unrelieved *hevel* going on here. This whole situation is *hevel*.

If we put Solomon's idea here into super plain, even crude English, he is stating that human reality is snafu. If you don't know that acronym, I'll spare you the uncomfortable web search results. It's a World War II phrase that, in its gentler formulation, means "Situation Normal, All [Fouled] Up." The original, of course, used a much cruder F-word.

Solomon states that the world is broken. It is all snafu. That's not a new idea. Solomon said it roughly three thousand years before rude World War II acronyms were invented.

If everything is such a mess, what should we do with this information?

How are we supposed to live in such a broken world? How are we supposed to deal with personal tyrants in our lives when we don't have power, the world isn't fair, and we don't know what the wise thing or time is?

Here is Solomon's advice:

> *15 So I commend enjoyment because there's nothing better for people to do under the sun but to eat, drink, and be glad. This is what will accompany them in their hard work, during the lifetime that God gives under the sun.*
>
> ECCLESIASTES 8:15

This again. This is the seventh time in this book that Solomon has returned to the recurring theme that the best thing to do in this crazy *hevel* of a life is to find enjoyment in simple moments.

Modern awareness of mindfulness teaching has come through diverse sources, including the Positive Psychology movement, general Zen Buddhism teachings, and in particular, the work of Thích Nhất Hạnh and others. Turning the clock back to other ancient, non-Buddhist sources reveals Hinduism's dhyana practices, Islam's Sufism, Judaism's Kabbalah, and other religions and philosophies that touch, to varying degrees, on this idea of contemplative focus as a central value, practice, or mental discipline for managing life's complexities.

Modern Christianity tends to ignore this vein of wisdom. Perhaps some Christians fear being corrupted by exposing themselves to ideas made more popular by other schools of thought. Based on my own experience of Christianity, Christians want to work and do and rush and distract—that famous Protestant work ethic in practice—instead of slowing down and listening to the teachings found in the Bible on this idea of mindfulness.

As far back as Exodus, Leviticus, and Deuteronomy, the Jewish legal texts taught people to slow down, reflect, and find gratitude through the practice of festivals and celebrations and shared meals. Take Jesus as an example: he constantly broke bread with his community in quiet settings, asked his followers to focus and notice details, and went off for times of solo prayer. All these practices from Jesus echo and expand on these principles of mindfulness.

Solomon's teaching here is part of a continuum in scripture—never mind societies outside of the Judeo-Christian tradition—that reminds us, again and again, to slow down and enjoy each moment, meal, drink, and relationship. We are reminded to be glad for what we have, even if it's just a crust of bread, because life is full of a lot of trouble, and moments of pleasure are to be savored and not rushed past. This teaching exists throughout the Bible. Solomon isn't done with Ecclesiastes yet, and he's already talked about this theme of enjoyment seven times.

What did you have for breakfast today? Did you savor it or barrel through it?

To paraphrase that Chesterton quote from the previous chapter: Solomon's advice here has not been tried and found wanting. It has been found foolish and left untried. Give it a try.

42

THE WORLD IS BROKEN ON PURPOSE

FOR ME, CHILDHOOD swimming lessons were comprised of a rope my father tied across a deep and fast stream. He sent me across the stream on my own, thrashing with one hand on the rope, trying to keep my face above the waves. Once I could do that reasonably well, he removed the rope. Thus, swimming became a game of managing the current and avoiding rocks rather than learning any kind of actual technique. It worked, but not well. To this day, I'm not a great swimmer. I'm as likely now to become a competitive pole vaulter as a recreational swimmer.

But I love water. It draws me.

A few years after that one-and-done stream swimming lesson, I stood on the west bank of the Sacramento River with a friend I'll call Billy. We were both fourteen years old and overloaded with testosterone, which our still-developing brains had not yet learned how to manage.

At a place near Princeton, California, the great river flowed. This was not a stream but a truly massive body of water.

"Let's swim across," Billy said.

I looked across the river. There was no reason to swim across. Our side had a gravel beach that salmon fishermen used to park their coolers and other gear. What we could see of the far bank, across the sun-dazzled water, was an unwelcoming vertical wall of eroding earth and rock and exposed roots topped by an ugly scrubland inhabited by opossums and magpies and not much else.

"Let's do it," I said with genuine enthusiasm because, well, we were fourteen. That age's mismatch between surging hormone levels and a lack of good sense is just one of the many things I want to ask God about one day.

Halfway across, I saw that the water's surface had formed a strange oval shape upstream. That oval was upstream but slowly moving downstream. Something below the water was eliminating the waves at the surface and creating a large pool of calm that slowly approached us.

Billy was a proper swimmer, and he was out of the path of that flat oval before it reached our position in the river. It moved slowly around me as though with sinister intent, and then, just as I marvelled at the strangeness of the experience, it pulled me under. I fought the undertow hard and thought I'd made it out, but I'd barely breached the river's surface, gasping for air, when it pulled me under once more. I fought and found air for a second time but was immediately pulled back down again. The forces at play had me by the legs and would not let me go. My limbs became dead weight. When the undertow finally released me, I found the surface again but could not stay there. I was sinking for what I believed would be the last time. My lungs burned and my brain screamed, but my voice was soundless, and my body began to surrender to exhaustion and accept the end.

A US Marine on leave was salmon fishing on that same stretch of the river. He saw me go down multiple times and understood what was happening. He dropped his rod, stripped to his shorts, swam out, and rescued me. I never got his name, but I'm alive today because of him.

The following summer, Billy and I fished Butte Lake together. Fishing was slow.

"Let's swim across the lake," Billy said.

There was no more reason to swim across Butte Lake than there had been to swim across the Sacramento River. A sensible person would have said "no."

"Let's do it," I said.

We left our fishing gear and cooler on the shore and began churning across the vast still water. We made it halfway when my left arm and left leg cramped up. I could no longer swim. Billy found a floating log and steered it toward me, and I half floated, half paddled with one good arm the rest of the way. At one point, a giant hairy spider appeared from a crack in that log, and I felt torn between drowning and being bitten by what might have been one of California's dangerous species. In the water, I was at eye level with the creature's thousand piercing orbs. The spider and I both made it to shore, after which I immediately lost track of it. Had it gone into a crack in the log or escaped somewhere along the shore? I didn't know. I knew I couldn't swim back on my own, and I wasn't going to take another chance on the spider. My friend swam back and continued fishing. I spent some time trying to find a solution before resigning myself to a long walk. I spent the rest of the afternoon walking around the rocky shoreline in just my shorts. I stumbled and broke one toe a few hundred yards into this trek and limped the rest of the way in a lot of pain. We taped the toe at home that night and called it a day because that's what we did in California in the 1980s when your medical plan's deductible was $5,000 per person, per incident.

Water, however, continued to pull me. I wanted something from it, even though it seemed uniquely focused on trying to injure or kill me.

After moving to Vancouver, I had a rough afternoon one day and decided to walk to Kitsilano Beach to sort out my mind. When I got there, I kept walking along the shoreline until I got to Granville Island, where I rented a kayak. From the rental dock, I paddled west, working off whatever had been troubling me. The physical workout and soothing movement of the kayak as it rode the Pacific Ocean swells was not a cure, but it was a salve. Finally, worn out and comforted to a degree, I turned back around. I was shocked by how far I'd gone. I could not see the paddle shop or even Granville Island at all. English Bay was a dot on the horizon. I'd been unknowingly paddling out with the tide. There had never been a tide on my childhood lakes, and I was an ocean novice. I paddled back toward shore for hours and did not seem to make any progress at all. I began to fear that I would be pulled out into the Georgia Strait and then into the Pacific Ocean proper and no one would know what had become of me. What felt like hours more passed just to get back into the bay proper, and it took another hour from there to get to the island. At the dock, I could hardly pull myself up and out of the kayak. My legs wobbled on the dock, and my hands shook as I secured the craft to its mooring post.

Once I'd checked in at the office and got my deposit back, I staggered up Kitsilano Beach, found a snack shop, bought a chocolate milk, downed it without taking a breath, moved up under some trees for shade, and fell asleep in my shorts, sandals, and T-shirt. I slept for hours, oblivious to the world.

I still love water. It still draws me. I'm smarter about its dangers now, and it hasn't tried to kill me for decades, but I still go to it hungry. And I leave hungry as well. It draws me but never satisfies me for long. Deep down, it's not really what my soul craves any more than it craves a different square kilometer of sky while I dangle from a parachute. That's not the *yithron* my soul seeks. These things are just Algonquin signs pointing me onward.

Solomon has talked about this phenomenon of unsatisfied hunger before, and he brings it up again in the next verses.

> *16 Then I set my mind to know wisdom and to observe the business that happens on earth, even going without sleep day and night*
>
> *17 I observed all the work of God—that no one can grasp what happens under the sun. Those who strive to know can't grasp it. Even the wise who are set on knowing are unable to grasp it.*
> ECCLESIASTES 8:16–17

This should bring to mind Ecclesiastes chapter three:

> *10 I have observed the task that God has given human beings.*
>
> *11 God has made everything fitting in its time, but has also placed eternity in their hearts, without enabling them to discover what God has done from beginning to end.*
> ECCLESIASTES 3:10–11

In chapter three, people were hungry for something more—the eternity God himself embedded within them—but they were deliberately thwarted in their quest. In chapter eight, people are unable to understand what God is up to: "Even the wise who are set on knowing are unable to grasp it" (8:17b). Again, our deepest inner hungers are thwarted by design. Stubborn insistence on finding satisfaction doesn't work. The deck is stacked against us.

These two passages are important keys to understanding Ecclesiastes. People hunger for something they cannot have, at least not here, in this life, which is the only time and place that Solomon is concerned with. Life under the sun is his focus, and under the sun, humanity's ultimate satisfaction is denied to them. As a result, everything is *hevel*. We are relentlessly hungry for what we cannot have.

I still love canoeing and kayaking, wading and just sitting along a shoreline. My friends will tell you I don't bother much with swimming anymore. But water still calls me, even though it has nearly killed me three times. I love it, but like a good meal, I need it again after I've enjoyed a beautiful time on or around it—there's never been a perfect day on the water that satisfied me for the rest of my days.

What I have learned to do, however, is to enjoy it for what it is: water. It's just a lake, a stream, a river, or an ocean. I listen to the waves and enjoy the way light dances across them like I enjoy music or a sunset. There's always a slight sadness afterward, a wistful feeling, a not-quite-fulfilled feeling, as though there was something out there that I hadn't quite paddled far enough to reach. There was something more out there that I'd missed. If I'd gone around just one more bend in the river or if the sunset had been delayed by just another thirty minutes, I would have discovered something that I've been seeking all these years. I almost had it, then I didn't. I know now that these experiences, this *hevel* feeling, is just another road sign. These experiences are gifts pointing me onward, not a failure to take from the experience something it never had the power to provide. The Algonquin signpost will never be Algonquin itself.

Ecclesiastes 3 tells us that God made life this way on purpose so that we wouldn't be entirely distracted by his creation but instead would always move past it and seek him. Ecclesiastes 8 tells us that people—even the wealthy and wise—who devote themselves to pursuing earthly fulfillment fail. That fulfillment is not here to find. This life is populated with road signs only.

C.S. Lewis again speaks eloquently about this experience.

> *Creatures are not born with desires unless satisfaction for those desires exists. A baby feels hunger: well, there is such a thing as food. A duckling wants to swim: well, there is such a thing as water. . . . If I find in myself a desire which no experience in this world can satisfy, the most probable explanation is that I was made for another world. If none of my earthy pleasures satisfy it, that does not prove that the universe is a fraud. Probably earthly pleasures were never meant to satisfy it, but only to arouse it, to suggest the real thing. . . . I must keep alive in myself the desire for my true country, which I shall not find*

till after death; I must never let it get snowed under or turned aside; I must make it the main object of life to press on to that other country and help others to do the same.[95]

The world is broken on purpose.

Theologians or the religiously conservative might react negatively to that last line. They might blame the brokenness of our world on the fall of humanity and quote passages from Genesis. I'm not talking about the sinful parts of the world. Those clearly come from something that Genesis speaks to. But even that original sin, a sin committed in God's perfect garden, was a sin responding to a certain *hevelness* in life. Adam wasn't fulfilled alone—he needed an Eve. Eve wasn't fulfilled with Adam—she wanted more and tried to find it in a forbidden tree. Adam saw wrong happening right before him and did nothing to prevent it. The world was *hevel*, even in the Garden of Eden. The first people had wanted more than even Eden could provide.

Hevel is part of the world's original design.

Good heavens. What are we supposed to do with that information?

---

95   C.S. Lewis, *Mere Christianity* (New York: Macmillan, 1952), p. 129.

43

GOD TAKES PLEASURE IN YOUR PLEASURE

I WAS FIFTEEN years old when I bought Sheena Easton's album *A Private Heaven*. Her previous album, *Best Kept Secret*, was my introduction to her music. *A Private Heaven*, however, proved to be a problem. The second track on side one of the vinyl was called "Sugar Walls," and it was unabashedly sexual in nature. I might have got away with it in my house by being careful when I played it, except the televangelist Jimmy Swaggart blew up the radio with diatribes against Easton and "Sugar Walls" in particular. Swaggart was more present on TV than radio, and we didn't have TV at home, so the album might still have escaped parental scrutiny, except the following year, the Parents Music Resource Center was founded, a conservative Washington group that created things like Parental Advisory stickers. Al Gore's wife, Tipper, was one of its founders, as was Susan Baker (wife of, at the time, Treasury Secretary James Baker). The group made Easton's album and "Sugar Walls" an early target for their media blitz.

Caught, I had to insist that I never played that track.

"Destroy it," my father said. If Jimmy Swaggart and Washington's conservatives were outraged, then the viny had to be broken into pieces. Unlike the misplaced outrage regarding "Stairway to Heaven," the politicians and televangelists may have had a point regarding "Sugar Walls," but even at fifteen, I recognized that the level of alarm politicians expressed and the actions people took might have been better expended on child poverty or helping victims fleeing abuse than a Scottish singer's racy pop lyrics. Regardless, Easton was the moment's evil, and I had to face the music.

"How about I take a knife to that one track?" I countered. This kind of compromise could sometimes work with my father if he was alone in the debate. Previously, I'd been forbidden to fish on Sundays. In response, I'd done an amateur study of the New Testament and succeeded in making a weak theological argument that my father accepted. Fishing on Sundays was back on the calendar. Likewise, rock music had been banned on the grounds that its beats were rooted in pagan African rituals and were therefore subliminally corrupting. As wth the supposedly satanic background to "Stairway to Heaven," I didn't understand the anti-rock argument either. My father was a big jazz fan, so when I countered that jazz was a music with African roots as well, he relented. Talking back to my mother like that would get you hit, and debating with my father in front of my mother was likewise a recipe for trouble. But sometimes you could reason with the man in private.

A Private Heaven mostly survived Tipper Gore, Susan Baker, and Jimmy Swaggart. The "Sugar Walls" track, however, did not. A sharp knife grooved the vinyl so that it couldn't be played again, which in effect destroyed the album because if you didn't get the needle up in time after the first track, or if you set it back down too early trying to hit the third track just right, you risked damaging the needle. I don't think I ever played the album again. As far as Easton was concerned, I'd won the battle and lost the war.

What did not occur because of that experience was any kind of increased wisdom or discernment regarding musical or other entertainment choices. Whether or not Easton was popularizing female sexual objectification—a kind of audio pornography if you will—or was merely expressing erotic love poetry that maybe wasn't necessary for a fifteen-year-old boy to immerse himself in never came up for thoughtful discussion. Instead, the lesson imparted was that the album was bad and I was bad for buying it. The deeper lesson I absorbed was another proof point that Christianity was a lot of useless rules that made me feel bad and took away fun things and, in this particular case, ruined a perfectly good record. As a result of this episode, vinyl was cut, but nothing changed in my heart or character.

Eventually, I grew up and learned how to think for myself, not just about music and religion but also about how to teach the heart rather than just enforce rules. When my son hit his teenage years, I focused my energy on training his developing brain to think clearly about values, and I avoided censuring his specific choices. As far as I can tell, the process of teaching Jackson values and how to think rather than simply imposing rules to follow has created a young man with, well, values and the ability to think. Those are skills that work across albums, genres, time, and even subjects. He doesn't need me looking over his shoulder if he's got his heart right to begin with.

However, living a life based on rules, and parenting based on rules, is easier. All you must do to personally grow or train others is to make a list of rules, hand them over to your child or employee, enforce them, and measure the resulting guilt with a steady hand and maybe a scowl or two. There's nothing to it really. It's the kind of lazy religion and lazy leadership a low-end AI could do for you. But rules are rigid by nature, and rigid things are brittle. The human heart needs more.

Solomon was also concerned with how to think clearly about the things we should value rather than trying to define rigid rules for us to follow.

> *¹ So I considered all of this carefully, examining all of it: The righteous and the wise and their deeds are in God's hand, along with both love and hate. People don't know anything that's ahead of them.*
>
> ECCLESIASTES 9:1

The Hebrew here is a bit difficult because it does not specify who is loving or hating, and likewise, who is the person or persons being loved or hated. In other words, both the subject and object are missing. Both love and hate await, and that's it for clarity. The vagueness here is intentional because life itself is a very uncertain affair. That's why teaching rules (certain Sheena Easton albums are not allowed) don't produce real lasting change. Rules are limited and limiting. Life, by contrast, is a wild and unruly thing that needs more than rules to navigate its unexpected twists and turns.

What is coming in your future? This verse leaves open many possibilities. Recognizing that uncertainty is important as you think about how to live your life. You may love or hate what comes next. Or others may love or hate you. The original Hebrew even suggests that God will love or hate you or your choices. The point of this ambiguity is to highlight that the future is indefinite—after "consider[ing] all this carefully, examining all of it," that is Solomon's open-ended conclusion.

Remember Solomon's earlier lines about kings trying and failing to be loved by the populace? Do you also remember his comments on wise people who had earned a nation's respect but were forgotten afterward? Solomon investigated all these scenarios and came up with a few proverbs and words of advice along the way, but the bottom line, after having examined "all of it," is that no person knows how their story is going to end. Only God knows.

The reality of this life is that even if we live well (i.e., follow all the rules), our stories might end badly—meaning our lives might end in a car accident, from a disease, or after we've endured some other terrible fate. That is what the words "love" and "hate" are getting at. We might have a happy ending in this life or a terrible one; we "don't know anything that's ahead." Having a clear-headed understanding of that reality is sobering but also helpful. The truth is trustworthy, even if it's uncomfortable. As a result, trying to map out life based on rigid rules won't work in the long run.

Solomon continues to expand on this idea in the following verses.

> *2 Everything is the same for everyone. The same fate awaits the righteous and the wicked, the good and the bad, the pure and the impure, those who sacrifice and those who don't sacrifice. The good person is like the wrongdoer; the same holds for those who make solemn pledges and those who are afraid to swear. 3 This is the sad thing about all that happens under the sun: the same fate awaits everyone.*
>
> ECCLESIASTES 9:2–3A

Put in plain modern terms, everybody dies. I, with my "Sugar Walls" track, and some person three farms over who only listened to the Bill Gaither Trio were both doomed to eventually die in the end. Of course, Solomon's poetry is prettier, but that's his point.

Solomon, however, is not done with this dark turn. He goes on to offer us this grim line next.

Moreover, the human heart is full of evil; people's minds are
full of madness while they are alive, and afterward they die.
ECCLESIASTES 9:3B

Okay. So not only does everybody die, but Solomon's assessment is that humans are pretty terrible beings while they're alive—their hearts are "full of evil"—and then they die. He seems to think that we're all a lost cause. Does this guy hate all of humanity?

It would start to seem so, but then he contradicts himself in the next few verses.

⁴ Whoever is among the living can be certain about this. A
living dog is definitely better off than a dead lion, ⁵ because
the living know that they will die. But the dead know nothing
at all. There is no more reward for them; even the memory of
them is lost. ⁶ Their love and their hate, as well as their zeal,
are already long gone. They will never again have a stake in
all that happens under the sun.
ECCLESIASTES 9:4–6

Uhm. So people are terrible, and then they die, but living people are better than dead people because at least the living people know that they're terrible. Then they die. And everyone will forget them. "Their love and their hate, as well as their zeal," vanish. Whatever happens after the dead are gone is irrelevant to those that have passed because "they will never again have a stake in all that happens under the sun."

Solomon seems to be saying here that being alive is better than being dead for the sole reason that, while you're alive, you can focus on how much of a bad person you are before you wink out and become irrelevant to the planet.

Maybe Solomon's ideal state would be those who had never been born at all.

He did actually come to that conclusion three chapters ago. In chapter six, the remedy to this troubling situation was learning to enjoy the good things in life. Of course, Solomon balanced that out by cautioning against excess and so on, but in the grand scheme of things, he made it clear that if you've already been born, it's a tough gig, so learn to enjoy the things you can.

Now, in chapter nine, his conclusion is the same. Here he talks about uncertainty regarding how life will turn out and the general evil that tends to characterize human thinking. However, the conclusion on how to manage this situation is the same as it was three chapters ago.

> [7] *Go, eat your food joyfully and drink your wine happily because God has already accepted what you do.*
>
> ECCLESIASTES 9:7

God has already accepted us? I thought Solomon said we were evil and had no idea whether love or hate awaited us.

The translation here is to blame for this confusion. I'll lean on my translator's handbook for a clearer presentation of the author's point.

> *So then, eat your food and drink your wine with joy because this is what God intended you to do.*[96]

The Message translation of the Bible might be a bit overly liberal with its treatment of this verse, but it does bring clarity to the mood the Hebrew is trying to relay. Here is how The Message puts it:

> *Seize life! Eat bread with gusto, Drink wine with a robust heart. Oh yes—God takes pleasure in your pleasure!*

Life is *hevel.* What awaits any individual human in this life is a complete mystery. Trying to figure it all out ahead of time is impossible. Things don't turn out the way you think they should. So why did God put us here, then? Solomon's answer to that question is that we are here to enjoy ourselves to the degree that we can, with what is available to us, despite the *hevelness* of life.

For real? Yes, for real. Solomon knows this is an unexpected teaching, so he elaborates on his point.

---

96   Graham S. Ogden and Lynell Zogbo, *A Handbook on Ecclesiastes* (New York: United Bible Societies, 1998), p. 331.

> *⁸ Let your garments always be white; don't run short of oil for your head. ⁹ Enjoy life with your dearly loved spouse all the days of your pointless life that God gives you under the sun—all the days of your pointless life!—because that's your part to play in this life and in your hard work under the sun. ¹⁰ Whatever you are capable of doing, do with all your might because there's no work, thought, knowledge, or wisdom in the grave, which is where you are headed.*
>
> ECCLESIASTES 9:8–10

Remember, it is not a pointless life. It's a *hevel* life. Life is important but fragile, ephemeral, essential, fleeting, and seemingly endlessly repetitive. God's direction amid this *hevel* existence is to enjoy your meal, dress well, keep up basic grooming, and enjoy your spouse because "that's your part to play in this life and in your hard work under the sun."

But shouldn't we always strive, labor, and push toward our life goals and feel guilty about any shortcoming that are exposed along the way? Shouldn't Solomon at least have included hard work in his list of values to help us manage life better?

Solomon anticipated our criticism and offered this response.

> *¹¹ I also observed under the sun that the race doesn't always go to the swift, nor the battle to the mighty, nor food to the wise, nor wealth to the intelligent, nor favor to the knowledgeable, because accidents can happen to anyone. ¹² People most definitely don't know when their time will come. Like fish tragically caught in a net or like birds trapped in a snare, so are human beings caught in a time of tragedy that suddenly falls to them.*
>
> ECCLESIASTES 9:11–12

So enjoy dinner. Wear decent clothes, get together, and spend a nice evening with your spouse. These are things that, in the moment, can be enjoyed. The rest, the future—we just don't know.

Solomon isn't preaching for us to embrace sloth here. He'll talk more in this book about hard work and diligence, but it is important to know that hard work and diligence might pay off or they might not. They definitely won't pay off if we don't at least try, but even if we try, we don't know how things will turn out. You might do nothing useful your whole life and then win a lottery ticket when you most need it. You might work hard and save your money and then trip over a health crisis or financial calamity that you never overcome. Life just isn't reasonable.

Dinner, though, the meal that is right in front of you? It's there. So enjoy it, and do the same with so many of life's other small and immediate but admittedly temporary pleasures. Don't try to find ultimate fulfillment in those things. But do enjoy them when you can. According to Solomon, nothing is better in this life under the sun.

There is a lot of truth in these words. The poor or the super wealthy may have different qualities of clothes, fineness of foods, or sophistication of spouses, but they enjoy the same things. Shrimp used to be the poor man's food, as was lobster, and things with sugar were the domain of only the elite classes. Now shrimp is quite expensive, lobster is listed on the menu as costing that dreaded market price, and sugar is classed as junk food. The irony is that, in seasons past, the poor man eating shrimp might have looked down on his meal, kids on Canada's East Coast were mocked for their lobster sandwiches as conclusive proof of their poverty,[97] and the rich rejoiced in their rare access to sugarcane products. Solomon isn't making an argument in favor of any particular menu item. His wisdom ignores the variability of era-dependent tastes and styles, and he calls us to focus on the present—what we can enjoy now, not what might come later.

Can we take action on that today? Yes, we can.

Will we? That's up to you.

Note that Solomon here is not talking about the kind of eating that is just endless craving in mind-numbing service to sugar or other addictions. Likewise, if your fashion sense is a shopping addiction or a better-than-my-neighbor exercise in superiority and pride, that's not what Solomon is getting at either. And clearly, Solomon isn't talking about alcoholism when he says you should savor your drink.

A mechanic may value an excellent pair of coveralls. A ballet dancer may have a pair of tights they prefer. If you're going to a barn dance and have just

---

97   I owe my second editor, Christine, for this local insight.

the right calico dress for the occasion, wear it! Enjoy your food, drink, and clothing, and find joy in your spouse. These are things that God intended for you to enjoy. Some of us who are addicted or overrun with a hunger to constantly accumulate or consume or best our neighbor need to learn how to simply enjoy experiences beyond any competition or runaway compulsion. I take the trend toward minimalism and other forms of aesthetic simplicity to be modern movements seeking to right the wrongs of human excess. The drive can be noble. For some, properly managed, it's a movement in the same direction Solomon is counselling as long as it doesn't become an aesthetic trap as controlling as its opposite.

I'll quote another bit from Sinéad O'Connor, this time the title of a song from her second album: "I Do Not Want What I Haven't Got." That's a good mental place to aim for. Unfortunately, Solomon's ultimate point defeats O'Connor's aspiration. We'll never achieve her ideal state: life will never relinquish its inherent *hevel* qualities. It is, however, true that the closer we get to enjoying what we have versus being consumed by what we don't, the better off we are. And that enjoyment is best focused on the basics: food, drink, clothing, and relationships.

As The Message translation puts it: "God takes pleasure in your pleasure." I don't know about you, but with my early religious training, I still find that to be a startling teaching. I was pretty sure God didn't want me to enjoy anything in my life. In fact, he wanted the opposite. He created things specifically for me to enjoy them. So it's worth paraphrasing The Message's translation: God doesn't take pleasure in the accumulation of your rules— God takes pleasure in your pleasure.

Learn to enjoy the good things that life makes available to you as a gift from God. It really is true: he takes pleasure in your pleasure. This isn't a new rule to follow. This is your maker trying to establish within you a healthy relationship with reality.

44

ENJOY LIFE BUT GET YOUR WORK DONE AS WELL

IMAGINE SOLOMON, AT this point in his work, still seated at his royal desk in his limestone and cedar palace. He is looking over Jerusalem's hills, rooftops, and gardens, wondering how to get his final points across this late in his writing. Despite God blessing him with great wisdom, Solomon made a grand mess of his life. The problem was not that he did not know what was wise but that he did not do what was wise. He knows this now, experientially as well as intellectually, and he wants to communicate a way to live differently. What will connect with the people he wants to reach?

Imagine further that the door opens and a servant comes in with fresh water or wine chilled in a deep cellar. The servant is in the latter months of her first pregnancy. Solomon doesn't notice. He accepts the refreshment with his mind elsewhere. The servant leaves. The king has his mind on himself. This is his work and his attempt to leave a legacy that will help others avoid his mistakes.

Sweat beads on his neck and trickles down his back. The king takes hold of the stone cup and drinks the cool beverage drawn up from deep cellars where coolness still lurks. The land of Israel is a mercilessly hot place in the summer months, and he enjoys the refreshment, reminding himself of his own words to enjoy these small things.

But what about his kingship? How can he enjoy himself when he had so many opportunities in life and foolishly squandered them with sin and bad choices? If only there had been someone to set him straight. A humble, simple man who could have guided his kingship.

The aged king shakes his head. That wouldn't have helped. Kings like him don't listen. He starts writing.

> *[13] I also observed the following example of wisdom under the sun—it impressed me greatly: [14] There was a small town with only a few residents. A mighty king came against it, surrounded it, and waged a terrible war against it. [15] Now there lived in that town a poor but wise man who saved everyone by his wisdom. But no one remembered that poor man.*
>
> ECCLESIASTES 9:13–15

It's unclear in our English translations whether Solomon is referring to an actual historical event or is instead describing a fictional parable-like scenario. In Hebrew, the nature of these verses is likewise not certain, but the language does tilt toward a parable versus a historical account. Additionally, verse fifteen could also be translated to say that the wise man did not save the town. Instead, he could have saved it, "[b]ut no one [remembered to listen] to that poor wise man."[98]

> *[16] So I thought, Wisdom is better than might, but the wisdom of commoners is despised and their words aren't heeded.*
>
> ECCLESIASTES 9:16

I'm sure we can all relate to Solomon's point. The powers that be often don't listen the way we wish they would. Solomon goes on to say,

> *[17] The calm words of the wise are better heeded than the racket caused by a ruler among fools.*
>
> ECCLESIASTES 9:17

It is a good thing to listen and respond well to wise words, but as the previous verse describes, those words are often ignored.

---

98   Adapted from Brown, *Ecclesiastes: Interpretation*, p. 97 and from Longman, *Book of Ecclesiastes*, pp. 234–235.

One of Solomon's accomplishments as a ruler was the accumulation of a terrifying arsenal of chariots, warhorses, and charioteers. In the tenth century BCE, this was the pinnacle of military might. First Kings 10 tells us that Solomon had fourteen thousand such chariots and twelve thousand horsemen to run them and fill out the supporting cavalry. He imported his horses from Egypt, one of the premier horse breeders in the ancient world. Solomon did this despite an injunction in Deuteronomy 17 against doing those exact things. With this backdrop in place, his next verse is particularly poignant.

> [18] *Wisdom is better than weapons of war, but one incompetent person destroys much good.*
>
> ECCLESIASTES 9:18

Solomon had no excuse for violating God's direction and amassing his overkill arsenal from a forbidden source. God told Solomon, possibly in the months before penning Ecclesiastes, that his actions in this regard would cost him his legacy and the future of his kingdom.[99] After Solomon's death, but because of his life, the land of Israel fractured into two competing and sometimes warring factions. The chariots, warhorses, and horsemen Solomon accumulated were eventually used to divide Solomon's kingdom and kill fellow Jews.

This brings us to the end of Ecclesiastes chapter nine, but Solomon did not originally divide his work into chapters. So as we flow into chapter ten, the king continues with his impassioned theme.

> [1] *As dead flies spoil the perfumer's oil,*
> *so a little folly outweighs wisdom and honor.*
>
> ECCLESIASTES 10:1

God gave Solomon wisdom, but Solomon deliberately immersed himself in folly anyway. It doesn't take much foolishness to ruin a life, and Solomon bathed in it. He was very clear on what he had done to ruin his life and nation.

---

99   1 Kings 11:10–12.

² The mind of the wise tends toward the right,
but the mind of the fool toward the left.

ECCLESIASTES 10:2

Solomon is not making a modern-day comment about liberal versus conservative politics. His point is that the difference between wisdom and foolishness is obvious. They are opposites of each other. The king had no excuse. God gave him wisdom, and he acted foolishly anyway. An honest confessor, Solomon records his thoughts this way:

³ Fools lack all sense even when they walk down the street;
they show everyone that they are fools.

ECCLESIASTES 10:3

Imagine the king having written that line and pausing to take another drink. His face must have burned with shame. He might have been the king, but everyone who saw him knew he had lived like a fool. Just look at his seven hundred weddings and three hundred mistresses. He was a walking advertisement for, at best, ridiculousness. Fine robes and bodyguards only impress fellow fools. Perhaps not even them.

But what does this king think a subject ought to do when the head of state is such a fool? Here is Solomon's advice:

⁴ If a ruler's temper rises against you,
don't leave your post, because calmness alleviates great offences.

ECCLESIASTES 10:4

Hmm. When dealing with a foolish ruler—king, boss, supervisor—stay calm. Remaining calm doesn't fix offences, but it can help manage them. It can dial them down. In the words of a British World War II slogan, "Keep Calm and Carry On."

Similarly, therapists, marriage counsellors, and career coaches often describe how we need to respond to challenging situations rather than react to them. At times, that work is an uphill struggle, but it's the good path. At many stages of his career, Solomon was a foolish king, but he knew that a calm approach would have worked better during his reign than more aggressive alternatives.

I've had personal experience with this dynamic as both an employee and employer. I remember several occasions when I grew angry with someone on my staff over some imagined offence, and that person responded with a wise calm. Those individuals ignored my tone and the specific words I used, and instead spoke calmly into my tension. As a result, we were able to calmly resolve the issue at hand without greatly offending both sides.

When I've been the foolish one—the impatient or misunderstanding manager—I've been very grateful for these wise staff members. Their actions not only prevented me from escalating my error but, more significantly, made me trust them more because of the calm wisdom they demonstrated. As a result, those relationships blossomed. In direct response to their proven maturity, I've made sure to find or make future opportunities for those individuals. Those moments of unnecessary tension—which I'd caused, to my shame—were the key to discovering a staff member's depths. I've used my own failures in these moments, and their wise responses, as evidence to support their later promotions. My mistakes became a gift to us both, but only because calm wisdom prevailed. Ecclesiastes 10:4 is gold for employee-employer relations.

Remember that pregnant servant who supplied Solomon with his cool drink on a hot day? Imagine that she returns to the room, removes his empty glass, replaces it with another, then quietly departs again. Solomon remains oblivious. He's a king. He's used to servants coming and going. He ignores her.

He considers just the page before him and then continues writing.

> [5] *There's an evil that I have seen under the sun: the kind of mistake that comes from people in power.*
>
> ECCLESIASTES 10:5

Oh, this is interesting. Solomon is about to get confessional again. As king, he sees a unique kind of mistake that people in power make.

⁶ Fools are appointed to high posts, while the rich sit in lowly positions. ⁷ I have seen slaves on horseback, while princes walk on foot like slaves.

ECCLESIASTES 10:6–7

Perhaps those in power sometimes make bad decisions due to nepotism, bribes, misguided favors, or poor talent spotting. As a result, a nation, company, committee, or volunteer group can wind up with apparent boneheads in charge.

Instead of building on this point, Solomon appears to change topics abruptly. However, he will return to this idea of bad leadership momentarily. First, though, he circles back to the generally unpredictable nature of life.

⁸ Whoever digs a pit may fall into it,
and whoever breaks through a wall
may be bitten by a snake.
⁹ Whoever quarries stones may be injured by them;
whoever splits logs
may be endangered by them.

ECCLESIASTES 10:8–9

Digging pits, opening walls, quarrying stones, and splitting logs are all legitimate but physically demanding activities. Some commentators think that the phrase "whoever breaks through a wall" is referring to thievery, but it could also be referring to renovations. Also note that the other three activities are wholesome and useful: for example, pits can be dug for burying waste, building naturally cold cellars, storing water, and so on. Given the positive qualities of the other items, Solomon likely intended for us to read the entire list as positive. But all these productive activities come with risks. Injuries can occur. Sitting at home and doing nothing is safer, but things won't get done if we just sit at home. We wouldn't even have a home to sit in if someone hadn't put in the effort to build it to begin with.

The remedy for these dangers is a bit of proper preparation.

10 If an axe is dull
> *and one doesn't sharpen it first,*
> *then one must exert more force.*
> *It's profitable to be skillful and wise.*

11 If a snake bites before it's charmed,
> *then there's no profit*
> *for the snake charmer.*

12 Words from a wise person's mouth are beneficial,
> *but fools are devoured by their own lips.*

ECCLESIASTES 10:10–12

Okay, so sharpen the axe before splitting the logs. The implied message here is that skill and wisdom are helpful throughout life. Digging pits, renovating homes, and quarrying stones are productive activities that can likewise be safer and easier with some thinking and planning ahead.

In the same way, taking some time to think and plan before speaking is a good idea. There isn't a name for lumberjacks who don't sharpen their axe before swinging it or for snake charmers who don't bother to charm the snake before working with it. There is, however, a name for the sort of person who talks without thinking. That person is called a fool, and they wind up "devoured by their own lips." Solomon builds on this theme in the following three verses.

13 Fools start out talking foolishness
> *and end up speaking awful nonsense.*

14 Fools talk too much!
> *No one knows what will happen;*
> *no one can say what will happen in the future.*

15 The hard work of fools tires them out
> *because they don't even know the way to town!*

ECCLESIASTES 10:13–15

Solomon started this section discussing bad leadership and then moved on to matters of conscientious work, such as sharpening an axe before using it. Next, he drew a parallel between those who plan their work poorly and those who plan their words poorly, defining that careless talker as a fool. Now, having spent a few verses expounding on the behavior of fools, Solomon returns to the subject that started this section: lousy leadership.

> [16] *Too bad for you, land,*
> *whose king is a boy*
> *and whose princes feast in the morning.*
>
> [17] *Happy is the land*
> *whose king is dignified*
> *and whose princes feast at the right time for energy,*
> *not for drunkenness.*
>
> [18] *Through laziness, the roof sags;*
> *through idle hands, the house leaks.*
>
> ECCLESIASTES 10:16–18

Householders must keep their roofs repaired or they will sag and leak. Likewise, kings—and by extension, parents, business owners, team coaches, and so on—need to tend to the basics of their profession, or their enterprise will fail. As any parent knows, you can't start raising your children when they're sixteen.

Solomon has counselled for us to embrace wisdom and the joy of a good meal well eaten, but here he reminds us that everything has its time and place. Feasting is not how you should start your day. You're supposed to enjoy yourself "at the right time for energy, not for drunkenness." Solomon's injunction to learn life's simple pleasures is not a new more modest hedonism. Instead, he directs us to mindfully enjoy the good things in life while still maintaining a sense of responsibility for the work that life requires of us.

So enjoy lunch, but fix your roof as well. Life is not a one-or-the-other affair—both matter.

About that pregnant servant—we'll come back to her. She's still busy about the palace, but her presence will finally intrude upon Solomon's awareness and inform a subtle change in his material. More on her to come.

45

ENJOY LIFE BUT STILL MIND THE BUDGET

A FEW YEARS before Ed and his construction project, my summer jobs were largely with local farmers. Here was my routine that hot California summer: I worked the night shift nursing job, ate breakfast at home, and then, depending on who had work for me, either went off to the fields (soybeans or rice) or the orchards (walnut, almond, or prune plums). After work, I went home for dinner and a shower, and then went back to the night shift job. One of my memories from that season is taking a frozen jug of water with me in the morning that would be empty by the end of the day. Between evaporation and sweat, a gallon-sized block of ice did not last in that heat.

At the time, though, it wasn't the round-the-clock work schedule or the heat or the water consumption that captured my attention the most but one specific farmer. He might have been the richest man I've ever worked for. He certainly had one of the biggest swimming pools I've ever seen.

I never dipped so much as a toe into that pool, and I don't think he did either. It was for his preteen daughters.

However, even as a teenager, I could tell that the pool was an act of landscaping in lieu of fatherhood. He was known to spend no time with the girls, he expressed no interest in them, and while they seemed to enjoy the pool, you'd have been hard-pressed to catch any hint of a family connection among the group. When they were around, he didn't even give them orders. They were invisible to him.

Some parents see their children as problems and solve those problems with neglect or abuse. Others treat money as the answer and buy their children off with things or activities, but the effect is the same. Maybe the spoiled have it worse. I imagine that when a lack of love is masked by an excess of stuff, it can be hard to sort out your own head later.

The man's later divorce and alienation from his children should not have come as a surprise. It seemed obvious to me, even as a silent but observant teenage laborer, that this wasn't going to end well, no matter how big the guy's pool was. He held the view that work and money were the solution to everything. I wonder if he ever had a change of heart after reality intervened.

Solomon says something in this next verse, though, that at first sounds like he agrees with that rich farmer's priorities.

> *¹⁹ Feasts are made for laughter,*
> *wine cheers the living,*
> *and money answers everything.*
> ECCLESIASTES 10:19

We should be sufficiently into the groove of Solomon's writing style here to understand the bit about feasts and wine, but "money answers everything"? Really? Would we expect Jesus, Paul, or someone of that caliber to say such a thing? This seems like the attitude of a secular Wall Street type—or my occasional California employer—rather than a truth presented in scripture.

As with most verses in the Bible, context matters. What came before this?

> *¹⁸ Through laziness, the roof sags;*
> *through idle hands, the house leaks.*
> ECCLESIASTES 10:18

Oh. I see. Solomon is not selling the farmer's message that money takes precedence over family or that money can serve in lieu of relationships. He's offering a full list of ingredients for how to navigate a complex and broken world. In that context, money is a useful tool.

To be clear on this point, let's look at the flow of the message. Here is what he's communicating:

- See how nations can fall into disorder when those in power feast and drink at the wrong time (10:16–17).

- So get your act together when it comes to basic household maintenance (10:18).

- Enjoy the food and drink we've been talking about (10:19a).

- And remember, you have to pay for all of this stuff (10:19b), which takes us back to the point about getting our act together.

All Solomon is saying here is that, at the scale of both nations and households, we need to stay on top of our businesses, enjoy life, and keep the finances in order. All three are important. That's good advice.

I could offer ten pages of commentary and input from my translator's handbook on how to tease these few verses apart and mine them for additional micro-nuggets of linguistic or contextual jewels, but the bottom line across all sources comes down to this three-part conclusion:

- Do your work.

- Enjoy life.

- Keep on top of the budget.

Whatever role we play in life—as politicians, managers, farmers, parents, spouses, and so on—we are at a high risk of poorly balancing these competing demands on our time and attention. We enjoy life and forget to fix the roof or balance the budget. We work and watch the money closely while our lives themselves fall apart. I like the image of a tightrope walker. One second, the performer is leaning a bit too far to the left; the next, they're too far right—constant adjustments are required.

It is interesting to note that for those who live their lives and do their work in the public eye (for example, politicians, bosses, and celebrities), the pressure to get it right is the same as for the rest of us. They too must make constant adjustments. Their challenge, however, is that their failures are subjected to extra layers of scrutiny, criticism, and publication. It goes with the job, so perhaps we're not too worked up about that point, but Solomon, ever the practical man in helping us navigate a broken world, cautions us to not be careless when we think about this detail. Here is how he puts it:

²⁰ Don't curse a king even in private; don't curse the rich in your bedroom, because a bird could carry your voice; some winged creature could report what you said!

ECCLESIASTES 10:20

Solomon is not saying this out of sympathy for the rich, who make mistakes. He's simply being pragmatic and advising us to protect ourselves from the fury of those in power. He's going so far as to warn us about even gossiping with ourselves, alone, in private, in bed. Once again, Solomon here is just offering practical real-world advice rather than purist ideals. If you don't say foolish things you won't pay a foolish price.

At this point, imagine Solomon putting down his reed pen and asking himself, "Where do I go from here?"

He knows there are people who will err too far on the side of work and money while other folks will spend all their time on pleasure and fail to be responsible. Should he say more about this, or would he be overstating his point?

He doesn't have a real editor to consult. He's the king. He answers to himself.

He doesn't have a word processing program that tells him his word count. Even if he had, he wouldn't have had a publication plan to suggest when he should start to wrap things up. The copyists of his day were called scribes, and they'd make copies of whatever he told them to produce, regardless of its length. Again, he was the king, and people did what he told them to do.

Solomon did have the Holy Spirit guiding him, but that was an invisible force in his life. He didn't even have a theology of the Holy Spirit yet, as he was writing a thousand years before Jesus arrived and the language of the Holy Spirit showed up in the book of Acts. So Solomon probably felt a little lost at this stage of his writing.

How do you conclude a book about the *hevelness* of life and the unending, inevitably unsatisfiable quest to find *yithron*—meaning and lasting benefit—in this *hevel* of a life? How do you wrap that up in a nice literary bow?

I picture Solomon settling into bed that night with the sleepy sounds of the palace and the city drifting into his room. The buildings were made of stone, and the windows would have been glassless and open to let cool night air in. Even the king heard everything. He tossed and turned. He may or may not have had one of his seven hundred wives with him or, if not one of them, then maybe one of his three hundred concubines. He's made a ridiculous mess of things, and though working on Ecclesiastes gives him some satisfaction, the reality is that he's an old man with many regrets. At this stage of his life, his whole situation—and that of his vast family—is clearly a wreck. Sleep that night probably did not come easily.

Imagine that when he got up the next morning, he had his morning refreshment, attended to whatever administrative or leadership duties the day required, and then returned to his writing table. And the question remained: where should he go from here? How should he wrap up this book?

He sighs. He picks up his reed pen, dips it in ink, and starts to write.

> [1] *Send your bread out on the water because, in the course of time, you may find it again.* [2] *Give a portion to seven people, even to eight: you don't know what disaster may come upon the land.* [3] *If clouds fill up, they will empty out rain on the earth. If a tree falls, whether to the south or to the north, wherever it falls, there it will lie.*
>
> ECCLESIASTES 11:1–3

Perhaps he paused, looked at those words briefly, and thought, "What do I mean by that?"

He wouldn't have said, "What is God trying to say through me?" because the theology for that kind of clarity is still far in the future. Plus, Solomon repeatedly stated that his focus in this book is very much on this world.

"So, what am I trying to say?" he murmurs.

The original Hebrew suggests that Solomon may be focusing on trading here. The land of Israel has an extensive coastline along the Mediterranean, which supports this idea. Likewise, various Middle Eastern proverbs from the region, both ones from Solomon's time and from later dates, use a similar image of "bread upon the waters" to refer to trade. So is Solomon following up his previous advice on money management by recommending that people invest in trade?

The Hebrew could also be referring to charitable donations. Verse two makes the case for this interpretation even stronger, referencing disasters and a what-goes-around-comes-around ethos.

Whether Solomon is counselling us to invest in a business or donate to a charity (or both), verse three nicely rounds out these ideas by referencing how life is full of inevitable and unpredictable but final things. When a tree falls in a particular place, that's where it falls. It doesn't change its mind later and move to a more comfortable spot. Time flows in one direction. Some things work out, and some don't, so diversify and be generous.

The banker in me gets him. Solomon dips his reed in ink again and adds another line.

> [4] *Those who watch the wind blow will never sow, and those who observe the clouds will never reap.*
>
> ECCLESIASTES 11:4

Hmm. Got it. This fits Solomon's previous advice on managing money prudently. If you always hesitate to invest your time, money, or effort into anything, you'll never get anything done. This is the forward-looking version of Solomon's previous instruction to tend to a leaky roof.

He pauses again and then hears someone approach.

Remember that pregnant servant? Imagine that she walks into the room once more. It's her first time in his chamber today. In Solomon's era (and even a thousand years later in Jesus's day), it was normal for girls to be engaged at twelve and married at thirteen or fourteen. A sixteen-year-old maiden was nearly a spinster, and a twenty-year-old single woman had serious social-status problems to contend with.

So imagine this servant as a very young woman. Picture her refilling Solomon's cup, padding about the room in open-toed sandals or closed-toe slippers, her belly showing and probably becoming uncomfortable, yet she keeps working.

Solomon finally notices. The man knows a thing or two about pregnancies—at least, from the male perspective. With a thousand bedmates and no birth control, the number of children he conceived would probably be a crime in the modern era.

This isn't creepy Solomon anymore, though. Instead, this chastened old man understands how badly he's blown it in life. He's like that farmer I used to work for but after his wife and children left him. How did you fix a lifetime of those kinds of mistakes?

In chapter ten, he admonished his readers not to follow his example but to learn to enjoy life with one dearly loved spouse. He now understands too late that marriage is a quality, not a quantity, thing. And you can't substitute things for the time that relationships require. I used to tell my son that it takes ten years to build a ten-year friendship. Likewise, my wife and I have commented to one another that it takes twenty-five years of marriage to find the growth and oases that only come after consciously growing a marriage for a quarter century. Starting over is sometimes necessary, but starting over restarts that twenty-five-year clock. With so many weddings and affairs to attend to, I wonder if Solomon ever got past even the one-year stage of a relationship.

So, the old man who has been talking about investments and money management sees his servant and finally notices she's pregnant. That pregnancy humbles him. He might be the king and the father of countless children, but he doesn't really understand much about the miracle of life or the social environment that a new life ought to be born into. He didn't have a healthy model in his own childhood to learn from and did no better himself.

And so he returns to his page.

> [5] *Just as you don't understand what the life-breath does in the fetus inside a pregnant woman's womb, so you can't understand the work of God, who makes everything happen.*
> ECCLESIASTES 11:5

A smile crosses the old man's face. He suddenly realizes how he wants to end this book. Part of his conclusion is that we need to accept that, no matter how wise we become, we'll never fully understand the work of God. Even Solomon, who was the king, understands that it is God "who makes everything happen."

His smile broadens further when another thought strikes him. He keeps smiling as he writes his next line down.

> [6] *Scatter your seed in the morning, and in the evening don't be idle because you don't know which will succeed, this one or that, or whether both will be equally good.*
> ECCLESIASTES 11:6

I can imagine Solomon wanting to laugh out loud at that line. What he's done is mixed investment diversification language with a sly commentary on sex and conception. The Hebrew idiom at play here—the "scatter your seed" bit—is pure sex. But in context, he's also referring to farming and, by extension, investments as well. Solomon knows that every bit of bedtime fun doesn't produce an heir, and every investment doesn't pay off, just as not every seed planted in soil grows a viable shoot. He's mixed it all together here and had a little fun with language. Sometimes, a writer can have fun with his writing, regardless of how badly dour commentators mangle his irreverent flow later. If we haven't learned to read Solomon's unorthodox and occasionally irreverent approach to inspecting the world by now, we haven't been paying attention.

He continues writing.

> [7] *Sweet is the light, and it's pleasant for the eyes to see the sun.*
> [8] *Even those who live many years should take pleasure in them all. But they should be mindful that there will also be many dark days. Everything that happens is pointless.*
> ECCLESIASTES 11:7–8

Not pointless. You know that by now. Everything is *hevel*: temporary, uncertain, ephemeral, transitory, mysterious. But large parts of it, as he points out here, are also enjoyable.

Solomon is telling us to live life while we have it. The sun shines every day, and every day it offers opportunities for pleasant experiences. Learn to notice those things. Learn to take pleasure in them. Solomon tells us that "those who live many years should take pleasure in them all."

So if we take issue with Solomon having a little fun mixing investment advice with sex idioms, Solomon's counsel is to relax. Don't follow his hedonistic example, but don't be a prude either.

The young servant leaves the room, and Solomon hears her go. His eyes are on the page, but he hears her leave, and she remains on his mind. In her absence, he writes a line just for her and young people like her.

⁹ Rejoice, young person, while you are young! Your heart should make you happy in your prime. Follow your heart's inclinations and whatever your eyes see, but know this: God will call you to account for all of these things.

ECCLESIASTES 11:9

In other words, go and live your life while you're alive. Have fun. Take pleasure in the joys you find in the world. But don't go overboard and ruin your life. Pleasure itself is *hevel*, so don't expect to find *yithron*—lasting benefit—in these things. But rejoice in them for what they do offer. They are like sunshine on your face. It feels good. Don't burn your face, but do enjoy the sun while it shines.

Youth, however, can be a time of high anxiety for many. Some families are better than others at preparing the young to step into adulthood. Even with good preparation, early adulthood is fraught with new, frightening uncertainties. Will I get into the right school or get a good job? Will I be able to support myself? Where should I live? Should I get married, and if so, will I make good choices? How will children fit into my future?

When I was young, I heard the phrase "honeymoons are wasted on the young" and thought that was such a weird statement. Now in my mid-fifties, I get it. In retrospect, I was a ball of insecurity, uncertainty, and stress as I was trying to figure out my place in the world and who I would spend my life with. Solomon's advice to me, then, and to people like me, is:

¹⁰ Remove anxiety from your heart, banish pain from your body, because youth and the dawn of life are pointless too.

ECCLESIASTES 11:10

Hevel. It's all *hevel*. Given that truth, enjoy the moment, each moment, for what it offers. Don't worry about the rest.

PART NINE:

CONCLUDING THOUGHTS

46

LIVE CONSCIOUSLY BECAUSE LIFE IS SHORT AND YOUTH IS TEMPORARY

LET'S RETURN TO our creative image of Solomon writing in his palace. As he penned Ecclesiastes chapter eleven, we left him alone in a room, jotting down a few words of wisdom for the young mom-to-be who had just refilled his water jug and left him in peace.

However, these chapter divisions did not appear in Solomon's original manuscript or in any other copies of it for over a thousand years afterward.

With this in mind, let's go back to that scene. The pregnant young servant has just exited Solomon's writing chamber. The king has shared some words of wisdom, colorfully expressed some ideas regarding his key themes of *hevel* and *yithron*, and reminded his young readers to enjoy life but to also keep God in mind in all that they do.

Now imagine that the room goes quiet. Solomon has just penned some good advice, but as he and we are all too aware, it was not advice he followed in his youth or even middle age. Solomon's writing chamber had no ticking clocks or hum of appliances to break the silence. Perhaps somewhere in the palace, dishes clattered or voices rose briefly. Maybe a cart passed on the street outside. But inside Solomon's chamber, the king is still. The combined weight of his wisdom and regret sits heavily upon him.

Slowly, he dips his reed in the ink jar again. As he starts the next lines, the servant remains in his mind, but now he writes to his younger self as well. There's a lump in Solomon's throat where regret swells. That regret spreads and tightens his chest. His bony wrists tremble. He closes his eyes, perhaps utters a silent prayer, and then begins writing again, a message to the future but one also to his unhearing past.

> *¹ Remember your creator in your prime,*
> *before the days of trouble arrive,*
> *and those years, about which you'll say, "I take no pleasure*
> *in these"—*
>
> ECCLESIASTES 12:1

Oh, how the old king wishes his words could go backward in time and not just forward. How he wishes that his proud young self could read those words and have the willpower to act on them, make different choices, and invest his wealth and wisdom in things that would mean something later. Instead, he squandered both his wealth and his wisdom. As a result, though, he now has tales to tell and lessons to impart, so God is revealed as sovereign over even a king's failures. Still, Solomon wishes his life could have been a positive example, not an object lesson on what not to do.

He sighs. He cannot write backward through time, so he'll send a message forward. He wants the young to understand that even youth is *hevel*—temporary, fleeting, important but ephemeral, and oh-so fragile. Breath. It's all breath.

So he tells the young to remember their Creator:

> *¹ Remember your creator in your prime,*
> *before the days of trouble arrive,*
> *and those years, about which you'll say, "I take no pleasure*
> *in these"—*
>
> *² before the sun and the light grow dark, the moon and the*
> *stars too,*
> *before the clouds return after the rain;*
>
> *³ on the day when the housekeepers tremble and the strong*
> *men stoop;*
> *when the women who grind stop working because they're*
> *so few,*
> *and those who look through the windows grow dim;*

⁴ when the doors to the street are shut,
  when the sound of the mill fades,
  the sound of the bird rises,
  and all the singers come down low;

⁵ when people are afraid of things above
  and of terrors along the way;
  when the almond tree blanches, the locust droops,
  and the caper-berry comes to nothing;
  when the human goes to the eternal abode,
  with mourners all around in the street;

⁶ before the silver cord snaps and the gold bowl shatters;
  the jar is broken at the spring and the wheel is crushed at
  the pit;

⁷ before dust returns to the earth as it was before
  and the life-breath returns to God who gave it.

⁸ Perfectly pointless, says the Teacher, everything is pointless.

ECCLESIASTES 12:1–8

I'm going to guess that most readers got Solomon's basic point at their first reading, even if they didn't completely grasp all the symbolism buried in the king's poetry. When not only the sun goes dark but the moon and stars do as well (12:2), it is the end of the world. The poetic images in the following verses express the same general idea. Whether Solomon means the actual end of the world or simply the end of one person's world—their sickbed, their death, or their funeral—the basic point remains the same: things come to an end, and then you face God, so get things right with him before it's too late.

But when is it too late? Should we wait literally until our deathbed before getting right with God? No, of course not. This section started with the instruction to remember God in our youth, and Ecclesiastes has made the point repeatedly that chasing other things just makes the *hevelness* of life worse. "Don't do what I did" is Solomon's point in plain confessional language.

The king, however, is a bit of a rascal. Can we say that about an author of scripture three thousand or so years after his death? The historical fiction writer in me wants to call that an anachronism—a bit of modern language inappropriately inserted into an ancient scene.

But he was a character that today we might call a bad boy. A thousand women, wild parties, foreign love affairs, and an unending supply of money will tend to create that persona. Someone raised in prison won't suddenly have polished social graces when freed in old age. Likewise, Solomon may be a chastened man, but there's inevitably a bit of his old self still found in his mannerisms and character.

However, Solomon wasn't just a bad boy. He was also an academic, respected in areas as diverse as zoology, botany, architecture, literature, engineering, and other disciplines.

Put the bad boy and the scholar together in one figure, give him a pen, and you wind up with a guy who, while wrapping up a book on the meaning of life, gets a little cheeky, even comedic, when describing the otherwise serious and depressing matter of death.

This is where most modern readers get the basic idea of these verses but miss the nuances embedded in the poetry. Let's look at what this old king has done with these verses.

> *¹ Remember your creator in your prime,*
> *before the days of trouble arrive,*
> *and those years, about which you'll say, "I take no pleasure*
> *in these"*
>
> *² before the sun and the light grow dark, the moon and the*
> *stars too,*
> *before the clouds return after the rain;*
>
> *³ on the day when the housekeepers tremble and the strong*
> *men stoop;*
> *when the women who grind stop working because they're*
> *so few,*
> *and those who look through the windows grow dim;*
>
> ECCLESIASTES 12:1–3

Solomon is doing a whole bunch of things at once in this passage. I'll refer you to the libraries of commentaries available in quality bookstores to unpack everything the wily writer is up to here. To keep things simple, I will track only one course through Solomon's poetry. My take will not be perfect because a perfect take would be complete and exhaustive—and exhausting. Like a joke, if you must explain it too much, it's not funny anymore. So we'll keep it simple.

One way of reading Solomon's imagery here is to imagine a person as a house—a very old house nearing the end of its serviceable years. In this house, the maintenance crew of housekeepers and strong men are falling behind in their work. They are trembling and stooping. Things are not working as well as they should. Chores are piling up. The years are starting to show. Remember, the house here symbolizes a person. Any reader past forty is probably beginning to feel their years more acutely than they had in previous decades. Things don't heal as quickly or bounce back as fast. After fifty, I feel it even more. The experience of aging is relative, but it remains one directional, and my internal maintenance crew is definitely slowing down.

Strong men in this context might also be referring to literal strength—a weaker back, arms, and legs. The fun of this poetic imagery is you can play with the images yourself—you're allowed. That's part of the interactive nature of poetry.

Continuing with this narrow image of the house as a person, think of the grinding women in this house as a person's teeth. They don't work like they used to because there are so few of them. Remember, this is before modern dental hygiene, crowns, cavity fillings, and dentures. People would pull a tooth and hope it didn't get infected. That was about it for dentistry. Being king didn't improve the king's dental situation in the tenth century BCE. Solomon, sitting at his desk, was probably largely toothless at this point. He was not exactly the dashing figure he'd like to remember himself as.

In this house, those who look through the windows can only see the outside world dimly. There were no eyeglasses or cataract surgeries in Solomon's day. The man probably had to hold his paper at arm's length or keep his face pressed close to the page while he wrote. His eyesight was becoming a problem.

⁴ when the doors to the street are shut,
when the sound of the mill fades,
the sound of the bird rises,
and all the singers come down low;

ECCLESIASTES 12:4

In ancient Israel, houses mostly had single doors. They might have had a front and a back door, and so on, but all of them would have been single doors. In Hebrew, this verse is explicitly referencing the double doors to the street—in other words, ears. With fading hearing, it becomes hard to hear the sounds of industry (the mill). In the same way, the pleasing sound of singers fades, but frustratingly, chirping birds will still wake you up in the morning. We could go on at length about the clever accuracy of this observation: hearing loss affects various pitches differently, and high pitches, in particular, can become acutely irritating while lower- and mid-range pitches are missing. I suspect that Solomon is speaking from experience here. The more a person's hearing fades, the more startling the higher pitches become.

Solomon continues with this imagery.

⁵ when people are afraid of things above
and of terrors along the way;
when the almond tree blanches, the locust droops,
and the caper-berry comes to nothing;
when the human goes to the eternal abode,
with mourners all around in the street;

ECCLESIASTES 12:5

The first bit of this passage seems to speak to the fragility of advanced old age and the fears that can accompany that stage of life. Solomon's era was not a period with accessibility standards and safety protocols. Tools or materials could fall from work sites above. Steps might be uneven. Railings were not standardized if they even existed at all. Traffic and marketplace activities were chaotic. Even fetching water from the local well was fraught with opportunities for injury.

The second part of this verse uses three examples from nature to expand on this theme. First, almond tree blossoms are white, so this image is prob-

328

ably referencing white hair, an age signifier that does not discriminate between sexes or races. But what about this business of drooping locusts and caper-berry failure?

Let's start with the locust reference. This line is not referring to any plant by that name but is instead referring to the grasshopper-like insect. The Hebrew describes the locust as dragging along or creeping slowly. The image in Hebrew does not make it clear if the insect is injured or overweight from overfeeding (locusts were great crop destroyers in Solomon's era and remain a problem even in modern times). Either way, the point is that a creature of destruction has passed its zenith.

I am guessing that both images applied to Solomon. He was a destroyer of opportunities and had almost nothing left of his old ambition and energy. Likewise, the destroyer called Time has done its work on his muscles and bones; he's injured, worn out, and nearing the end of his life. In his 1980s synth-pop hit "Tower of Song," the Canadian singer Leonard Cohen expresses similar sentiments. He goes so far as to talk about his gray hair and how "I ache in the places where I used to play." That kind of bodily candor might offend more conservative readers, but Solomon would have understood and approved. His poetry and Cohen's were similarly raw in places.

What we encounter here in this line about locusts is the difficulty and beauty of poetry. Solomon tells us that "the locust droops," and we get two paragraphs' worth of meaning packed into those three words.

Okay, now what about this bit about caper-berries? First, the word translated as "caper-berry" here is obscure. This is the one and only time it occurs in scripture. The root of this word suggests that it means "desire," although "caper-berry" is also a legitimate translation option. Rather than picking between these choices, it helps to recognize that the caper-berry in ancient Jewish lore symbolized energy and was used as a euphemism for sexual desire. So the king, with his seven hundred wives and three hundred official mistresses, in an era before erectile dysfunction drugs, discovers that his desire now comes to nothing. The man sacrificed his youth on the altar of sex to the point of engaging in Astarte worship, and then in his later years, he could not enjoy what he'd gathered for himself.

If you find this imagery and twist offensive, it may be helpful to understand that Solomon wrote this in poetry, at least in part to be discreet, but also for an audience that would have known what he was talking about.

Like decomposing a joke, something gets lost when you need to explain it. However, it's better we lose something by explaining it than completely miss the point altogether. Solomon is not making generic observations. His reflections on old age are intensely personal—and intimately informed by his biography.

He concludes this bit by referencing humanity's eternal abode, which for him is a rare acknowledgement of something beyond this life. Having mentioned it, he concludes with two memorable verses that sum up humanity's exit from this life.

As he does so, however, he's aware that he's nearly at the end of his book. As a result, he concludes in an interesting way, using the same Yoda-like language technique he employed at the start of the book. Let's look at that passage next.

47

DON'T WAIT: REMEMBER GOD WHILE YOU ARE YOUNG

THERE IS A trick writers often use to create a sense of closure by linking the end of a story back to its beginning. Tolkien's *Lord of the Rings* is a massive trilogy spanning many lands, but it begins and ends in the Shire. The Bible itself does something similar, beginning and ending in a garden with the tree of life alongside a river. Sometimes, the link is not in geography but meaning: for example, typical mystery novels pose a question at the beginning and answer it at the end. Here's a more subtle literary version of this technique: the writer uses a unique phrasing at the beginning and end of the book to tie them together.

Solomon uses this last technique in Ecclesiastes. He wanted his readers to remember God

> *6 before the silver cord snaps and the gold bowl shatters;*
> *the jar is broken at the spring and the wheel is crushed at*
> *the pit;*

> *7 before dust returns to the earth as it was before*
> *and the life-breath returns to God who gave it.*
> ECCLESIASTES 12:6–7

In our English translations, the magic in verse six that ties this ending back to the beginning of Ecclesiastes is missing.

Previously, we discussed how Solomon used a Star Wars-style, Yoda-like phrasing at the beginning of Ecclesiastes when talking about the cyclical nature of time.

Here is the retranslation we already discussed in chapter five, which is deliberately awkward in English but gets across the feeling of the original Hebrew:

> *Goes round and round to the south, goes round and round to the north; goes round and round and goes round and round the wind.*
>
> ECCLESIASTES 1:6

The weird Yoda thing happening here is that the sentence's subject appears at the end: "goes round the wind," not "the wind goes round." That's not how English typically works.

Ecclesiastes 12:6 works the same way. Here's how it would read if we retranslated the passage into bad English to better capture the feeling of the Hebrew text.

> [6] *before it is snapped the silver cord and it is broken the bowl of gold and it is shattered the pitcher at the fountain and it is broken the wheel at the cistern*[100]
>
> ECCLESIASTES 12:6

The emphasis here is on the sudden action, with the snapped, shattered, and broken, things appearing as secondary.

The original Hebrew is also much more unified in its language than many English translations, which appear to lose the poetic imagery in service of other translation objectives. In particular, the items in this verse are all related to wells. The wheel, for example, is referring to a pulley at a well (not a wheel on a cart). Similarly, the silver cord is referring to a chain at a well. Why translators did what they did here is a mystery, even to the authors of my translator's handbook and related commentaries. So here is the verse again with both the Yoda cadence and proper specific items:

---

100 Graham S. Ogden and Lynell Zogbo, *A Handbook on Ecclesiastes* (New York: United Bible Societies, 1998), p. 430.

⁶ before is snapped the silver chain and is broken the golden bucket and is shattered the jug for drawing water and is broken the pulley at the well[101]

ECCLESIASTES 12:6

This is another verse that, like a joke, loses something when it's over-explained. If you're anything like me, the passage might not touch you at first. Give it a year or a decade, and suddenly the words land differently. It took a long time of sitting with this verse for me to deeply understand it. That pattern is not unique to Bible verses—many things take a long time to penetrate my thick skull. But I get it now.

The basic idea here is that the wellspring of Solomon's life has not run dry—the underground source of water still flows—but his ability to draw up its refreshment is ending, after which "dust returns to the earth as it was before and the life-breath returns to God who gave it" (12:7).

Solomon is telling us to remember God now. Don't wait. As you age, it will become harder to access inspiration or refreshment not because what you need isn't there but because your tools to access it will start to fail. And once you're in the grave, your regrets will be too late.

Okay, so remember God while we're young. Getting old is no picnic, and we must not wait until we're old before we try to get close to God.

What next, Solomon? How do you sum all of this up?

⁸ Perfectly pointless, says the Teacher, everything is pointless.

ECCLESIASTES 12:8

Let's rewrite that properly.

> *Perfectly hevel, says the Teacher, everything is hevel.*
> *Complete breath, says the Teacher, everything is breath.*

Life is elusive, mysterious, enigmatic, temporary, and repetitive but oh-so important. It's all *hevel*, designed on purpose to drive you to seek God.

---

101 Author's own translation, adapted from Ogden and Zogbo, *A Handbook on Ecclesiastes*, pp. 429–432 and Longman, *Book of Ecclesiastes*, pp. 272–273.

48

LIVE WELL NOW

THERE IS SOMETHING bittersweet about endings. If the tale was good, the meal fine, the relationship deep, or the career a joy, then its conclusion is a time for both celebrating the experience and mourning its conclusion. Endings matter.

Solomon is careful as he ends Ecclesiastes. He's written quite the book, and he likely knew ahead of time that parts of it would be misused or misunderstood. He probably didn't expect later translators to do such a bad job of handling *hevel*, but even without that detail, he has said enough to stir controversy even among his own people reading in their native language.

With these issues in mind, he goes thoughtfully into his concluding verses, aiming to end with something memorable and applicable. There is no point in writing a book like Ecclesiastes if you don't want people to learn from it. The whole point is to teach us how to avoid his bad choices.

> *9 Additionally: Because the Teacher was wise, he constantly taught the people knowledge. He listened and investigated. He composed many proverbs. 10 The Teacher searched for pleasing words, and he wrote truthful words honestly.*
>
> ECCLESIASTES 12:9–10

Solomon's phrasing was sometimes a bit crude—at least for some readers' tastes—particularly on matters relating to sex. Sometimes he contradicted himself because life is not always one thing. Sometimes reality runs cross-

ways with itself, and Solomon said what was needed and pulled no punches about the disconnections he observed. Sometimes life offers us injustice and even failure despite our good intentions or right actions. Solomon was king, and even he, as we saw, was frustrated at times by the bureaucracy he was responsible for. The world is broken. Genesis gives us that idea in theological terms. Solomon laid it out practically, as he observed it, and then gave us instructions he wished he had followed in his own life.

Next, he tells us something important about how to respond to wise words—whether they come from Solomon himself or others.

> *11 The words of the wise are like iron-tipped prods;*
> *the collected sayings of the masters*
> *are like nails fixed firmly by a shepherd.*
>
> ECCLESIASTES 12:11

Wisdom literature prods us in a particular direction. The prods (or "goads," as given in other translations) are steering tools. They deliberately create discomfort—sometimes even pain—to keep an animal on a path or get it back on course after it has strayed.

In the original Hebrew, the word "nails" here seems to be modifying the phrase "iron-tipped prods." In other words, the iron tips are specifically what the shepherd has nailed firmly into the wood. The head of the nail would have been the part to contact the sheep, goat, or cow—not the pointy tip—so the shepherd's aim is not to cause serious injury. Instead, the shepherd's goal is to get the animal's attention. That's how wisdom literature works. It should make us uncomfortable at times, but the point is to help us, not injure us.

However, Solomon then gives the reader a warning about wisdom literature:

> *12 Be careful, my child, of anything beyond them!*
> *There's no end to the excessive production of scrolls. Studying*
> *too much wearies the body.*
>
> ECCLESIASTES 12:12

Here, Solomon is warning against two different dangers.

The first danger is that of going beyond wisdom into something else entirely. If you've ever been exasperated at supposedly secret knowledge (misleading diet fads, outlandish conspiracy theories, and so on), you understand what Solomon is getting at. Don't go beyond wisdom. Be careful with your learning. Curate your sources.

Likewise, serious and respectable study on a solid subject can also go too far. Solomon is not saying that the production of scrolls is the problem. The excessive production of said scrolls is his concern. Too much study can wear a soul out, just like consuming too much food or drink can be a health problem. Unrelenting academia is not a healthy way to live. Solomon's warning here doesn't discount the value of wisdom and learning—he has affirmed the importance of wisdom throughout Ecclesiastes. He has, however, designated it as part of the *hevelness* of life and warns us not to wreck ourselves on its shoals. The non-academic might shrug at this advice, but the professional student should acutely recognize the danger. Get out of the lab or library regularly. Modern medicine and psychology both attest to the value of this advice.

And now, having provided these concluding disclaimers, Solomon wraps up his book with two more verses.

> [13] *So this is the end of the matter; all has been heard. Worship God and keep God's commandments because this is what everyone must do.* [14] *God will definitely bring every deed to judgment, including every hidden thing, whether good or bad.*
> ECCLESIASTES 12:13–14

I love that Solomon did not start Ecclesiastes with this formulaic pronouncement. He puts these two verses at the end of his book, as closing comments after a lifetime of opportunity, investigation, and pursuit that have taken him in nearly every conceivable direction. After Solomon was equipped with all the fame and wealth a man of his generation could hope to have, supplied with God-given wisdom to manage it all, and still left with sufficient personal independence to squander it, this is his conclusion: Worship God. Keep God's commandments. Recognize that everything eventually comes before God for final judgment.

Solomon's wealth, fame, and wisdom did not insulate him from that reality. In his old age, looking back on a lifetime of regrets, Solomon thoroughly understands the *hevelness* of life and the lack of *yithron* to be found anywhere under the sun. It wasn't that he didn't try hard enough or lacked the resources to explore every option on his *yithron* quest. The problem was that what he sought in this world was not there to be found. The search is intended to lead us to God, not deeper into a hedonistic, intellectual, or other rabbit hole. The ultimate end of every man and woman will be to meet their maker and give an account.

Most sermons on Ecclesiastes will again jump straight to Jesus and the Gospels here, which is arguably one valid course to take. I'll decline that route here. Even though Solomon wraps up his book with concerns about eternity, he only touches on it briefly and at the end. The heart of what he has been getting at is life under the sun, not eternity. Existence in this life is *hevel*. It's all *hevel*. Utter *hevel*. Complete *hevel*. Endlessly repetitive *hevel*.

Truly understanding that and how to live this *hevel*-filled life, regardless of eternal destinations, was Solomon's goal. When we live our lives day by day, hour by hour, minute by minute, heaven seems far away. We need tools for us now as well as hope for eternity.

Ecclesiastes is about how to live now.

God set eternity in our hearts without giving us the ability to understand it all, and he did so on purpose (Eccles. 3:11). His purpose was twofold.

His first purpose was to force us to enjoy the little things now without getting sucked into the greed associated with materialism, accomplishments, recognition, or other temporary rewards. Modern-day psychological language would phrase this idea as God directing us toward intrinsic rewards rather than extrinsic rewards. If you investigate those two ideas through online searches or good books, remember Solomon said it first. Modern psychology just documented it in its happiness and well-being literature and provided supporting technical language.

God's second purpose in setting things up this way was to turn us to him. Nothing, not even intrinsically rewarding things, will give us *yithron*—lasting benefit. *Yithron* exists in God alone. Our hungers are like C.S. Lewis's road signs, pointing us onward. Take pleasure in the moment—in the sign—but for heaven's sake, don't fail to reach your destination because you got distracted by the mileage marker.

49

UNFINISHED BUSINESS

I IMAGINE SOLOMON putting down his quill as the sun begins to set, satisfied that Ecclesiastes is now complete, but he's not ultimately satisfied. How could he be? Writing Ecclesiastes did not banish the *hevelness* and missing *yithron* from his life but simply recorded it.

Plus, beyond *hevel* and *yithron*, one other matter is bothering the king.

I imagine Solomon sitting back and turning his mind inward to unpack an uncomfortable feeling that gnawed at him. As he lets his thoughts settle and he strives to expose the source of his discomfort, imagine that pregnant servant surfacing again in memory. His thoughts, however, are not really on her. She is of the generation coming while his is going. She reminds him, though, of something—of someone. She brings to his mind his first true love. There was, believe it or not, such a woman.

What happened to her later in life? We don't know. Did she die young? Perhaps in childbirth or due to some illness or accident? Was her exit from his life part of why he made so many bad marital and other decisions ever after? The historical record does not tell us.

But she did exist, and for a time, she was very important in Solomon's life. In fact, she was the most important person in his life. He wrote a whole book about her, describing her impact on his world. I'll explain that in a minute.

For now, imagine the old king looking once more at his just-completed manuscript. He thinks about his seven hundred weddings and so many mistresses, and then his mind returns to that one woman. Deep regret lives there. His legacy, he knows, will not be her. He will be remembered for the ridiculous thousand he courted afterward.

But that pregnant servant reminds him of his one true love and the season in his life before corruption ruined what had once been filled with wonder. He'd like to set the record straight, to write something about love and sex that honors what God had made beautiful before sin and excess turned it ugly. Such a book could be an antidote to Astarte's temple prostitutes and serve as a positive guide for young people as they navigate the most hormone-inflamed periods of their lives. It would also serve as a king's sorrowful requiem for someone he truly missed.

Imagine if Solomon had stayed with that woman or not lost her to whatever took her from his life. Imagine if he had known the wisdom of Ecclesiastes when he'd been young and followed it, and the couple had built a good marriage together. Imagine if they'd reached that twenty-year anniversary and then their fortieth and been devoted to growing their relationship the entire time instead of Solomon taking one thousand other detours. How different would his legacy be?

I imagine Solomon picking up a new sheet of papyrus. His old hand shakes, and he hesitates. Then he pushes the ink jar away and sets the blank page down. He brushes the reed pen aside. It rolls off the table and falls to the floor. Not today. He can't write that book today. It hurts too much. But soon, he will. He will write that book one day. But not today.

In my speculations on the king's state of mind as he thought about beginning his next book, the old sage wasn't quite ready. But he would be. Soon he would be. When he finally does write it, it'll be carefully preserved and called sacred. It is now preserved in our Christian and Jewish scriptures. We call it, depending on your Bible's translation choices, The Song of Solomon or The Song of Songs. Ecclesiastes is about the *hevel* of all *hevels*. His next book is about the song of all songs, the greatest song of them all: a book about love.

One day, I'd like to complete a nonfiction trilogy: *Even the Monsters* on Job, *Something More* on Ecclesiastes, and then a piece on the Song of Solomon—the Song of Songs. God willing, I will.

In the meantime, may C.S. Lewis's idea of signposts and Solomon's lessons on *hevel* and *yithron* guide you. May your next sunset, sandwich, or song fill you with joy, even if only for a moment. May you have the power to savor the gift of enjoying both your small pleasures and your work without these things swamping you or distracting you from your ultimate destination: the place where all the signposts are pointing. It's why Solomon wrote his book. It's what you were made for.

AFTERWARD

In the introduction, I described the conversations I had with my son Jackson and my friend George as well as my own journey through life that led me to write this book. So how did Ecclesiastes help?

For my son, well, that's his story to tell. Let me just say that I'm a proud father as I see him mature into a young man. He has wisdom that I never dreamed of having at his age. He is a young man making good use of what he's learned and been given, and I'm immensely proud to be his dad.

For George, his road has been rockier. Ecclesiastes stabilized his journey. However, as with any of us who bring years of unaddressed baggage and regrets into later adulthood, late-life pressures don't lighten the load. I don't connect with him often, but it's an increasing pleasure when I do. His growth has been an inspiration, but again, it's his story to tell in his own time, so I'll leave his tale to him.

For myself, I learned so much from Ecclesiastes, I can hardly contain it. From Ecclesiastes 5:8–10, I learned to stop being surprised at the injustices that are so common in the world. For my personality, that means spending more time on taking practical actions and less time sitting in angst, alarm, and what psychologists call "catastrophic thinking." That lesson has been good for my mental health. I doomscroll a lot less.

From Ecclesiastes 3:11–14, I discovered that the hole I've tried to fill since I was a child just isn't fillable. It's a road sign pointing me onward. For me, that's been very helpful as I navigate daily life. I enjoy my dinner a lot more. I also eat a lot less of that dinner now that I'm not subconsciously trying to fill myself with some form of *yithron* that food is just not designed to give us. The same goes for life's other pleasures.

I don't doubt that God deliberately brought my aunt and my cousin and the rest of my extended family into my life as I was three-fourths of the way through writing this book. I was finally ready. The research for this book made me ready, and at exactly the right verse, lightning struck.

The list of personal benefits Ecclesiastes has given me goes on and extends into the future. One thing I discovered from writing this book is that I'm not very good at having fun. That's an embarrassing admission, but a childhood of isolation and Dickensian labor followed by decades of medical grinds and work and sleep deprivation and striving seem to have robbed me of the natural ability to just relax to the degree that Ecclesiastes recommends. Ecclesiastes 4:6 says, "better is resting with one handful than working hard for two fistfuls and chasing after wind." I've been a two-fistfuls guy for too long. I've now engaged a therapist to help me change gears. She's got her work cut out for her, and thus so do I.

Another step my wife and I are taking is finding more nursing support for our daughter's medical condition. Our goal is to do a better job of living life rather than just surviving it. We recently spent the better part of a thousand dollars of our available nursing budget to attend a friend's all-day twenty-fifth anniversary celebration. By contrast, we did nothing but deal with the daily medical drama for our own twentieth and twenty-fifth anniversaries. Our friends' invitation was for a weekend getaway, but we could only afford nursing for the one day—but better one day than no time at all. So we went, and it was a special day.

A thousand dollars for just a day's coverage is, of course, not sustainable. But never celebrating anything with others as a couple is also not sustainable. Ecclesiastes taught me the value of consciously creating better balance in our life. The sacrifices and grind-it-out days persist, but we're both learning to prioritize fun as well. That's not easy with our strange circumstances, but it is a God-given direction that is already providing benefits.

I wrote this book for Jackson. But also for George and myself. And for you. My prayer is that, through this book, the message of Ecclesiastes lives and grows in your life. May that message help you see and delight in life's road signs when they appear but still recognize them for what they are—just signs. Not the destination.

Wherever and whenever you live, I look forward to meeting you at our common destination. When that day comes, I hope to sit somewhere quiet and compare notes with you on the signs that got you there and the ones that guided me. I've got a few folks I'll want to introduce you to as well. We'll have a party. I am certain the food will be amazing.

ACKNOWLEDGEMENTS

Something More was not a solo effort, and I am very grateful for the many people that have helped me over the years as I put this book together.

The book's title is the result of several dinner-table discussions with my wife, Carolyn, and son, Jackson, while Jackson was still in high school. We bandied about many names before landing on *Something More*. I have no record or memory of who said those two words first. Probably Jackson.

My inspiration to write this book came from many sources. Certainly Jackson and George were pivotal, as I described in the book, but before them, my friend Tim Smith paid me a visit that forced me to rethink how I was living my life. My time with him led to my original deep study of Ecclesiastes, which formed the basis for this work.

Amelia Winters has been with me for all my Paper Stone Press publications (she's credited as Amelia Wiens in previous volumes). For *Something More*, she brought an even deeper and tougher persona to the table, and it's the first time we've had arguments about parts of her feedback. In the end, she was right. For one section, I had to reinterpret things I'd told myself for years about my own biography, and in another case, I had to change how I looked at the interpretation of a particular verse. The feedback hurt (writers can be a bit sensitive about their work), but she was brave and articulate, and the book is better for her strong and knowledgeable hand.

Christine Gordon Manley is a seasoned editor but one new to me. She stepped in partway through my rewrites and brought a completely different lens and tool kit to the table. I was initially aghast at her feedback since it required me to rewrite major sections of almost every chapter, create new chapters, and reorder and divide up material to a degree that was overwhelming. Her feedback added nearly six months to my publication timeline, but the result was more than just an incremental improvement. I loved the result of her guidance. It is also worth noting that she's also gifted at performing literary surgery while keeping a writer's fragile ego in view. Her cuts come with kindness and a follow-up salve that leaves the patient able to go on notwithstanding what feels like outpatient organ replacement. If you think I'm exaggerating the internal discombobulation an editor can wreak on a writer's insides, well, then you're not a writer. Thank your maker you're spared that vulnerability!

S. Robin Larin is always the last editor to see my work before it goes to press. Her skill, diligence, and thoroughness are sometimes as overwhelming as Amelia's or Christine's bigger-picture input. Robin's editorial focus has moved on from proofreading, but for this project, she made an exception and agreed to take it on. Robin always gets the work when I'm certain it's perfect and has even passed the layout and typesetting phase. What then comes back from Robin makes me feel like a novice still in middle school. She has saved me from many a self-inflicted embarrassment.

A special thank you to three fellow authors who took the time to read an early draft of *Something More* and offer detailed encouragement and criticism. They are Marilyn Kriete, Fred Faller, and Thyra Root. These three are like creative siblings to me, though we've never met in person. I look forward to remedying that deficiency one day. In the meantime, thank you for your friendship and engagement when I've sent up a cry from the creative wasteland. Your responses gave me the help I needed to do better or be strong enough to carry on. Writing is a lonely activity, but even writers need community, and you've been part of mine.

I am also grateful to others who read and commented on select portions of the text without seeing the manuscript as a whole. My Aunt Louise and cousin Julie reviewed and made minor corrections to chapters thirty-eight and thirty-nine. Brock Peters is a Canadian editor based out of Manitoba whom I consulted on the introduction and chapter one, and I enjoyed our dialogue a great deal. His insights and feedback were useful not just for the select chapters he reviewed; they also shaped how I thought about later material in the book.

A special thank you to my therapist, Leslie Pashuk. She read the book in draft form at about the same time Christine Gordon Manley was preparing her feedback. The combination of editorial surgery (Christine) and the input of a registered therapist and theologian (Leslie) were profoundly helpful tools as I tackled the final version of *Something More*.

A book like this needs many eyes and points of view. It touches on history, psychology, theology, ancient language interpretation, and many other areas of intellectual specialty. I try as best as I can to source these inputs from a growing library of academic materials, but there is something invaluable about wise humans talking to you live and helping you see areas of error or places for improvement. Thank you to all my teachers and guides, only some of whom are mentioned here. You are all valuable to me.

LIFE LESSONS SUMMARY

Chapter 1

- Before making a cake or building a life, make sure you've got an accurate recipe.

Chapter 2

- Everything in life is fleeting, enigmatic, temporary, essential, life-giving, fragile, repetitive, and mysterious.

Chapter 3

- People need more than heaven to look forward to. We need lasting benefit (*yithron*) now, in this life.

Chapter 4

- Grim endurance of life's challenges is not enough to grow a healthy human heart.

Chapter 5

- Life and nature demand that we understand *hevel* and find *yithron*.

Chapter 6

- The quest to find meaning in our lives will take effort.

Chapter 7

- Accepting that some things are crooked and letting them go is a necessary step to grasping what will provide lasting benefit.

Chapter 8

- Being lighthearted isn't bad, but failing to take life seriously enough can produce unnecessary suffering.
- Pleasure and laughter will never provide *yithron*.
- Adding alcohol to life won't improve its outcome.

Chapter 9

- Building projects are more commendable than partying, but from a *yithron* perspective, they are equally empty.
- A party is a party, and a building is a building, and neither one fills an empty heart.

Chapter 10

- Pleasure—positive pleasure, like a vast music library, or sinful pleasure, like sexual objectification and abusive relationships—is temporary, fleeting, and transitory.

Chapter 11

- The benefit of wisdom over foolishness is not immediately obvious given that everyone winds up dead in the end regardless of whether they were wise or foolish.

Chapter 12

- Work is as much *hevel* as any other part of life. A better job won't satisfy what the soul craves.

Chapter 13

- All work—even a prestigious, lucrative, life-saving career—might be necessary, even important, but is always ultimately ephemeral. Temporary.

Chapter 14

- There's nothing better for human beings than to eat, drink, and experience pleasure in their hard work.

Chapter 15

- The pursuit of milestone achievements is not a path to real joy. That path makes you subservient to the whims of others and is a curse from God. It's an easy path to be tricked into pursuing, but it's a dead end.

Chapter 16

- Everything needs to have its place and be limited to its proper proportions.
- There's a right time for the things we experience in life, and not every moment is the right time for every experience.
- Enjoying the simple things in life is good, but our pleasure needs to be taken in stride and not made central in our lives.

Chapter 17

- Birth and death are outside of our control. This fact should teach us how little control we have in life.
- Sometimes we need to start things, and sometimes we need to end them. Both are valid events in their place.
- Sometimes change is what is needed, even if that change is hard.

Chapter 18

- Both mourning and celebrating (dancing) have their appropriate time.
- Sexual and non-sexual physical affection also have their own appropriate times.
- Learning these appropriate times—customized to your culture, relationships, and personal history—is an important part of healthy maturity.

Chapter 19

- Losing things, giving up on dreams, and facing other harsh realities have their appropriate place and time.
- Likewise, peace, love, and other positive experiences are important parts of the human experience.

- Consciously thinking about what times are missing in life is a good practice to ensure a balanced life path.

Chapter 20

- Everything is beautiful in its time, but that beauty is not absolute or complete.
- Enjoy the simple things in life: eat, drink, and enjoy the results of our hard work.

Chapter 21

- Enjoy the little things, but don't worship them. Keep signposts as just signposts and not the destination. Keep *yithron*—lasting benefit—as your goal.

Chapter 22

- Identify broken things that hurt and put them in perspective so they don't overwhelm you.
- There is a time for judgment. Not every wrong has to be (or can be) immediately solved.
- Learning to find enjoyment in life despite life's flaws takes effort. Learning to enjoy your lunch and job while existing in a world prone to injustice is a next-level life skill.
- Sometimes the long view is the right perspective. We have to recognize that God will deal with injustice in his time, not ours.
- Sometimes the right perspective is a narrower focus—on lunch or the one friend who really cares about you.

Chapter 23

- Competition is ubiquitous and also empty. It is just breath (*hevel*).
- Enjoy life with one handful rather than chasing two handfuls. Don't chase the wind.

Chapter 24

- Going through life self-focused and alone is not healthy.
- Real friendships, though, require effort. They don't happen on their own.

Chapter 25

- Friends are not just emotionally meaningful; they are also practically valuable.
- Friendships, however, will not solve the *hevelness* of life.

Chapter 26

- Do a lot of listening when you pray and not so much talking.
- Too many words lead to foolishness, and fools produce too many words.

Chapter 27

- Don't be naive about injustice in society.
- When we don't let injustice surprise us, we're better able to remedy problems we encounter.
- Injustice benefits no one in the long run.

Chapter 28

- Money can be a barrier to happiness.
- Take pleasure in the journey, not the prize at the end.

Chapter 29

- We will never satisfy the eternity lodged within us in this life, but we can learn to enjoy the moment.

Chapter 30

- The more we try to outwit God, the less successful we will be at finding the *yithron* (lasting benefit) that our souls seek.

Chapter 31

- Go to the funeral and comfort those who mourn.
- Real joy is a by-product of substance not froth.

Chapter 32

- It is not a small thing to give or take a bribe. It corrupts the heart of both the giver and the taker.
- Starting is easy. Finishing is hard. Finishing is better.

- Patience gives the worth of a thing time to materialize.

Chapter 33

- Don't let the past become your focus.
- Enjoy the moment but then keep moving forward.

Chapter 34

- If you think you know what's going on or think you're in control, think again.
- God does what God does, and people are powerless to thwart him. God makes good and bad things "so that people can't discover anything that will come to be after them" (Eccles. 7:14).
- When times are good, enjoy them. When times are bad, trust God.

Chapter 35

- Avoid overdoing it in the areas of righteousness and wisdom.
- You can't be perfect, so get on with life and don't sweat missteps.
- Live your life the best you can, and course correct as you go, always aiming for better.

Chapter 36

- Absolutely everybody makes mistakes.
- On the road to growth, we need to filter our internal and external critics.

Chapter 37

- Men and women are not from different planets.
- Human beings are all from Earth—God made us upright and we make a lot of mistakes.

Chapter 38

- Family matters. That mattering can be positive or negative.

Chapter 39

- Sometimes all a hurting soul needs is to know they have an aunt who loves them and always has.

Chapter 40

- There is a right time and way for every matter, and the wise will know that time.
- There is no point in arguing with a dictator.
- Gentleness carries with it next-level authority.

Chapter 41

- Sometimes oppression hurts the oppressed, sometimes it hurts the oppressor, and sometimes it hurts both.
- The world is not predictable and does not run on a formula.

Chapter 42

- We are relentlessly hungry for what we cannot have.
- This life is a life of road signs. The destination is not found here.

Chapter 43

- No person knows how their story is going to end. Only God knows.
- Life is important but fragile.
- Learn to enjoy the good things life offers as gifts from God.

Chapter 44

- Calmness doesn't fix offences, but it can help manage them.
- In addition to enjoying the small things in life, thinking and planning and being responsible are also part of a well-lived life.

Chapter 45

- Keep the finances in order.
- The sun shines every day, and every day it offers opportunities for pleasant experiences. Learn to notice those things.
- Invest your time and energy wisely.

Chapter 46

- Even youth is *hevel*—temporary, fleeting, fragile, and important but ephemeral. Breath. It's all breath.

Chapter 47

- Life is elusive, mysterious, enigmatic, temporary, and repetitive but important. It's all *hevel*.
- Don't let *hevel* distract you into missing a connection with God.

Chapter 48

- Be careful with your learning.
- When we live our lives day by day, hour by hour, minute by minute, heaven seems far away. We need tools for our present and hope for eternity.

Chapter 49

- Regrets expose additional wells of missing *yithron*.
- Not everything can be solved in one book—not by Solomon, nor by us.

www.ingramcontent.com/pod-product-compliance
Lightning Source LLC
Chambersburg PA
CBHW061134120626

46546CB00005B/1778

THE MIRROR'S TOUCH BOOK II

FIVE MUST DIE

Jackie Notter

Climate Publishing
Seattle

Written by Markus Taylor under the pseudonym Jackie Notter.
Editor: J. Lopez, Mistress Editing
Editor: Kim Wahl
Italian translation: Francesca Petroni

Cover: Trif Book Design
Blurb: Jake Carney

ISBN: 979-8-218-44447-1